Biblical Origins

The Political Intent of the Bible's Writers

Biblical Origins

The Political Intent of
the Bible's Writers

S. David Sperling

with Tara S. Keiter

Vidonia Publishing

Published in the United States
by Vidonia Publishing
2022

ISBN: 979-8-9867647-0-2

The present work is an updated and expanded revision of
The Original Torah: The Political Intent of the Bible's Writers
published by New York University Press in 1998, ISBN: 0-8147-8094-6.
Paperback of above was published in 2003, ISBN: 0-8147-9833-0.

Enjoy life with a woman you love. (Ecclesiastes 9:9)
For Jennifer, the love of my life.
S.D.S.

For my mother, Brenda K. Bhavnani, with whom I share
my passion for reading and religion.
T.S.K.

FOREWORD

When I was a child, my parents ended every dinnertime with a teaching based on a biblical verse. There were many important moral and ethical teachings from these lessons. But sometimes I was troubled by what I was taught. I rejected the idea that a serpent spoke to the first humans in the Garden of Eden, and I was unsettled with a God who would drown creation in a great flood; save for one family and the animals on the ark.

Although I was raised to believe that the Bible reflects God's infallible and unchanging communication with humanity, I had trouble accepting every word a literal truth, as the traditional Christian religion of my parents required. When I grew older, I left the faith of my childhood and lived for many years without any formal religious affiliation. Yet I never lost the sense that I was part of something bigger than myself, part of a larger pattern in our universe.

As an adult, I discovered that Judaism offered a way to explore the Bible's ancient teachings and stories in a rich and meaningful way. This new perspective on the Bible came into clear focus for me when I enrolled in rabbinic school. As one of my teachers, Rabbi Martin A. Cohen, said: "Our sacred tradition evolved out of human searching. If we understand the human condition, we can understand the Divine."

I am seeking to understand: to understand myself, to understand my fellow humans, and to understand the human quest to discern God. I seek to understand my purpose in this world, a purpose reflected in the essential when we ask, "Why am I here?" and "What's it all about?"

Now I am the senior rabbi at a congregation whose members come from a wide variety of religious experience. No matter their background, I have seen my congregants pondering these same essential questions. And at the occurrence of major life events (marriage, birth of children, divorce, illness, death), I have witnessed a yearning for the comfort and sense of community that religion brings—even for those people who consider themselves doubters.

For both believers and non-believers, religion holds an important place in human experience around the world and, for a large percentage of the world's population, the words in the Hebrew Bible are held in high esteem. However, without guidance, it is inevitable that many nuances of the Bible will be missed. As a student in rabbinic school I was fortunate to have as one of my guides Professor of Bible, Dr. S. David Sperling. After ordination, I was even luckier that we got married. As well as being my husband, he continues to be my teacher, and, with this book, he brings his insightful inquiry of the Torah, or the first five books of the Bible.

In a 1787 letter to his nephew, Thomas Jefferson counseled, "Question with boldness even the existence of a god; because, if there be one, he must more approve the homage of reason, than that of blindfolded fear." I agree with that statement. My education and experience have led me to believe that we cannot understand the Torah unless we seek to understand the lives and concerns of the people who created it. Like us, the creators of the Torah sought to understand the world and their place in it. By studying and questioning we honor the human quest to understand the Divine. Some people may find the journey to understanding leads them to a truer version of themselves, and others may find the journey brings them a truer connection to the Divine.

Rabbi Jennifer Jaech
July, 2022

CONTENTS

AUTHOR'S NOTES

In the year 525, a monk named Dionysius Exiguus gave us the commonly known A.D. (anno Domini, "[the] year of The Lord") and B.C. ("before Christ") system. The B.C.E. (Before the Common Era) and C.E. (Common Era) expressions, which have become popularized in academic and scientific publications, embrace the year 1 starting point that is today's most widely used civil calendar, but secularize them by removing the reference to "Christ" or "Lord."

Scripture translations provided by the author have been so noted. Other scriptural quotations come from the JPS Hebrew-English Tanakh (2nd edition, The Jewish Publication Society. Philadelphia, P.A. 1999), but have been slightly edited to be consistent with the author's own translating format.

Readers can find a time line, a genealogy of the kings of ancient Israel and Judah, and a map of ancient Israel and Judah in the Appendix of this book. For print-at-home documents, please request a PDF from Tara Keiter at tkeiter@me.com, subject: Biblical Origins—Appendix.

PART I
THE BEGINNING
(Genesis 1:1)

Overview: The Bible is popularly viewed as one singular and unified document, but discrepancies and inconsistencies point to multiple authors over approximately eight centuries. By combining the biblical text with archeological, linguistic, and extra-biblical evidence, we get a fuller picture of the movement of the Israelite people and their motivations in preserving the biblical traditions.

1. Through the Generations

Every generation inherits a world it never made; and, as it does so, it automatically becomes the trustee of that world for those who come after. In due course, each generation makes its own accounting to its children.
Robert F. Kennedy (1925–1968), politician

When she was eight years old, my daughter Deborah came home from her Jewish religious school and asked me, "Since no one could have known what really happened, why were the stories in the Torah made up?" That question marked the beginning of a journey for me: a quest to document known scholarship about the people who lived and wrote in biblical times. And then to synthesize this difficult material in a way that is more easily accessible to a wide range of people.

Who am I to answer the question? I've been studying the Bible my entire life, or at least since I started school at the age of 5. I grew up in Brooklyn and was educated in the *yeshiva*—or traditional Jewish K–12—where all my parents' friends sent their boys. After high school, I graduated from Brooklyn College, where I studied philosophy and history, and then attended The Jewish Theological Seminary, where I was ordained as a rabbi. I continued my education by earning my Ph.D in Ancient Semitic Languages from Columbia University in New York, and then began my career in academia. For more than 40 years, until my retirement in 2019, I enjoyed a rewarding career as a professor of Bible at the Hebrew Union College-Jewish Institute of Religion (HUC-JIR) in New York.

My work is driven by a deep desire to make sense of the Bible. I wanted—and still want—explanations for myself. When I have studied all the available information and I feel that I might have hit upon the motivating force of the writers, I am passionate about sharing my theories with others. Luckily, as a professor I have had colleagues and students with whom to share my thoughts.

The ability to understand the origin of the Torah stories is an essential part of the training of rabbinic students at HUC-JIR. In an effort to consolidate information into one comprehensive text for my students, in 1998 I published *The Original Torah: The Political Intent of the Bible's Writers* (New York University Press). Today, my *Original Torah*, which was intended for an academic audience, is more than twenty years old. This updated and expanded revision of the book, renamed *Biblical Origins*, makes note of more recent scholarship and with the help of a co-writer, Tara Keiter, attempts to make the work more accessible to a wider audience.

When I use the word "Bible" I am specifically referencing the "Hebrew Bible," which is the body of literature more commonly known as the "Old Testament." All Christian denominations—Catholic, Protestant, Eastern Orthodox and Oriental Orthodox—incorporate the ancient Israelite texts that comprise the canon (collection of sacred books) of the Hebrew Bible. However, the ordering of the books may differ, and some ancient writings which were excluded from the canon of the Hebrew Bible are included as additional books in some Christian Old Testaments.

When I use the name "God" I am referring to the deity known variously as Adonai, Elohim, El and Yahweh. But these terms are not strictly interchangeable. A more accurate translation of the word Adonai is "Lord." A more accurate translation of the words El and Elohim is "God." And Yahweh—which is actually the proper name of Israel's god—can be more accurately translated as "Eternal," and is the translation I will use in this text.

For the purposes of this book, I will focus on the very narrow definition of the Torah in its sense of the first five books of the Hebrew Bible: Genesis, Exodus, Leviticus, Numbers, and Deuteronomy. Neither the English term "Pentateuch," based on a Greek word for a case containing five scrolls, nor the more descriptive "Five Books of Moses" adequately conveys the emotive content of the Hebrew word "Torah," which literally means "teaching," "instruction," and/or "law." Many Jews will use the word "Torah" to refer to the entire Hebrew Bible, or even to the whole body of sacred Jewish lore rooted ultimately in the Bible. This includes the vast body of Talmudic literature which is the primary focus of the traditional Jewish academies, or *yeshivas*.

In a synagogue setting, the Torah is called the *sefer torah*. The word "sefer" comes from the same Hebrew root as the word "scribe." The *sefer torah* is written on a scroll, even though the far more convenient book format has been available for almost two millennia. It is written in the ancient Jewish system of lettering without vowels. For example:

Cn y rd ths sntnc? Add vowels and you have "Can you read this sentence?" Now imagine an entire collection of writings that have no vowels—that is the *sefer torah*. As if this were not enough, the *sefer torah* continues to be handwritten by a scribe (*sofer*) with a quill pen on parchment, in an age when one could easily print the text of the entire Torah at home with the press of a button.

The iconic aspect of the *sefer torah* becomes most obvious in its use during services. Every synagogue houses the scroll in a chamber— referred to as the "Holy Ark"—at the front of the sanctuary where the Torah, like the cross in a church, is designed to be visible to the entire congregation. Congregants stand when the *sefer torah* is lifted high from either of its two perches: inside the Ark or from the podium where it will be read. In many congregations, the *sefer torah* is paraded around the sanctuary and congregants turn to follow its progress so that their backs are never toward it. In recent years it has become common at bar and bat mitzvah ceremonies—Jewish coming-of-age ritual of 13-year-olds—for the *sefer torah* to be "handed down through the generations." Grandparents pass the scroll ritually to the parents, who will then pass it to the teenager. The symbolism is lovely, but the reality is that the grandparents and parents are, usually, handing down the scroll without much knowledge of its contents. Most adults, if they learned to read from the *sefer torah* for their own bar or bat mitzvah, have not practiced and have lost that ability. Thanks to more recent religious school experience, the 13-year-old may be the only one of these three generations with the ability to read any part of the *sefer torah*.

Contemporary, critical, scholarly study of the Bible contrasts sharply with its iconic role. Instead of wholly accepting the Bible as something to be uncritically revered, scholars seek to understand it. Scholars attempt to comprehend what meaning the writings had for the ancient writers. What was happening in their world? What was happening in the world around them? What messages were they trying to convey to their people? And how did these messages help to unify a people?

Some may clamor that I am seeking to debunk the Bible, but the opposite is true. The best way to honor our sacred text is to seek to understand it on its own terms. One cannot understand the Torah without trying to understand the lives and concerns of the people who created it. The creators of the Torah sought to understand the world and their place in it. All religious traditions grow out of the human searching for meaning, and the Torah is no exception.

Although the Torah text is more than two millennia old, thanks to modern archaeological and historical research it has become increasingly possible to recover the historical circumstances of much of its composition. This, in turn, enables scholars to make some very confident statements concerning when particular traditions of the Torah originated.

Biblical Origins is an attempt to appreciate the significance of the Torah by humanizing these iconic writings. Through study of the Bible, study of the literature from contemporaneous cultures, and study of what historians and archaeologists know, we may be able to figure out the motivations of the writers against the background of the times in which they wrote.

2. Scholarly Study of the Bible

A thorough knowledge of the Bible is worth more than a college education. Theodore Roosevelt (1858–1919), U.S. President, 1901–1909

Study of ancient Israelite culture is not an easy task. First, we lack reliable texts. Students of the literature of Babylonia and Assyria, for example, regularly have the opportunity to study documents on the original clay tablets on which they were written. There are no surviving texts of the Torah from the biblical period. Biblicists only have copies of copies of copies. Indeed, before the discovery of the Dead Sea scrolls at Qumran in 1947, the oldest known complete biblical texts date from the 10th century C.E. But even the texts found in Qumran are copies of texts created centuries earlier. For example, the scientific methods of radiocarbon dating and paleography (the study of ancient writing systems) have dated the Great Isaiah Scroll—one of the seven texts discovered at Qumran—to approximately 100 B.C.E. However, the text contains references to events as early as the 8th century B.C.E., hundreds of years earlier.

A second problem is linguistic. Linguists discern the meaning of a word when they find the same word used in a variety of ways. By looking at the word in different contexts, they can better understand its exact meaning, register, form, and more. However, almost every newly unearthed Hebrew text from the biblical period contains a word or phrase not previously encountered. This has led to huge gaps in our understanding of biblical language, making precise translation challenging. Bible translators use their expertise to attempt to get at the true meaning of a word, but the fact of imprecision is evidenced, for example, in the Jewish Publication Society translation of the Hebrew Bible (1999) which has a considerable number of words noted as, "meaning of Hebrew uncertain." The larger the body of ancient texts, the greater the odds of achieving linguistic precision. Again, in contrast to the literature of Babylonia and Assyria—written in an early writing system known as cuneiform, and of which we have a great many examples to compare—the Hebrew Bible offers scholars only a very small corpus to study.

We also recognize, linguistically, that language changes over time. For example, 150 years ago prayer books referred to God as being "terrific," which at that time indicated that God was terrifying—as in *scary*. Today's readers may agree that God is "terrific," but the modern meaning of the word is an informal description meaning really good, or excellent. Sometimes an old word is appropriated to describe something new. 100 years ago, a mouse was simply a small, furry rodent. Today an author could write, "I used my mouse to select it," and readers would understand what was meant. 100 years from now, a new meaning might be attached to the word.

A third problem is that we often cannot gauge the importance or impact of the writers in their own time. That is, the prophet Ezekiel may have been listening to God, but we cannot tell whether anyone was listening to the prophet Ezekiel!

Still another difficulty is the sparse corroborating documentary record of Israel's earliest history. We know what the Bible stories tell us about Israel's early history, but which of these stories has been verified by sources outside of the Bible? Not much has been discovered. The earliest reference outside the Bible to a group called "Israel" comes from an Egyptian source dated to approximately 1220 B.C.E. There is not another mention until 400 years later, in 9th century B.C.E. texts from the neighboring kingdoms of Moab and Assyria, when King Omri of northern Israel turns up in a Moabite text and his son Ahab in an Assyrian document. Also dating from the 9th century B.C.E. is a pictorial representation of King Jehu paying tribute to a king of Assyria. Only after that do the number of references to Israel, its rulers, and its political history in outside sources begin to get respectable.

Of particular value to scholars are ancient Hebrew documents from Israel and Judah from the 8th to 6th centuries B.C.E., as well as the archives of a 5th century B.C.E. Jewish colony in southern Egypt at the site known as Elephantine. Although the amount of non-literary material (contracts, inventories, etc.) excavated from Israel from the biblical period has grown tremendously since 1967, we have few instances of the "ideal" archaeological situation where an artifact is accompanied by a clear identification on the order of "Palace of Solomon, King of Israel, built in his fifteenth year."

Contemporary scholarship is virtually unanimous that before 922

B.C.E. there were ethnically diverse tribes of people living in the area of current day Israel who banded together, eventually becoming what scholars refer to today as a "united kingdom." In roughly 922 B.C.E., these tribes divided themselves into what is now commonly known as the northern kingdom, Israel, and the southern kingdom, Judah. Beginning in approximately 740 B.C.E. and lasting twenty years, successive rulers of Assyria invaded the northern kingdom of Israel. The Assyrian strategy when they conquered a land was to remove local inhabitants from the land and replace them with other groups. The Assyrian conquest resulted in traditions about "the Ten Lost Tribes of Israel."

The southern kingdom of Judah survived. Research shows that some of the people from the defeated northern kingdom migrated to the southern kingdom and brought their stories and traditions with them. Knowing that stories from both the northern and the southern kingdoms have been integrated into the one Bible can explain some of the inconsistencies in the text.

Readers may find the timeline in the Appendix of this book to be a helpful visual aide. It attempts to show the movement of the Israelite people, and to highlight the impact neighboring cultures had on the course of Israelite people and the stories they told. One important point as we move forward: We have no direct evidence of the existence of characters best known to readers of the Bible, including—but not limited to—Abraham, Sarah, Isaac, Jacob, Esau, Moses, Joshua, Deborah, Gideon, David, Goliath, and Solomon.[1]

3. Sacred Scripture & the Prophet Isaiah

Then I heard the voice of the Eternal saying, "Whom shall I send? Who will go for us?" And I said, "Here I am; send me." Isaiah 6:8

Documentary and linguistic issues are real, but these difficulties pale beside the most formidable obstacle: the fact is that the Bible is sacred Scripture. As such, Jews and Christians have distorted the Bible in two ways. First, they have made Scripture "relevant" by imbuing it with their own ever-changing beliefs and values, rather than concentrating on what a biblical text might have meant when it was written.

Second, they have tended to treat the Bible monolithically, as a singular and unified document. They have referred to what "the Bible says" rather than appreciating that biblical writers might differ among themselves, or from later religious Jews and Christians. The very first chapter of the Bible provides an excellent example:

> Then God said, "Let us make a human in our
> image, after our likeness." (Genesis 1:26,
> translation by the author)

This is a direct translation from the Hebrew as found in the Torah. If there was only one God in existence, to whom was God referring when he used the pronouns "us" and "our?" Jews who read the *Iliad* are not troubled by the grammatical plurality of the Greek gods because they don't expect Homer to be a monotheist. As monotheistic readers of the Bible, however, they expect Genesis to agree with the monotheistic teachings of Judaism. In fact, if the author of Genesis chapter 1 had wanted to score a point for monotheism the passage would have read differently—perhaps something like the following:

> Then God said, "Let me make a human, in my
> image, after my likeness."

There are real, monotheistic biblical writers but the author of Genesis 1 is not one of them. For example, the book of Isaiah makes monotheistic statements and is fully able to use the proper pronouns:

> I am Deity and there is no other. I am God and
> there is none like me. (Isaiah 46:9, translation by
> the author)

Also found in the book of Isaiah is a statement in direct opposition to the claim of Genesis 1:26 that humans are after "our likeness" or "our image." In fact, Isaiah voices disapproval of the notion that humans are fashioned in the divine likeness.

> To whom, then, will you liken God or what
> likeness compare with him? (Isaiah 40:18,
> translation by the author)

Over time, monotheism came to predominate in Judaism. Once monotheism had become the official Israelite religion, it seemed natural to read it into all scriptural passages and not get bogged down in the details of pronouns. Genesis 1 would express the same sentiments as Isaiah, and the pronoun problems would be glossed over.

Before we continue, it is important to provide a little background. The entire book of Isaiah is purported to be the words of the prophet Isaiah, who lived during the 8th century B.C.E. This does not mean, however, that there was a prophet, Isaiah, hunched over his parchments writing down his thoughts to be saved and studied for the three millennia to come.

Instead, think of the schools of the ancient Greek philosophers, like Socrates, Plato, and Aristotle, to name a few. At a time when literacy levels were very low and mass media did not exist, people would gather to talk and share ideas. A man named Isaiah likely existed, but his words do not make-up the entire book of Isaiah. In the words of H. G. M. Williamson (born: 1947), who taught Hebrew at the University of Oxford, the book of Isaiah is a compilation of passages from multiple authors, "like a tapestry, with many hands contributing to a greater unity."[2]

The original, 8th century B.C.E. teachings are most notably found in chapters 1–39 and are referred to by scholars as First Isaiah, or Proto-Isaiah. The Proto-Isaiah passages contain commentary on what was witnessed during the devastation of the Assyrian invasion of the northern kingdom (740–720 B.C.E.). Evidence to support the historical authenticity, or historicity, of the passages is found in the details that synchronize nicely with extra-biblical accounts of King Hezekiah of Judah and Sennacherib of Assyria.

Chapters 40–55—referred to as Second Isaiah or Deutero-Isaiah—share the spirit of Isaiah but are certainly written by a different hand. Scholars date these passages to the 6th century B.C.E. because of the clear reference to King Cyrus of Persia, a historical figure from that time, who is hailed as the "victor from the East" that the Eternal has "summoned to His service" (Isaiah 41:2). In case there are any doubts about the reference, Cyrus is specifically named in Isaiah 44:28 and Isaiah 45:1. The monotheistic passages mentioned above come from this period.

The final set of writings, known as Third Isaiah or Trito-Isaiah, are a collection of prophecies that seem to have been created in Jerusalem after the Babylonian exile, sometime after 539 B.C.E. While likely contemporary with Deutero-Isaiah's work of the 6th century B.C.E., chapters 56–66 have a slightly different flavor leading scholars to believe they come from a different hand. Someone thought these prophecies were worth preserving and they were appended to the end of the book of Isaiah.

When the 8th century B.C.E. Proto-Isaiah says, "For the Eternal has spoken" (Isaiah 1:2), he is specifically talking about the God of Israel known variously as the Eternal, Elohim, El and Adonai. The Assyrians worshipped Ashur, and other gods. The Babylonians worshipped Marduk, and other gods. The Philistines worshipped Dagon, and other gods. The Moabites worshipped Chemosh, and other gods, etc. People worshipped their gods in the hope that these gods would be willing and able to provide abundance in both crops and family, as well as protection against enemies and bad luck. Though people believed in the existence of many gods, they tended to worship only the ones who presided over the region in which they lived.

Any belief that a neighboring god might be more powerful than their own would amount to a political and theological crisis for Israelite leaders. Instead, Proto-Isaiah asserted that the Assyrian devastation was proof of the superior power of Israel's god: The fall of the northern kingdom came about because the Israelites were not upholding their end of the bargain by worshipping God properly. Israel's god actually *is* the most powerful god; so powerful that he is able to use the Assyrians as his tool to demonstrate his displeasure with the Israelites when they cavorted with their neighbors and worshipped other gods. On this interpretation, the writers could declare that the 720 B.C.E. final destruction of the northern kingdom was evidence of the might of God.

After 130 years of relative peace in the southern kingdom of Judah, the people learned of the westward advances of the Babylonian armies and, rightly, became afraid. They knew the stories their grandparents told them about the defeat of the northern kingdom. Perhaps, once again, their God was reprimanding them for not properly worshipping him.

When Judah was invaded by the Babylonians early in the 6th century B.C.E., the center of Judah's religious worship, the temple built by King Solomon (10th century B.C.E.), was utterly destroyed. By 586 B.C.E., the Babylonians forced many Israelite leaders into exile and installed either their own people or pro-Babylonian Israelites to administer the Babylonian system of government (see 2 Kings 25:22). The Babylonians left the "common" people in place to work the land, tend the flocks, and pay taxes to the conquerors. The exile of nonconforming leaders was intended to prevent people from rallying together to plot rebellion.

Then, in 539 B.C.E. Cyrus of Persia defeated the Babylonians and invited the exiled Israelite leaders to return (see Ezra 1:2–4). Under the theory that "the enemy of my enemy is my friend," the defeat of the Babylonians cast the Persians in the role of hero to the Israelites; a fact evidenced by glorious accolades heaped upon Cyrus in Deutero-Isaiah. The earlier Proto-Isaiah passages in the book of Isaiah were known in the Israelite community, and through judicious editing were used to political advantage. The words in the book of Isaiah were edited to give the impression that they were a prophecy about the impending Babylonian invasion, and also a time to, in the words of H. G. M. Williamson, "look forward to the imminent arrival of Cyrus as the one who will let them go back home to Jerusalem, where the temple will be rebuilt."[3]

In a span of less than 200 years, the Israelite nation experienced devastation, conquest and exile, defeat of an enemy, and finally, return home. During this upheaval, many leaders felt a strong desire to save as much of their community and culture as possible. They gathered histories, parables, poems—anything that related to their culture—so that they could preserve it and, just as we do in the synagogues today, pass it down to their children and to future generations.

This was no small feat. Plenty of other cultures have come and gone over the millennia. Along with the Babylonians, Assyrians, and Philistines, there were also the Seven Enemies of the Israelites: the Hittites, the Girgashites, the Amorites, the Canaanites, the Perizzites, the Hivites, and the Jebusites. And there were the Midianites, Moabites, the Cushites, the Kenites, and the Phoenicians. Most of these peoples have been lost to history. The concerted effort of the Israelites to preserve their culture may be a key reason why the Jewish community continues to exist today.

4. Impact of Other Cultures on Israelite Belief

For they are full [of practices] from the East, and of soothsaying like the Philistines; They abound in customs of the aliens.   Isaiah 2:6

King Cyrus II of Persia, a.k.a. Cyrus the Great (reign: 559–530 B.C.E.), was unlike some previous conquerors in that he encouraged the Jews to worship their own God and govern themselves, as long as they swore fealty to Persia and paid taxes. Cyrus welcomed the leaders who had been exiled by the Babylonians to return to their homeland. Most chose to stay away because they were comfortably settled in their new land, but others returned.

Those who migrated back to Israel had been changed by their experiences in exile. Although we can imagine that they were excited to come "home" to live among "their people" in their homeland, this was not a homogeneous group. People had lived in Babylon, or in Egypt, or in other communities. They had adopted practices from other cultures which would not be quickly shaken off. Residents of Israel—perhaps initially delighted to have their kinsmen come home—might have been appalled by how these returnees had adopted "alien" traditions.

Leaders would have made an effort to reestablish this disparate group as one people. One way to do that might have been to get the message out that God would not like this blending of customs. By building upon the already popular teachings of Isaiah, adding a dose of editing and a little revisionist history, the leaders might say something along the lines of, "Isaiah has already warned us what would happen if we didn't follow God's commandments and look how we were conquered! Now we have a chance to do it right. Let me refresh you on the rules."

This brings us back to the conflict between Genesis 1 and the writings by Second Isaiah, or Deutero-Isaiah. In a 1968 quarterly publication for Jewish studies, *Tarbiz*, Bible scholar Moshe Weinfeld (1925–2009), who taught Bible at Hebrew University of Jerusalem, asserted that it would be difficult to find two more opposed theologies of creation in the Bible than in Deutero-Isaiah and Genesis 1. That assessment is still well founded.

In Genesis 1, God's creation is completely good. In contrast, Deutero-Isaiah teaches that the creator God is the "maker of good and creator of evil" (Isaiah 45:8). Only when we have dated these texts and set them in the historical period of their composition can we begin to understand the reason for the discrepancy between Genesis 1 and Deutero-Isaiah. The biblical writers of these texts—two different people—were attempting to come to grips with the religious currents of their own time.

We now know that both Genesis 1 and Deutero-Isaiah were composed during a period in which virtually all world Jewry was governed by the Persian Empire of Cyrus the Great, which was led by followers of the Zoroastrian religion. The highest divinity in the Zoroastrian religion was the benevolent creator Ahuramazda, whose name literally means "Lord Wisdom." In a royal inscription roughly contemporary with Deutero-Isaiah and Genesis 1, King Darius the Great of Persia (reign: 521–486 B.C.E.) praises his god in the following words:

A great god is Ahuramazda
Who created this earth
Who created that heaven
Who created humanity
Who created happiness for humanity. [4]

The Persians conceived of the deity Ahuramazda as the god who created everything good in the world, making him, by definition, a god to whom evil or suffering was never attributed. But something had to be responsible for the bad things in life. Zoroastrianism was a dualistic system of worship that attributed the source of all evil to the archfiend Angra Mainyu.

Genesis 1 and Deutero-Isaiah, each in opposition to the other, provide a Jewish account of the creation in response to the dominant religious currents of their time. The writer of Genesis 1 accepted the Persian notion that the creation was completely good, but maintained that its goodness was due to Elohim, the Hebrew divinity more commonly referred to today as God. In contrast, Deutero-Isaiah insisted that the Hebrew God was responsible for both good and evil, an ancient Israelite teaching that had always been taken for granted but now needed to be articulated in the most forceful terms—stressing the monism, or unity, of Deutero-Isaiah's God to counter the influences of Persian dualism on Jewish belief. When we understand the historical circumstances and the intellectual currents of the Persian period, we can begin to appreciate the significance of the controversy between Genesis 1 and Deutero-Isaiah.

5. To Honor and Understand

I have a fundamental belief in the Bible as the Word of God, written
by those who were inspired. I study the Bible daily.
Sir Isaac Newton (1643–1727), scientist

The more we understand about the background of the writers and
the times in which they lived the more we can understand about their
agenda, allowing us to further humanize the Torah and its stories. The
Hebrew Bible is divided into three parts, the Torah being only the first
part. The entire Hebrew Bible is also referred to as the Tanakh, which
is an acronym for the three divisions: 1) The Torah, or **T**eaching,
which is the Five Books of Moses, 2) the Prophets, or **N**evi'im, and 3)
the Writings, or **K**etuvim.

The writings from the *Prophets*, the second section of the Hebrew
Bible, are mostly set in the land of Israel. Chronologically, the *Prophets*
covers a manageable period, from the beginnings of Israel through the
demise of the Israelite states of Israel and Judah. Many of the events
referred to in the *Prophets* are corroborated by extra-biblical sources,
some of which name, and even describe, biblical locales and
personalities. As a result, we can translate the chronology of the books
in this section into our own terminology and to say, with confidence,
that the *Prophets* covers events between $14^{th}/13^{th}$ century and the 5th
century B.C.E. In contrast, the Torah, beginning with the creation, is
set long before the rise of the Israelite states and largely outside the
land of Israel, in what are now, Iraq, Syria, Turkey, Armenia, Egypt,
and especially, Jordan.

When it comes to chronology of the Torah our quests for specific
detail are constantly frustrated, making it difficult to surmise what
political realities may have motivated the writers. The writers of Torah
literature often fail to provide the kind of information necessary to
establish a chronology for both the Hebrew characters and their gentile
(non-Hebrew) contemporaries. To cite the most notorious example,
we have inspiring, detailed stories about Joseph, the eleventh son of
Jacob, but very little that can be corroborated as fact.

The birth of Joseph is mentioned in Genesis 30 and by Genesis 37
the Joseph story has taken a dominant position, which continues all

the way through the end of the book of Genesis (Chapter 50). Joseph rose in prominence in the Egyptian court, becoming a trusted and powerful advisor to Pharaoh. But even though the interactions between Joseph and Pharaoh figure prominently in the story, we are never told the name of the pharaoh whom Joseph served, nor are we told the names of his Egyptian successors who were the pharaohs of the enslavement and the Exodus. Had any of these specifics been provided they would enable us to assign a date to this part of the Torah, or at least to the time period in which this story is set.

Another problem with Torah literature is that we cannot reasonably rely on the Torah's own internal chronology. The lifespans attributed to Torah characters run the gamut from contradictory to fantastic. Consider the Hebrew patriarch, Abraham who lived 175 years. Or Noah, who lived 950 years. Or, longest-lived of them all, Methuselah, who lived to the age of 969! And with fantastic chronology of her own, Abraham's wife Sarah may have only lived 127 years but she was able to give birth to her son Isaac at the age of 90.

The story of Ishmael, the son of Abraham and Hagar, presents us with contradictions. We are told that Abraham was 86 years old (Genesis 16:16) when Ishmael was born, and Abraham was 100 years old when his son Isaac was born (Genesis 21:5). After the birth of Isaac, Sarah demanded that Ishmael and Hagar be sent away, meaning that Ishmael must have been at least 14 years old. Genesis 21 tells us that Abraham placed Isaac *on Hagar's shoulder* "and sent her away," and when it appeared that Ishmael would die from thirst, Hagar placed Ishmael under a bush and walked away, so as not to watch him die (Genesis 21:14–16). A mother carrying her healthy, 14-year-old son on her shoulder and, later, placing him under a bush and walking away so as not to watch him die from thirst seems like unlikely behavior for a teenager and his mother.

6. Decoding the Torah

If Scripture were to describe the downfall of an empire in the style
adopted by political historians, the common people would not be stirred.
Baruch (Benedict) Spinoza (1632–1677), philosopher

The book of Leviticus ends with, "These are the commandments that the Eternal gave Moses for the Israelite people on Mount Sinai" (Leviticus 27:34). Having received the Ten Commandments, and after a kerfuffle about the Golden Calf which you may remember from the 1956 Cecil B. DeMille epic movie *The Ten Commandments* or the 1998 DreamWorks animated movie *The Prince of Egypt*, the Israelites were ready to wander through the wilderness on their way to Canaan: the land that would become their home.

The book of Numbers begins with Moses taking a census of the people (hence, the name of the book). There is a list of tribal leaders designated by God to assist Moses in dividing the land of Canaan among the Twelve Tribes of Israel. Biblical chronology would lead us to calculate that Moses would have lived in the 14th or 13th century B.C.E. However, a verse from Numbers casts doubt on that dating:

> Of the tribe of Zebulunites a leader, Eli-zaphan,
> son of Parnach. (Numbers 34:25, translation by
> the author)

A more likely time for the composition of this verse is revealed by the name of Eli-zaphan's father. "Parnach" is the well-documented Persian name, Farnaka, which would not have been known to the Israelites leaving Egypt and trekking through the wilderness in the 14th or 13th century B.C.E. As far as we know, Jews did not come into contact with Persians until the 6th century B.C.E.; therefore, Numbers 34:25 can be dated no earlier. But just because the verse cannot be historically accurate does not mean it has no value. First, Numbers 34:25 is an early witness to the Jewish practice of adopting foreign names. Second, and much more important, by using the clue provided by the date of the text, we may find that the chapter in which it is embedded does not have a 14th or 13th century agenda, but instead a 6th century agenda. In fact, the chapter turns out to be part of a blueprint for Jewish political and religious organization under Persian rule.

The detail "Parnach" is emblematic of how we must approach the Torah if we want to understand it. As I will explain in the next chapter, the archaeology of the past fifty years demonstrates that the Torah's two fundamental claims appear to be unhistorical: 1) Israel was never enslaved in Egypt, so consequently there was no Exodus and no trek through the wilderness, and 2) the people "Israel" did not come from outside the land, meaning there was no conquest.

This leads us to conclude that the entire Torah does not have a 14th or 13th century agenda, and certainly none that reaches further back into the second millennium B.C.E. Instead, the stories in the Torah reflect religious-political concerns of the Israelite-Jewish communities between 1100 and 400 B.C.E. I suggest that, to advance their own platforms, the authors of the Torah set their tales in times and places far removed from their own. In other words, the narratives of the Torah are best described as *allegories*—narratives contrived to signify a second order of meaning from what they present on the surface.

Allegorical interpretation of the Hebrew Bible is not new, of course. From antiquity to modern times, many readers of the Bible have construed the Garden of Eden, Noah's Ark, and the book of Jonah as allegories because these tales seemed scarcely credible. The Song of Songs (also known as the Song of Solomon), in contrast, tended to be read as an allegory of spiritual love between God and the Jews, or between Christ and the church, because it was all too credible in its sexually explicit descriptions of human eroticism. Christian readers of the Hebrew Bible have commonly used typology—interpretations of types and symbols—to claim that events and persons in the Hebrew Bible prefigure events and persons referred to in the Christian New Testament. As St. Paul explains in his classic statement found in Corinthians:

> All these things that happened to them [the
> earlier Hebrews] were symbolic (Greek: *typikos*]
> and were written down as a warning for us. (I
> Corinthians 10:11, translation by the author)

To be sure, the methods of allegorical interpretation applied in the following chapters differ significantly in their fundamental assumptions from those made by most earlier allegorical interpreters. I begin with the premise that the Bible is a completely human document to be studied with the same tools that have been accredited in the study of other ancient human documents. In light of what we now know, it is clear that Paul was wrong in accepting that "all these things happened" in the way his Jewish Bible said they did. Nonetheless, the method I advocate in this study would have been impossible without the work of earlier Jewish and Christian allegorizers.

Like the philosopher Philo of Alexandria (20 B.C.E. to 50 C.E.), who allegorized the four rivers of Paradise by writing that they stand for four virtues, I am compelled to read the Torah allegorically because it cannot be read historically. If "historical" means that an event occurred in the time and place in which it is set, then nothing in the Torah is historical. Whether these events are constructed as fantasies about talking snakes (Genesis 3:1) and donkeys (Numbers 22:28) or, given more believable settings—e.g. a war led by Moses—is irrelevant.

Summary – Part I

- The lack of reliable texts and corroborating evidence makes study of the Bible difficult.
- Before 922 B.C.E. there were ethnically diverse tribes of people living in the area of current day Israel who banded together, eventually becoming what scholars refer to today as a "united kingdom."
- We know that sometime around 922 B.C.E. the northern kingdom of Israel separated from the southern kingdom of Judah.
- Around 720 B.C.E. the northern kingdom of Israel was conquered by the Assyrians.
- The Bible is often treated as one singular and unified document, but discrepancies and inconsistencies point to multiple authors over approximately eight centuries.
- The southern kingdom of Judah was invaded by the Babylonians and many Israelites were forced into exile by 586 B.C.E. The collection of Israelite histories, parables, and poems began in earnest around this time.
- Original writings in the book of Isaiah were from the 8th century B.C.E. and recorded impressions of the Assyrian conquest of 720 B.C.E. Later editing gave the impression that the writings were a prophecy about the impending Babylonian invasion, followed by the defeat of Babylonia by Cyrus of Persia. The edited writings reflected the reality of that later time.
- This was also a time when the writers made a clear move from polytheism to monotheism.
- The Persians defeated the Babylonians in 539 B.C.E. and the people of the diaspora were invited to come home to Israel.
- Some of the stories became part of the blueprint for Jewish political and religious organization under Persian rule.
- The authors made extensive use of allegory, setting their stories centuries earlier than when they were written.

PART II
INSCRIBE THIS IN A DOCUMENT
(Exodus 17:14)

Overview: Nowhere in the Hebrew Bible is there a claim that the events reported actually happened. Voices of doubt about the historical reliability of the Bible became louder in the 17th and 18th centuries. In the 19th century, Julius Wellhausen put forth a hypothesis that the Torah (the first five books of the Bible) is a compilation of documents from several sources—this is known as the "documentary hypothesis." Archaeology has added greatly to known biblical scholarship and has also provided evidence that the Torah is not a fact-based retelling of history.

7. The Torah and Joshua, In Brief

The holy canonical Scriptures in their original text are the infallible truth and are free from every error. That is to say, in the sacred canonical Scriptures there is no untruth, no deceit, no error, not even a minor one, either in content or words, but each and everything presented to us in Scripture is absolutely true whether it pertains to doctrine, ethics, history, chronology, topography, or onomastics, and no ignorance, no lack of understanding, no forgetfulness or loss of memory can or should be ascribed to the amanuenses of the Holy Spirit in their writing of the Holy Scriptures.

Johann Quenstadt, Professor of Theology, University of Wittenberg, Germany (1617–1688)

The narrative contents of the Torah are easily summarized: The account runs from "In the beginning…" of creation until the death of Moses, prior to the Israelite people crossing the Jordan River into Canaan. The account of settlement in the land is completed in the book of Joshua. The main events of the Torah and Joshua are as follows:

Genesis

The first book, Genesis, relates how God, called variously the Eternal or Elohim, creates heaven and earth and all that encompasses—what we now call *the world*. Dissatisfied with the behavior of his animal and human creatures, the same God obliterates most of them in a great flood. Only spared are the righteous Noah and his family, and enough animals to repopulate the entire earth (after allowing for sufficient ritual sacrifices by Noah). Ten generations later, through the line of Noah's son, Shem, God calls on Abraham to emigrate to Canaan, where a mutually beneficial relationship will be established. God will provide land, offspring, and blessings to Abraham and his descendants, the Israelites. In return, the Israelites will worship only God and follow his laws. A short time later, a famine in Canaan causes the grandchildren and great-grandchildren of Abraham to move to Egypt, where God has thoughtfully already installed one of their own to great power.

Exodus

The second book, Exodus, has the Israelites settled in Egypt and as having successfully multiplied. However, their population increases so much that the ruling Egyptians become afraid and treat the Israelites with extreme brutality, including infanticide. The Israelites cry out to God for deliverance, and God responds by inflicting ten plagues on the Egyptians, then drowning their army in the sea. Guided by two pillars, one of fire and one of cloud, as well as by the man Moses, the Israelites travel through the desert to Mount Sinai, where God descends from heaven and speaks to them. God takes the occasion to enter into a covenant with the Israelites, which certifies Israel as his people, and then God gives the Israelites the Ten Commandments and all manner of good laws. For their physical needs, God provides bread (manna) from heaven and water from stone. For their religious duties, God provides detailed instruction on the construction of a portable sanctuary where the Israelites may serve him. The same sanctuary also provides for atonement, which is frequently required—owing to Israel's tendency to be ungrateful and inconstant, as witnessed in the worship of a golden calf.

Leviticus

The third book, Leviticus, has the Israelites still in the desert, where they are given the needed instructions about who is to perform the divine service of the sanctuary and how and when to perform it. God's presence in the midst of the Israelites requires him to legislate detailed rules to maintain cultic[*] and ethical purity. With divine foresight, God also prepares the Israelites for life in the Promised Land, where they will need to know about such practical matters as land sales, slave purchases, accurate weights and measures, and the proper treatment of the less fortunate. But God's closeness to Israel also has its disadvantages: Israel is warned in no uncertain terms that its future tenure in the Promised Land is contingent upon avoiding the "way of

---

[*] "Cultic" is used in its original sense of "service" or "work" (as in the words "cultivation" or "agriculture") and should not be understood as the emotionally charged term it has become in popular usage. In this book, the term "cultic" refers to the system of religious service rituals directed toward a specific deity.

Egypt and the way of Canaan," and adhering to the divine statutes.

Numbers

The fourth book, Numbers, brings us to the second year of the wilderness journey, when a detailed census is undertaken. The Israelites are organized into the military units essential to an army on the march. Again, God gives them numerous laws to govern themselves in the Promised Land. To aid Moses and advise the Israelites, God appoints seventy elders to whom he gives divine spirit, akin to the prophetic spirit he had conferred on Moses. Despite God's manifold provisions, however, the ungrateful Israelites complain continually about the food and the leaders that they have been given.

The breaking point is reached when a party of twelve Israelites spies returns from a scouting trip to the Promised Land. Ten of the spies report that Canaan is populated by gigantic warriors living in massively fortified cities, meaning the Promised Land will be impossible to conquer. The Israelites, discouraged by the report and lacking faith in the divine ability to overcome the inhabitants of Canaan, express the wish to have died in Egypt or in the wilderness. In punishment, God announces that they will get their wish: the people will wander in the wilderness for forty years, until the entire Exodus generation has perished. Only their children will enter the Promised Land, along with faithful Joshua and Caleb, the two lone spies who dissented from the majority report. Although Moses and Aaron are not culpable in this matter, they fail to sanctify God publicly when he commands them to bring water out of a rock. As punishment, they too are barred from the land, sharing the fate of the rest of their generation. Despite these setbacks, God resumes his kindnesses by turning the curses of the seer Balaam into a blessing, and by giving the Israelites a victory over two powerful Transjordanian rulers: Sihon and Og.

Deuteronomy

The final book of the Torah, Deuteronomy, finds Moses on the east bank of the Jordan River (present-day Jordan) within sight of the Promised Land, but barred from it. Moses takes the opportunity offered by his impending death to deliver a farewell speech, in which he revises many of the narratives and laws contained in the previous four books. God's covenant with Israel is presented elaborately, echoing the wondrous blessings for adherence and the severe penalties for violation found at the end of Leviticus. The book ends with the new generation of Israelites poised to enter the Promised Land, following the death of Moses—who had died while still in his prime, at the age of 120.

Book of Joshua[*]

The book of Joshua, the first book of the section of the Bible called the Prophets (Hebrew: *Nevi'im*), completes the narrative begun in the First Five Books. As Moses's legitimate successor, Joshua leads the Israelites across the Jordan River. With God fighting for Israel, many of the formidable city-states of Canaan, including the great-walled city of Jericho, are destroyed. The newly acquired land is distributed among the tribes, and God's covenant is renewed. According to the book of Joshua, everything promised to the ancestors in the Torah is given to their descendants in their new land. Joshua dies contentedly at the age of 110.

---

[*] For our purposes, it does not matter whether we speak of the six books as a Hexateuch or of a more original tetrateuch (Genesis through Numbers) followed by a Deuteronomic history, of which Deuteronomy and Joshua constitute the first two books.

8. Mosaic Authorship

I freely acknowledge that the fundamentals of my faith make it
impossible for me to conclude that the Torah was not written by Moses,
and surely not that it was written after the time of Moses . . . We are
obligated to accept with complete faith that everything written in the Torah
is absolute truth.
Rabbi David Z. Hoffman (1843–1921)

How much of the narrative of the first five books of the Bible may
be considered historical—that is, in reasonable agreement with actual
events? Nowhere in the Torah, nor in the rest of the Hebrew Bible, is
there a claim that the events related actually happened.[5] Nonetheless,
for much of Jewish and Christian history, the factual nature of the
Bible was not questioned. Such original thinkers as the Dutch Jewish
philosopher Baruch (Benedict) Spinoza, the English political
philosopher Thomas Hobbes, and the French thinker Voltaire became
notorious for casting doubt on the historical reliability of the Bible;
and they were not the first such questioners. It is safe to say though,
until the 19th century most Jewish and Christian believers would have
agreed that the Torah and the rest of the Bible were factual.

The biblical figure Moses, according to the Torah, spoke directly
with God. According to many early Jewish and Christian sources,
Moses wrote down the Torah. By combining the notion that Moses
had a direct line to God with the claim that Moses was the Torah's
author, it was natural to conclude that the Torah was God's word—
and therefore the absolute truth. Accordingly, challenges to Mosaic
authorship would call into question the very reliability of the Torah,
even though nowhere in the text of the Torah is Moses named as its
author. Indeed, no Hebrew Bible source goes beyond what we find in
Malachi, the book that concludes the section of the Hebrew Bible
known as the Prophets:

Remember the Torah of Moses, my servant, to
whom I gave at Horeb laws and statutes for all
Israel. (Malachi 3:22 translation by the author)

Much of the books of Exodus through Deuteronomy could be accurately characterized as "laws and statutes," making the statement from Malachi fitting. However, that characterization would be inapplicable to Genesis, which recounts the creation of the world and the emergence of the Jewish people but does not set out laws and statutes. Likewise, Nehemiah 9, which is found in the section known as the "Writings" and summarizes the narrative of the Torah, says only the following about Moses, the statutes, and the laws:

> You decreed commands, statutes, and laws for them [the Israelites] through Moses, your servant. (Nehemiah 9:14, translation by the author)

Neither Malachi nor Nehemiah say anything about the Mosaic authorship of the Torah's narratives. And still, by the 1st century Jews took for granted that Moses had written the whole Torah. The Roman-Jewish historian Josephus (37–100 C.E.) devotes books 1–2:9 of his *Antiquities of the Jews* to a paraphrase of Genesis, accompanied by frequent comments in which he repeatedly refers to Moses as the author of Genesis. Similarly, the Alexandrian-Jewish philosopher Philo (20 B.C.E—50 C.E.) understood Genesis as the necessary introduction to the Mosaic laws:

> Moses . . . introduced his laws with an admirable and most impressive exordium . . . It consists of an account of the creation of the world implying that the world [cosmos] is in harmony with the law [nomos] and the law with the world.

The position that Moses wrote the Torah has been around for centuries. But people have periodically felt the need to proclaim the veracity of the statement by using the Torah itself. Consider the following "proof" adduced by the medieval Jewish scholar Moses Nahmanides. (1194–1270 C.E.), using a passage from Exodus 24 as validation:

> He [God] told him: "Come up to me on the
> mountain and while you are there I will give you
> the tablets of stone and the Torah and the
> commandment that I have written to instruct
> them." (Exodus 24:12, translation by the author)

The proof is as follows:

> The "tablets of stone" means the ten
> commandments; "the commandment" means the
> entirety of positive and negative commandments.
> Therefore "and the Torah" includes the stories
> from the beginning of creation . . . It is the clear
> and manifest truth that the entire Torah from the
> beginning of the Book of Genesis until "in the
> presence of all Israel" [the final verse of
> Deuteronomy] reached the ear of Moses from the
> mouth of God.[6]

Nahmanides's "proof" of Mosaic authorship is far from "clear and manifest" and will convince only those who need no proof. The Torah itself claims Mosaic authorship only for some specific sections. Most of the narratives about Moses refer to him in the third person, including those describing the man as uniquely humble (Numbers 12:3), or dead, buried, and lamented (Deuteronomy 34:5–8).

The claim of the Torah's Mosaic authorship persisted as long as it did because of subsequent religious developments. As we have seen, the author of Nehemiah 9 (5th–4th century B.C.E.) attributed all the laws and statutes of the Torah to Moses. Sometime before the 1st century C.E., the attribution had been imprecisely broadened to include the entire Torah. By the 1st century C.E. this imprecise attribution had become accepted, so that for such seminal figures as Philo, Josephus, Jesus, Paul, and the Jewish sage Rabban Yohanan b. Zakkai (30–90 C.E.), the Mosaic authorship of the Torah was a given. In fact, it had taken on the imprimatur of an article of faith to be defended and passed on to subsequent generations. Employing this given as a foundation, classical Christianity and rabbinic Judaism constructed massive theological and institutional edifices that, in their different ways, claimed to be the fulfillment of the "Torah of Moses."

9. J, E, P, and D

In the beginning God created man in his own image, and man has been trying to repay the favor ever since.
Voltaire (1694–1778), philosopher

The Age of Enlightenment—also known as the Age of Reason—ushered in an era of critical reasoning, which in turn led to scrutiny of religious authority. The 17th and 18th century skepticism of Spinoza, Hobbes and Voltaire (and others) came of age in the late 19th century and the notion of the Mosaic authorship of the Torah was vehemently, and irrevocably, challenged in ever-widening circles. By then, the solidarity and authority of institutional Christianity and Judaism had been undermined by scientific discoveries and newer scholarly approaches. Now authorship of the Torah could be viewed as an academic question rather than an article of faith, not just in universities but also in seminaries. In the earlier dogmatic context, internal contradictions and historical anachronisms had been viewed as challenges to the audience rather than as problems inherent in the Torah and its attribution to the single author, Moses.

In the newer academic context, these same contradictions and anachronisms were explained in a manner that attempted to do them justice. The origin of the Torah seemed much better explained by the hypothesis that it was not the work of a single author but a compilation of literary "sources" or "documents," which had originated at different times and places, some of them written many centuries later than the events they related. Of course, this theory—referred to as the "documentary hypothesis"—has generated enormous debate over the past two centuries.

Julius Wellhausen (1844–1918), who taught at the University of Göttingen in Germany, is the person most closely associated with the "documentary hypothesis." Wellhausen reached his central conclusion about the literary "sources" or "documents" by closely reading the Bible and comparing and contrasting the various texts, paying special attention to repetitions and/or jarring inconsistencies. Repetitions and inconsistencies in the Hebrew Bible act as hiccups in the text, alerting scholars to something that should be given extra attention and could be useful when trying to decipher how the Bible might have possibly come together. Here is an example from the very beginning of the Torah: According to Genesis 1, on the third day God said, "Let the earth sprout vegetation" (Genesis 1:11). Then a full three days later, on the sixth day of creation, God created all the living creatures of the earth. Also, on that same sixth day, "God said, 'Let us make man in our image, after our likeness. They shall rule the fish of the sea, the birds of the sky, the cattle, the whole earth, and all the creeping things that creep on earth.' And God created man in his image, in the image of God he created him; male and female he created them" (Genesis 1:26–27).

Genesis 2 tells a different version of the events. Genesis 2:3 says that God created earth and heaven, but there were no shrubs or grasses because, "there was no man to till the soil," (Genesis 2:5) . . . so "the Eternal God formed man from the dust of the earth. He blew into his nostrils the breath of life, and man became a living being" (Genesis 2:7). Then God planted a garden in a place named Eden and placed man in it—alone! God realized that Adam would need a helper, "So the Eternal God cast a deep sleep upon the man; and, while he slept, he took one of his ribs and closed up the flesh at that spot. And the Eternal God fashioned the rib that he had taken from the man into a woman" (Genesis 2:21–22).

These two stories are not in sync, and there are other examples of duplicated Bible stories with conspicuous discrepancies. It is certainly possible to explain away the differences creatively through *midrash*— rabbinic finessing of the biblical text—to reconcile contradictions. A *midrash* to reconcile the two stories of human creation, for example, presents the character Lilith as the first woman created. Drawing on a single sentence from Isaiah 34 about a female demon in repose, the rabbis claimed Genesis 1 describes the creation of Adam and his first wife, Lilith. But Lilith failed to become subservient to Adam and, being an unfit mate, she left. When God saw that Adam had become lonely, he created Eve in Genesis 2 to be his helpmate.

Midrash serves the purpose of smoothing discrepancies, but modern, inquisitive, academic minds perceived of another reason for the discrepancies. Inconsistent literary tone or word usage (e.g., the use of the term Elohim versus the Eternal, when referring to God), reveal that the Torah and the rest of the Bible are repositories of many traditions. Wellhausen identified at least four contributors to the final version of the Torah: The J source, the E source, the P source, and the D source, plus the Redactor, or "R" source.

J, or the Eternal

These passages come from a source that identifies God as the Eternal, in Hebrew: *Yahweh*. Wellhausen, as a German, would have used a "J" instead of a "Y" in his identification. Wellhausen believed that the J source contains some of the oldest material in the Torah.

E, or Elohim

These passages come from a source that identifies God as Elohim. These stories seem to have originated among the Northern Tribes.

P, or Priestly

These passages come from the Priestly source and are mostly about ritual sacrifice and the functions of the priests at the Temple, as well as genealogies.

D, or Deuteronomist

These passages offer codes of conduct for the Israelites toward each other, and toward God. It is possible these laws were created during the reign of King Josiah of Judah from circa 640 to 609 B.C.E.

R, or Redactor

This is the person (or people) who had the formidable task of putting these collected stories together and attempting to have them make sense—in a time thousands of years before computers! When we see awkward transitions, we could assume that a redactor was trying his best to make it smooth.

Still More Sources

It is now widely agreed that the Torah contains an "H" source, or Holiness (H) Code. The passages in H prescribe behavior designed to make the People of Israel "holy" just as God is holy. Much of this material has been interwoven with the P, or Priestly, source. But scholars have noted that the language is slightly different and has a heavy emphasis on the word "Holy," which makes them believe it originated from a different source.

American and Israeli scholars generally accept Wellhausen's hypothesis and continue to refine it. However, several European Bible scholars have questioned Wellhausen's source division, instead dividing the Torah into "P" material and "Non-P" material. Other scholars, influenced by recent trends in literary criticism, now speak of floating motifs that were combined in different ways by different authors and editors. Despite these differences of approach, it must be emphasized that no critical Bible scholar accepts the traditional notion of a Torah authored completely by one author, whether Moses or anyone else.

10. Evidence Unearthed

There are no secrets that time does not reveal.
Jean Racine (1639–1699), dramatist

Julius Wellhausen's critical analysis of biblical passages, and a lack of evidence to the contrary, led him to draw negative conclusions about the historical reliability of ancient biblical tales. In his 1878 book, *Prolegomena to the History of Ancient Israel,* Wellhausen asserted that literacy had not reached Syria-Palestine* before the 10th century B.C.E., meaning that stories set centuries earlier (e.g. Abraham stories, Jacob stories, Moses stories) were fabricated by later writers and had no value as evidentiary sources of information. Another assertion was that biblical names like Jacob or Daniel only became common after the 10th century B.C.E., so their use in stories set centuries earlier were anachronistic when used in such settings and were flags that the story was unreliable. (It would be as if I told a story about my Eastern European grandmother born in 1884 and gave her name as Britney. It rings untrue and you would doubt my story. For the record, her name was Shifra—later Americanized to Sophie.)

Although Wellhausen's statements were unverified by any actual evidence, they were readily accepted and went largely unchallenged for more than 50 years. They had the added benefit of enabling scholars to avoid struggling with otherwise puzzling Bible passages, such as the following:

> If I sent a pestilence into that land and poured out
> my wrath upon it with blood, to cut off humans
> and animals from it, even if Noah, Daniel, and

---

* Syria-Palestine encompasses modern-day Israel, Lebanon and Syria. In the 2nd century B.C.E., Hellenistic rulers replaced the name "Judah" with "Judaea (Judea)." In the 2nd century B.C.E., following the suppression of the Jewish revolt of 132-135, the Romans replaced the name Judea with "Palaestina." The region was referred to as Palaestina (Palestine) until 1948, when the Jewish state was declared.

> Job were in it, as I live, says the Eternal God, they
> would save neither son nor daughter; they would
> save only their own lives by their righteousness.
> (Ezekiel 14:19–21, translation by the author)

The references to the offspring of Noah, Daniel and Job puzzled scholars. Noah and Job were known to have children, but the biblical Daniel was a eunuch who never fathered a child. Using Wellhausen's assertions—the supposed lack of literacy in the area pre-10th century B.C.E. and that the name Daniel was an anachronism—scholars were able to dismiss this passage to the realm of "made-up stories," and unworthy of further scrutiny.

Wellhausen's book was published at a time when the field of middle eastern archaeology was in its nascent stages, but advances in the field would show that he didn't quite get it right. Ten years after the publication of Wellhausen's book, the discovery of hundreds of clay tablets of 14th century B.C.E. correspondence between Egypt and Canaan proved conclusively that there were literate people in Syria-Palestine well before the 10th century B.C.E. The discovery of the Amarna letters, unearthed in Egypt in 1888, should have laid to rest any doubts about scribal activity in the region. The evidence of early scribal activity continued to mount and Wellhausen, as a prominent and influential scholar, should have updated his theory, but he did not.

Further discoveries showed that the names of some of the biblical characters in ancient settings truly were ancient names. For example, the name "Jacob" was found in an 18th century B.C.E. site uncovered at Chagar Bazar* in modern-day Syria *and* on a 15th century Egyptian list compiled by King Thutmosis III of Egypt. Also found in modern-day Syria was the name "Ishmael" in 18th century texts from the ancient city of Mari, as well as the personal name "Israel" in 13th century texts

---

* Fun Fact: The expedition at Chagar Bazar was led by British archaeologist Max Mallowan, who was accompanied by his wife, the prolific murder mystery writer, Agatha Christie. According to a 2002 *Archaeology Magazine* article by Amy Lubelski, Christie made "herself useful by photographing, cleaning, and recording finds; and restoring ceramics, which she especially enjoyed." Christie once said, "An archaeologist is the best husband a woman can have. The older she gets the more interested he is in her."

from the ancient city of Ugarit.

Between the two world wars, Middle Eastern archaeology continued to expand and thousands of written documents from Syria-Palestine proved that ancient traditions, many of which bore directly on the Bible, could have been written down and preserved. This shedding of light on pre-10th century B.C.E. life in the region allowed archaeologists and Bible scholars to have a fuller picture of how the Bible might have come together, and puzzling passages—like Ezekiel 14:19–21, with its references Noah, Daniel and Job—could be analyzed with a new perspective.

To better understand the passage, we must first understand the stories around these characters. According to the book of Genesis, ten generations after God created Adam, Noah was born and he "was a righteous man; he was blameless in his age" (Genesis 6:9). God becomes displeased with the other people on earth and decides to "put an end to all flesh, for the earth is filled with lawlessness" (Genesis 6:13). God instructs Noah to make an ark and go aboard it with his wife, their three sons, their three daughters-in-law, and one male and one female of "all beasts . . . [and] creatures of every kind" (Genesis 7:14). God caused it to rain for forty days, until the water level rose above the mountain peaks and "All existence was blotted out . . . Only Noah is left, and those with him in the ark" (Genesis 7:23). After 150 days, according to Genesis 8:4, the water subsides and the ark comes to rest on top of an unnamed mountain in Ararat (present-day Armenia), but it took quite a while longer until there was enough dry land for Noah and his family to emerge from the ark—estimates total as long as 378 days of ark-living with his family and the beasts/creatures. After going to the effort of preserving every creature, Noah selects one of "every clean animal [and] offers burnt offerings on the altar" (Genesis 8:20). Then God creates a rainbow as sign of "my covenant between me and you and every living creature . . . so that the waters shall never again become a flood" (Genesis 9:15). At no point are we told what "righteousness" Noah's wife, sons, or daughters-in-law exhibit that causes God to save them along with Noah. In fact, Noah's middle son, Ham, gets into sexual shenanigans in Genesis 9, causing Noah to become angry and deliver a curse that Ham would be a slave to his brothers. (The Hebrew name "Ham" is similar to—but unconnected with—the Hebrew word for "brown," providing a pretext for people to claim that Ham had brown skin. The pretext was used, centuries later, as a "primary justification for slavery among Southern Christians" in the United States.[7])

Another righteous man is Job, whose story opens, "There was a man in the land of Uz named Job. That man was blameless and upright; he feared God and shunned evil. Seven sons and daughters were born to him" (Job 1:1). Job's children hold feasts where there will be abundant eating and drinking, with the possibility of overindulgence. Job fears that, "Perhaps my children have sinned and blasphemed God in their thoughts" (Job 1:5), and Job worries that God will punish them. Seeking to protect his children, Job tries "rising early in the morning, he would make burnt offerings, one for each of them" (Job 1:5).

A group of divine beings present themselves before God, and God takes the opportunity to boast about his righteous devotee, Job. Among these divine beings is the Adversary (Hebrew: *Satan*). The Adversary challenges God to wreak havoc on Job's life, in an effort to test whether Job would remain devoted in the face of nightmarish adversity. Some of Job's flocks are destroyed and others are stolen, his children die, and Job is stricken with all-over skin inflammation. Job's wife and three of his friends come to commiserate with Job and bemoan that God allowed these terrible things to happen. Job answers, "Should we accept only good from God and not accept evil?" (Job 2:10). He also says, "My lips will speak no wrong, nor my tongue utter deceit . . . until I die I will maintain my integrity. I persist in my righteousness and will not yield; I shall be free of reproach as long as I live" (Job 27:4–6). Because Job remains unwavering toward God, God "blessed the latter years of Job's life more than the former," (Job 42:12) with restored wealth and health, and seven sons and three daughters, of whom we are told, "Nowhere in the land were women as beautiful as Job's daughters to be found" (Job 42:15).

The tenor of the story is that, because of the righteousness of Job in the face of adversity, God replaces everything Job had lost. Yes, technically Job's first set of children died, but they were (rather easily) replaced, and it is notable that Job attempts to use his own righteousness to protect his children from any sins they might commit. Similarly, Noah's righteousness protects his family members. The Noah and Job stories cannot be dated with precision, but the settings of the stories are agreed to be "ancient times"—at least 2100 B.C.E. for Noah and 1500 B.C.E., plus or minus, for Job.

Now we get to the puzzling inclusion of Daniel. As we know, the righteous hero from the book of Daniel was a childless eunuch. Also, according to inner biblical chronology,* the "Daniel" in the book of Daniel would have been a younger contemporary of the 7th century B.C.E. prophet Ezekiel, and not a figure of the ancient past.

A solution to the puzzle was provided with the 1929 excavation of the ancient city of Ugarit—a city in modern-day Syria that had lain buried since the time of its destruction in about 1200 B.C.E. One of the significant finds at Ugarit was an epic about a righteous man named Daniel who resurrects his beloved son after the boy had been unjustly slain by the agent of a vengeful goddess. A more plausible conclusion is that the Daniel of the Ugaritic epic was the "Daniel" to whom Ezekiel was referring, not the Daniel of the biblical book.[8] The fact that the prophet Ezekiel refers to a centuries-old tale as an example indicates that he expected that his audience was familiar with the story. Although we do not know how this (at least) 13th century B.C.E. story was transmitted to the 7th century B.C.E. Ezekiel, we can be certain it was.

The field of Middle Eastern archaeology directed to the Bible, or "biblical archaeology," became alive with possibilities. The proof that a centuries-old tale was preserved and passed down through the generations opened the door that there were likely many similarly ancient tales also passed down—maybe even ancient tales about biblical heroes such as Abraham or Moses. The search for evidence of the existence of other biblical characters was on!

---

* "Inner biblical chronology" refers to a timeline constructed using biblical lifespans and significant events as markers of time. The timeline is highly speculative, as Bible narratives are often conflicting.

11. Biblical Archaeology

*Archaeology gives us an opportunity to study past civilizations and see
... 'Well, really, what were they thinking?'* Nathan Myhrvold (born:
1959), businessman, inventor and author

From the mid-1930s until the early-1970s, "biblical archaeology"
dominated biblical studies in the United States and Palestine (Israel,
after 1948). Biblical archaeologists began their explorations with a
positive attitude, giving the accuracy of Bible narratives the benefit of
the doubt. They believed that archaeological finds would shed light on
the Bible narratives, and they enthusiastically attempted to synthesize
the Torah's traditions with these archaeological finds. In the United
States, William F. Albright (1891–1971), who taught at Johns Hopkins
University, and G. Ernest Wright (1909–1974), who taught at Harvard
University, and in Israel the archaeologist Yigael Yadin (1917–1984),
were the most dominant figures in the 20th century biblical archaeology
movement. They believed that if the major historical claims of the
Bible were demonstrated archaeologically then inner biblical
inconsistencies and contradictions, as well as exaggerated numbers and
incredible wonder tales, would become minor annoyances at worst.
The following is a characteristic evaluation of Genesis by William F.
Albright:

> As a whole the picture in Genesis is historical,
> and there is no reason to doubt the general
> accuracy of the biographical details and the
> sketches of personality which make the patriarchs
> come alive with a vividness unknown to a single
> extra-biblical character in the whole vast
> literature in the ancient Near East.[9]

John Bright (1908–1995), who taught at Union Theological
Seminary, stated in his book *A History of Israel* that, "We can assert with
full confidence that Abraham, Isaac and Jacob were actual historical
individuals."[10] Yes, as a writer one can, of course, assert whatever one
wants. And Albright's note of "vividness" could just as easily lead to

the conclusion that Genesis was written by a talented writer of fiction, rather than by a historian.

Despite some encouraging archaeological finds and positivity on the part of scholars, greater validation would come from proof of pivotal narratives in biblical history, such as the Israelite enslavement in Egypt, the Exodus, the desert wandering, and the conquest period. When that evidence was not found, it became apparent that early biblical archaeologists made a mistake of equating antiquity—how long a story has been around—with historicity. That is, just because people have been telling the story of the Great Flood for thousands of years does not necessarily make it true.

Scholars who questioned the historical validity of the Bible used the lack of evidence to bolster their attacks on the overall credibility of the Bible. Note the following quotation from Niels Lemche in *The Anchor Bible Dictionary*:

> The simple fact [is] that the ancient Near Eastern sources from the 3rd and 2nd millennia B.C. do not contain a single direct reference to any of the features mentioned in the Old Testament narrative. There is not a single reference to Abraham the Patriarch, or to Joseph and his brothers in Egypt, or to Moses and the Exodus, or to the conquest of Canaan.

Assyriologist Friedrich Delitzsch (1850–1922), who taught at the University of Berlin, also called into question the historical character of the Bible by highlighting the obvious borrowing of traditions from neighboring cultures. In 1902 he gave a series of lectures, which were later published as *Babel und Bibel* (Babylonia and Bible), in which he argued that the Bible is not original because all the sources of the Hebrew religion were found in Babylonia. In 1921, he published *Die große Täuschung* (The Great Deception), which was blatantly anti-Semitic in tone and, as its confrontational title indicates, "an outright attack on traditionalist biblical historiography," according to scholar Joel Sweek of Lewis & Clark College. [11]

12. Bible Thumping

Many a night I woke to the murmur of paper and knew [Dad] was up, sitting in the kitchen with frayed King James—oh, but he worked that book; he held to it like a rope ladder.
Leif Enger (born: 1961) from his novel *Peace Like a River*

In Israel, nationalistic pride was a primary motivation to search for archaeological proof of Bible narratives. Israeli Bible scholars of much of the 20th century were mostly secularists for whom the Bible was a national book, as opposed to a spiritual guide. Living in the country where the Bible had its origins, these scholars viewed biblical history as the story of the beginnings of their people.

Interest in biblical archaeology did not flourish in the same way in Europe; an omission of scholarly interest that Israeli scholars viewed with antipathy, especially after the WWII destruction of European Jewry. European biblical scholarship—German scholarship, in particular—had tended to combine a late dating (post 6th century B.C.E.) for much of Torah literature with gratuitous statements about the degenerate nature of "Jewish" ritual practices advocated or described in these allegedly later biblical sections. This kind of scholarship could be accurately faulted on the charge of anti-Judaism (maligning the Jewish religion), or worse, anti-Semitism (maligning Jews as a people or a race).[12]

In the United States, in contrast, the enthusiasm for biblical archaeology was often religiously motivated. The movement did not develop roots among fundamentalist Christians and Orthodox Jews, as they believed the Bible needed no archeological validation. But biblical archaeology held particular sway among religious moderates. These were people who could not in good conscience reject either the credibility of the Bible or of the scientific method. For a while at least, it seemed that biblical archaeology offered them both.

A good example of how biblical archaeology could be practiced successfully is the story of Assyria's King Sennacherib's (reign: circa 704–681 B.C.E.) invasion of Judah. Chapters 18–19 in 2 Kings relate that Sennacherib had besieged Jerusalem but that the city was miraculously spared:

> That very night the angel of the Eternal set out
> and struck down 185,000 in the camp of the
> Assyrians; when morning dawned, they were all
> dead bodies. So King Sennacherib of Assyria left,
> went home, and lived at Nineveh. (2 Kings 19:35–
> 36, translation by the author)

A 7th century B.C.E. six-sided, clay prism that memorializes the military achievements of Sennacherib, including details of the siege of Jerusalem, was unearthed in Iraq in the mid-19th century. Written as if it were a first-person account, the text details the huge number of captives—young and old, men and women—as well as horses, mules, donkeys and camels taken by the king's army. Sennacherib even boasts that he locked up King Hezekiah in Jerusalem like a bird in a cage. What scholars have observed is the absence of one particular detail: The formula "I took that city"—which was regularly used in the royal Assyrian annals to describe the fall of a city to the Assyrians—is not found in Sennacherib's account of the siege of Jerusalem. Apparently, the Assyrian king's grandiose description of triumph deliberately glossed over the failure of the king and his troops to conquer the city. In a "win" for biblical archaeology, the comparison of the biblical and Assyrian accounts may be said to confirm the "general accuracy" of 2 Kings 18–19. It may be hard for our modern minds to believe that an angel of the Eternal slew the Assyrian troops (as quoted in the passage above), however, as was noted by the scholar John Bright, "some remarkable deliverance must be assumed,"[13] and the biblical account that Jerusalem was not taken may be characterized as "essentially historical."

The case of the siege of Jerusalem was a clear demonstration of the validity of evaluating biblical claims in light of archaeology. But critics of biblical archaeology, on the other side of the debate, had good reason to express their doubts. Unfortunately, in an effort to prove their position, some biblical archaeologists did not shrink from adjusting a detail or two on either the biblical or the archaeological side to maintain the "general accuracy" of the biblical account. When archaeological evidence threw doubt on a biblical story, more than one biblical archaeologist came up with unsubstantiated reasons for the discrepancy. For people who were looking to understand the Bible in a historically accurate way, making up new "history" was not going to fly.

The past four decades have given biblical archaeology a bad reputation in some circles. But this bad reputation is undeserved. It is not a mistake to apply archaeology in an effort to evaluate the biblical accounts. The mistake is in expecting archaeology to *verify* the biblical accounts. The examination of the Torah in light of archaeology has performed a far greater service then demonstrating "general accuracy"—it has pointed us to a better way to read the Torah.

The Torah devotes more than four books to the proposition that the Israelites came to Canaan after having been subjugated in Egypt for generations. The story we know follows the biblical narrative: Moses talked to God, played a role in securing freedom for the Israelites living in bondage, and led the Israelites during their desert wandering (finally reaching the Promised Land in the next part of the Bible). However, systematic excavation of Israel since 1967 has shown that the Torah's account of this early period of time is completely unhistorical.

According to Exodus 12:37, there were 600,000 Israelite men, plus the women and children, who wandered through the desert—a total number of more than two million people. As such, we would expect a large transient group to have left some indication of its presence in the desert. But archaeologists have found virtually no Middle or Late Bronze Age (roughly, 1550–1200 B.C.E.) presence in the central or southern Sinai. Likewise, there is at present no evidence for large-scale Israelite incursions—warlike or peaceful—into the Promised Land in the 13th–12th century B.C.E.[14] And if the Israelites had been living in Egypt for hundreds of years, as the Bible states, the early Israelite settlements in Palestine would have reflected some of the Egyptian material cultural aspects that they adopted, but there are none. The only reasonable conclusion at the present time is that Israel was never enslaved *in* Egypt. Instead, the Israelites were people who already lived in Canaan and worked in servitude *to* distant Egypt, somewhat like feudal serfs. Consequently, there was no Exodus and no trek through the desert. The people "Israel" did not come from outside the land and there was no conquest of a new land.

Two chapters ago we cited the Amarna letters, which include 14th century B.C.E. correspondence between Egypt and Canaan, as

evidence of scribal activity in Syria-Palestine. The clay tablets on which
the letters were written were found in Egypt, but were not written in
the ancient Egyptian language. The majority of the tablets are in
Akkadian—the language of ancient Mesopotamia, which had become
the international language of diplomacy. But those Akkadian Amarna
texts—which had been sent from locations in present-day Syria,
Lebanon, Jordan and Israel—also contain some 120 Canaanite words
and linguistic forms, which are witness to the native dialects of the
Canaanite writers. Biblical Hebrew shows no linguistic break with
these Amarna forms, which we would expect if the Israelites had
resided in Egypt for centuries. Combined with the evidence from
material culture, the linguistic continuity of biblical Hebrew and the
Canaanite dialects suggests the Israelites never spent this time in Egypt.
Everything points to the conclusion that the Torah's account of the
Israelites as outsiders is not historically accurate.

Summary – Part II

- Until the 19th century, most Jewish and Christian believers would have said that the Torah was written by Moses. But the Torah itself never claims that to be the case. In fact, most of the narratives about Moses refer to him in the third person, including those that describe him as uniquely humble, or dead, buried, and lamented.

- By the 19th century, authorship of the Torah could be viewed as an academic question. The origin of the Torah seemed much better explained by the hypothesis that it was not the work of a single author, but a compilation of literary "sources" or "documents" written over a span of several centuries. Sometimes the stories were set centuries earlier than they were written.

- Julius Wellhausen is the biblical scholar most closely associated with the Documentary Hypothesis, which posited that the Torah is a compendium from four distinct sources: The "J" or the Eternal source, the "E" or Elohim source, the "P" or Priestly source, and the "D" or Deuteronomist source.

- Wellhausen believed that there was no scribal activity before, roughly, 1000 B.C.E. This theory necessitated that any narratives referring to earlier dates must have been fabricated. However, archeological finds have proven scribal activity in the area dates as far back as 1800 B.C.E. There was ample opportunity to record for posterity significant Bible events.

- From the mid-1930s until the 1970s Biblical Archaeology provided scholars with a whole new world of information. Imagine the excitement when biblical narratives in the books of Kings were attested in non-biblical sources. Finally, hard evidence that the Bible is "essentially historical." However, some intellectually dishonest archaeologists overstated the evidence and tainted the field.

- Even so, it is not a mistake to apply archaeology in an effort to evaluate the biblical accounts. The mistake is in expecting archaeology to *verify* the biblical accounts.

- One account that has not been verified, and in fact the archaeology can only repudiate, is the Exodus narrative.

PART III
THE WORDS OF THE WISE AND
THEIR RIDDLES
(Proverbs 1:6)

Overview: Although the Torah is not historical, that does not mean that it has no historical value. Readers from ancient times, through medieval times, and up until today have understood that Bible stories could be read allegorically. We have to learn to extract the valuable information from these stories, such as likely timeframe of authorship, in order to better understand the true meaning of the allegories.

13. Allegory Using Bible Characters

He said. Th' Almighty, nodding, gave consent;
And peals of thunder shook the firmament.
Henceforth a series of new time began,
The mighty years in long procession ran:
Once more the god-like David was restor'd,
And willing nations knew their lawful lord.
    John Dryden (1631-1700)
    from "Absalom and Achitophel,"

John Dryden (1631–1700), the first Poet Laureate of England, was appointed by King Charles II in 1668. Although there are no official duties attached to the position, the holder is expected to create poetic works to commemorate events with national significance. Dryden's 1681 poem "Absalom and Achitophel" purports to recount the circumstances that led Prince Absalom to attempt to seize the throne of his father, David. In the biblical account on which Dryden drew (2 Samuel 15–18), the succession line to David's throne had not been clarified. Seizing the opportunity, David's son Absalom, aided by David's wise but disloyal counselor Achitophel, took advantage of the popular resentment of David and attempted to take the throne for himself.

The Bible-reading public of the latter half of the 17th century was well aware of the numerous parallels between the biblical tale and the prevailing political situation of England. The Puritan Revolution (1640–1660) had ended with the restoration of Charles Stuart as King Charles II of England. But the royal succession had not been settled because Charles had no legitimate heir. James, duke of York, was Charles's brother and could have been the successor. However, succession to the throne by James, an avowed Roman Catholic, might well have engendered a new religious war. The Whigs, led by the earl of Shaftesbury, gathered behind the succession of Charles's handsome illegitimate son, James Scott, duke of Monmouth, who allowed himself to be used against his father. In the manner of the biblical Absalom, Monmouth was sent on a triumphant procession through the country and, like Absalom, was enthusiastically received. But Charles had

Shaftesbury imprisoned when he realized that the Whigs had overreached themselves.

Authors have long used allegory as a way to address a controversial topic. If Dryden had written about these people directly, he might have angered people on either side of the debate. Dryden was able to mask his commentary by framing it in an allegorical story. Understanding the author's historical circumstances may give us clues to deeper meaning of the allegory. For example, if an author in 1915 wrote a play with a German-Jewish character named Adolph, we would not pay special attention to that character's name. However, if the author in 1943 had created a German-Jewish character named Adolph, we would surely raise our eyebrows.

Before Shaftesbury's trial, Dryden wrote "Absalom and Achitophel" in the hope of influencing the grand jury's verdict. Ostensibly, the poem is set during the reign of David. All the names of the protagonists are taken from the Bible. But as Dryden's audience knew, David stood for Charles, Absalom for Monmouth, Achitophel for Shaftesbury, and so on. They knew this first of all because, from the pulpit, their preachers had been comparing Monmouth with Absalom even before Dryden wrote the poem. Second, the events in the poem corresponded broadly to the biblical tale, but specifically only to the events of Dryden's own time.

The poem "Absalom and Achitophel" is an allegorical poem—one with a hidden meaning, often moral or political in nature. George Orwell's *Animal Farm* is an allegory about the Russian Revolution. Arthur Miller's *The Crucible* is an allegory about McCarthyism. Instead of stating the facts of the situation in a dry or didactic way, writers use allegory to present a moral in a way that is engaging to the audience.

Religion was a central part of people's lives in the 17th century, a time which did not come with as many distractions as today. The connection to religion might have been through church attendance or through reading the Bible at home, or both, as a way to socialize and pass time. Because of their Bible reading and the sermons they heard, many people would have already been familiar with the biblical tale of Absalom's attempt to usurp David's throne. While reading Dryden's poem, they would have nodded their heads in agreement with a story well-known and been able to draw their own conclusions. Or, even better, reached the conclusions the author was subtly directing them to draw.

When examining the historical narrative traditions of the Torah, it is helpful to keep the use of allegories in mind. In the manner of Dryden, the Torah's writers set their tales in a historical period far distant from their own—in the time period between the creation of heaven and earth, and the death of Moses—and outside the land of Israel. As we have seen, contemporary archaeological research has revealed that the Torah's settings are as fictional as Dryden's.

14. Allegory Within the Bible

For we walk by faith, not by sight.   2 Corinthians 5:7

We saw in earlier chapters of this book that the Torah is unhistorical, a finding that has led some scholars to conclude that the work has no historical value. But the fact that the Torah is unhistorical does not mean that it may not be used as a source of significant historical information. It is, rather, a question of how to extract the historical information. As we saw, the primary failure of the biblical archaeology movement was not in the application of archaeology to the Bible, but in the expectation that archaeology would prove the Bible to be essentially historical.

The most productive method of interpreting the Torah is to regard it as historical and political allegory. By comparing the Torah with other parts of the Bible, and by enlisting the written and unwritten data provided by archaeological sources, we can argue that the stories about the wholly fictitious characters Abraham, Jacob, Joseph, Aaron, and Moses allude to characters such as Saul, David and Jeroboam, who are more firmly anchored in history. Similarly, the theological constructs "Covenant" and "God" can be understood as allegorical reflections of historical and political realities. Over the course of two millennia, the Hebrew Bible has often been read allegorically.

First applied in ancient Greece to the poems of Homer and Hesiod, allegory was used in two different ways: 1) to find support for philosophical theories in the writings of the venerated poets of antiquity, or 2) to defend the same ancient poets from charges that their work was offensive or unreasonable. By the late 5th century B.C.E., philosophers were systemically finding *hyponoiai*, "hidden meanings," in the work of the great poets.

Despite the antiquity of the allegorical method, the verb itself, *allegorein*, "to speak allegorically" and "to explain allegorically" is late Greek. The Septuagint—the 3rd/2nd century B.C.E. translation by Jewish scholars of the Bible into Greek—never indicates that the written works are allegorical. However, one of the most influential adherents of early Christianity was Paul (circa 4 C.E.–64 C.E.), who assigned allegory to many passages of the Hebrew Bible.

Paul the Apostle, also known as Saint Paul, and Saul of Tarsus, was a Roman citizen who was born Jewish and educated in Jerusalem, where he was initially an adversary of the early followers of Jesus. However, on the road to Damascus, Paul had a vision of Jesus which impelled him to convert. Paul then made it his business to spread the teachings of Jesus to everyone who would listen, and he wrote numerous letters in support of the new faith. Many of his letters, referred to as "epistles," have been preserved in the New Testament.

At the time of Paul, ethical and moral behavior of Jews was imposed by both the law as written in the Torah, and by an entire body of Jewish laws and practices that had evolved by Paul's time. There were members of the Jewish community who followed the laws as stipulated. But there were also people—some born Jewish and others not—who might have been looking for something different; these were the people whom Paul sought to convert to the teachings of Christ.

Paul's Epistle to the Galatians provides us with an example of how Paul, when trying to guide new converts, made extensive use of allegory. Using the biblical hero of Abraham and the children he fathered with two different women, Paul explains that the mothers of these children should be understood to be allegorical mothers. He allegorized people who blindly clung to established Jewish laws and practices as the off-spring of Hagar—Abraham's slave and concubine—and the followers of the teachings of Christ as the off-spring of Sarah—Abraham's wife:

> It is written that Abraham had two sons, the one
> by a slave-girl, the other by free-born woman.
> The slave-girl's son was born according to flesh,
> but the one of the freewoman through God's
> promise. *Now this is an allegory*. The two women
> represent two covenants: the one from Mount
> Sinai, which is Hagar, has children born into
> slavery . . . But the Jerusalem above is the free-
> woman, and she is **our** mother. (Galatians 4:22–
> 26, emphasis added)

According to Paul, Hagar is the allegorical representation of the first covenant—the one made at Sinai—which bound Israelites to the Torah law. Children born of female slaves were also slaves, therefore it is as if those people who continued to observe the laws given at Mount Sinai were similarly enslaved. Paul has equated the law-observing Jews in the Jerusalem of his day—the children of the covenant—to the enslaved children of the gentile slave woman, Hagar. (Paul forms his argument by making the Jews into gentiles!)

Paul believed that the covenant of Jewish law was too punitive, having the effect of excluding people from the Jewish community. He appealed to potential converts by declaring that there was a second covenant—what Paul calls in 2 Corinthians the "new covenant"—which was represented by Sarah. Sarah was a free woman and, likewise, the adopters of the second covenant were free from the law. Those people who accepted the new covenant did so by expressing their faith in Christ, as opposed to by strict adherence to Jewish law. Their faith in Christ would earn them the grace of God, which in turn would earn them entry into the "Kingdom of God" (Galatians 5) after death.

Paul next uses a passage in the book of Isaiah to bolster his case. By all accounts, Isaiah 54:1 is not about a "barren woman" who has been "deserted," but is instead an allegorical passage about the exiled nation of Israel returning home and becoming a strong multitude of people who will oust their enemies from their land. Paul uses an almost word-for-word quotation of Isaiah 54:1 to apply his own allegorical reading to the Genesis narrative, equating the children of Sarah (the free-born wife of Abraham) with the barren and deserted woman of Isaiah 54:

> For scripture says: "Rejoice, O barren woman
> who never bore a child; break into a shout of joy,
> you who have never been in labor; for the
> deserted wife will have more children than she
> who lives with her husband." (Galatians 4:27,
> quoted from Isaiah 54:1)

Paul's associative reading of Genesis and Isaiah assures his audience that:

1) The people who became the Christians were spiritually "barren" until they accepted Christ.

2) Those who labor under strict Jewish law are not promised salvation, but those who put their faith in Christ will be saved.
3) The offspring of Sarah—the Christians—will come to outnumber the Jews.

But more is involved than the numerical superiority of those justified by faith over those who keep the law:

> Now we, brothers, like Isaac, are children of the promise. But just as then the one born according to the flesh persecuted the one of the spirit, so also now. But what does Scripture say? "Drive out the slave-girl and her son, for the son of the slave-girl shall by no means share the inheritance with the son of the free-woman." (Galatians 4:28–30)

This is an allegorical reading of Genesis 21, when the free-born Sarah finally bore a son to Abraham and insisted—regarding the slave Hagar and her son Ishmael—that Abraham:

> Cast out that slave-woman and her son, for the son of that slave shall not share in the inheritance. (Genesis 21:10)

In Paul's time, Christians were in the minority and had been persecuted by the Jews. In Galatians 4, Paul claims that Sarah required the banishment of Hagar and Ishmael because Ishmael (the son born "according to the flesh," e.g. born into slavery) persecuted Isaac (the son born of "the spirit") by openly mocking Isaac during a feast (Galatian 4:49, interpretation of Genesis 21:8). Paul invokes Genesis 21 to make an allegorical (and prescient) prediction of the ultimate expulsion of the Jews and their suppression by the Christians.

According to Paul, Christians (whether Jews by birth or not) who follow the law will not share in the inheritance, because in seeking their justification through the law they will have become obliged to all of it and therefore are—like Jews who have not accepted Christ—slaves:

(slave) children of the flesh rather than (free) children of the spirit.

15. Allegory Alongside Literal Reading

"Literal" teaches what has been done. "Allegorical" teaches what we ought to believe.   paraphrased from John Wyclif (1330–1384), philosopher, theologian and reformer

Although Galatians 4:24 is the only time in the New Testament that the use of allegory is specifically identified, allegory had significant value to Christian interpreters of the Hebrew Bible. Sometimes the allegorical meaning could coexist with the literal. At other times an allegorical interpretation was required to displace the literal. And sometimes, when crucial doctrines were at stake, one had to be careful not to displace the literal by the allegorical.

Both the Jewish philosopher Philo of Alexandria (20 B.C.E.—50 C.E.) and the Christian church father Augustine (354—430 C.E.) warned against those who take allegorical interpretation too far. They recognized that the authenticity of these characters of old could come into question, tearing down religious foundations. For example, Paul and the writers of what would become the canonical gospels taught that Jesus was the messianic savior whose coming, literally, had been foretold in Hebrew Scriptures. While Paul allegorized the offspring of Sarah and Hagar in the Galatians passages, the following passage in the New Testament book of Matthew would be meaningless if the audience did not believe that David had existed in real life.[*]

> Turning to the assembled Pharisees, Jesus asked them, "What is your opinion about the Messiah? Whose son is he?" "The son of David," they

---

[*] Allegorical interpretations are also known in Islam, particularly among the Batiniah, who some Islamic believers consider to be heretical. The *bāṭiniyya*, "inward interpreters," of the faith teach that every sacred text has a hidden meaning concealed in allegories and other symbolic tropes. According to them, scripture functions to reveal truths to those who know, or can be taught, the code, while concealing information from those they consider unenlightened. (See Kholili Hasib, "The Sect of Batiniah; Past and Present," *Kalimah* 14 (March, 2014).)

replied. "How then is it," he asked, "that David
by inspiration calls him, 'LORD'? For he says [in
Psalms 110:1], 'The LORD said to my lord, "Sit at
my right hand until I put your enemies under
your feet".' If David calls him 'LORD,' how can
he be David's son?" Not a man could answer him
in reply, and from that day forward no one dared
ask him another question. (Matthew 22:41–46)

In this passage, Jesus and the Pharisees share the belief that King
David received divine inspiration about the coming of the Messiah,
which he recorded in Psalms 110. The Pharisees claim that the divine
passage foretells of a Messiah who will invite David to sit at his right
hand. But Jesus counters their interpretation when he points out that,
if the Messiah were a son of David, David would never refer to his
own son as "Lord." Jesus has bested the Pharisees by pointing out the
inconsistency in their own interpretation. Of course, if there is no
David, there is no argument to be made.

In a similar vein, Paul needed to use Hebrew Bible "history" to
support some of his own theological arguments. If Abraham was the
"forefather of us according to flesh" (Romans 4–5; Galatians 3), then
Abraham required fleshly existence. Accordingly, even Paul's
allegorical interpretation in Galatians 4 does not deny the historical
existence of Hagar, Sarah, Ishmael or Isaac, for that could lead to the
denial of Abraham's historical authenticity.

Paul, a Jew by birth and education, used Hebrew scriptures claiming
that a Messiah will come as evidence that Christ IS that Messiah. At
the same time, because Paul maintained that salvation will come from
faith in the crucified and risen Christ, he needed to dismiss the
necessity of following the Jewish laws in those self-same scriptures.
Allegory was one effective approach, even when the word allegory was
not specified:

Your self-satisfaction ill becomes you. Have you
never heard the saying, "A little leaven leavens all
the dough?" The old leaven of corruption is
working among you. Purge it out and then you
will be bread of a new baking. As Christians you

are unleavened Passover bread, for indeed our
Passover has begun; the sacrifice is offered—
Christ himself. So we who observe the festival
must not use the old leaven, the leaven of
corruption and wickedness, but only the
unleavened bread which is sincerity and truth. (1
Corinthians 5:6–8)

This passage follows Paul's denunciation of certain sexual practices among members of the Corinthian church (1 Corinthians 5) and immediately precedes his condemnation of swindlers, idolaters, slanderers, and drunkards in that same community. In Paul's allegorical reading, the leaven that is to be purged stands for corruption and wickedness. The unleavened bread has two related allegorical meanings: the Christian who has purged himself of corruption, and the quality of sincerity and truth.

Just as the biblical Passover began with the sacrifice of a special Passover offering, so the sacrifice of Christ begins with the new festival ("our Passover"), or what Paul calls elsewhere, the "way of life in Christ" (1 Corinthians 4). Although Paul's remarks are not directly addressed to the question of whether Christians should eat only unleavened bread on Passover, his allegorical interpretation has the potential to nullify the literal Hebrew Bible prohibition against eating real leaven on Passover.

As we can see from these examples, Paul used allegory to reinterpret the Hebrew Bible in a way that would garner more support for Christianity. This allegorical—indeed political—reinterpretation of the text does little to shed light on the true intent of the Hebrew Bible's writers.

16. Prophets and/or Philosophers

*When a house is being built which is to be made as strong as possible,
the building takes place in fine weather and in calm, so that nothing may
hinder the structure from acquiring the needed solidity.*
Origen (3rd century C.E.), scholar and theologian

One of the most influential figures in early Christian theology was Origen of Alexandria (circa 184–253 C.E.). Origen was a prolific writer, many of whose writings laid the foundation of Christian theology. Of particular interest to contemporary readers is Origen's attempt to show that certain scriptural verses demand an allegorical, rather than a literal, interpretation. Numbers 12 is one such chapter, according to Origen:

> Miriam and Aaron spoke against Moses because of the Cushite woman whom he had married, for he had married a Cushite woman; and they said, "Has the Eternal indeed spoken only through Moses? Has he not spoken through us also?" And God heard it. Now the man Moses was very meek, more than all men that were on the face of the earth. (Numbers 12:1–3, translation by the author)

Origen points out that, while the story begins with Miriam and Aaron criticizing Moses for marrying a Cushite woman, it immediately shifts in verse 2 to a boast by Miriam and Aaron about their own prophetic ability. Were this section meant literally, verse 2 should have continued the criticism with Miriam and Aaron insisting that Moses should have taken an Israelite wife. By completely changing the subject to the uniqueness of Moses as a prophet in verses 6–8, the Bible impels us to read the passages allegorically. The story is allegorically stating that Moses is the "spiritual law" (*spiritalis lex*), and the Cushite woman is the gentile church. Miriam is the superseded Jewish law-observing people, and Aaron the priesthood according to the flesh.

Jewish scholars also dealt with the problems raised by allegory.

Ancient Jewish tradition, later adopted by Christians, universally accepted that the Song of Songs was allegorical. It appeared more seemly for a book of the Bible to speak metaphorically of God's love for his people than literally and explicitly of human eroticism (see Song of Songs—a.k.a. Song of Solomon— 4:5 and 7:4 "Your breasts are like two fawns," for example). But allegory could go too far. Critics of the medieval Jewish philosopher Moses Maimonides (1135–1204)—the most influential Torah scholar of his time, and quite possibly of all time—claimed that he treated all of Scripture as a philosophical allegory. Maimonides himself did not concede that characterization.

Other scholars were much more explicit. Zerahiah of Barcelona (12th century) argued, as had Origen, that in certain cases an allegorical reading was demanded. Using the example of Job—a man who remained steadfast to God in the face of unbearable suffering— Zerahiah elaborates on a Talmudic statement (Babylonian Talmud Baba Batra, 15a) that Job had never existed in reality. The opening verse of the book of Job demonstrated that it was not to be taken literally:

> There was once a man in the land of *Uz* whose
> name was *Job*. That man was blameless and
> upright, one who feared God and turned away
> from evil. (Job 1:1–2, translation by the author)

Zerahiah pointed to the transparency of the name of Job's homeland, Uz-land, which means "land of counsel." Indeed, Hebrew philologists have noted that the author of Job connected the very name "Job" (*Iyyov*) with the Hebrew word for "antagonism" or "hatred" (*eivah*), which is most appropriate for one antagonized by God and treated hatefully by him.[15]

Although readers of the Bible from Paul and Philo onward had sought allegorical meanings in Scripture, most had assumed that the allegorical meaning could coexist with the literal and the historical. Those in the faith communities who had their doubts tended to express them in subdued fashion. In contrast, Zerahiah's critique of the historicity of one biblical book is unique in its articulate character:

If our stated proofs that Job is an allegory are
insufficient for the party of fools, we will
continue with further proof that this book was
composed as an allegory. For should you say that
Job and his companions did indeed exist, one
might come along and ask you how the sequence
of respondents was composed. For were you to
say that these men all assembled and each one
spoke his words and transcribed them in his own
idiom; and then afterward Elihu spoke his words
and transcribed them, and then God came
afterward and spoke them, a questioner might
respond and ask further: "Then who incorporated
their words in a single volume once they had
spoken their words?" And should you say that our
master Moses found their words written but
disjointed and scattered, and collected them and
wrote them down—where did he find God's
words, and who collected them from God's mouth
and wrote them down?[16]

Zerahiah also provided a modernist argument from the standpoint
of style, noting that:

...if Job and his companions were . . . not
allegorical, individual differences of speech should
have appeared among them . . . Job is stylistically
uniform from start to finish.[17]

The implications of Zerahiah's allegorical analysis of Job were not
lost on the medieval philosopher Joseph ibn Kaspi (1279–1340), who
at first seems to have taken exception to Zerahiah's analysis. Kaspi
noted that by using the same method, one could read the entire Bible
as allegory and deny its historicity. He wrote, scornfully:

I am amazed that both ancient and modern
scholars have doubted [the historicity of Job

> simply because it lacks precise chronological and
> geographic date] . . . For if we characterize the
> tale of Job and his companions as an allegory
> written by a sage to instill wisdom and faith in
> the heart of readers, the same might be said of the
> rest. If so, we have no Torah or Prophets of
> Sacred Writings of any kind. So what concern is
> it of ours if some of our blessed predecessors did
> not know when Job lived or where?[18]

Kaspi's antipathy to allegorizing the Bible is consistent with his dictum that "all the words of the Torah and the remainder of the Bible are, in my opinion, to be accepted in their own meaning, like the books on logic and nature of Aristotle."[19] However, upon closer inspection, we can make a good case that Kaspi may not actually have believed every word in the Bible to be completely true. In his commentary on Maimonides, Kaspi wrote a far more revealing paragraph about his understanding of the Bible:

> In order that the masses should not think that the
> prophets made up what they said and that these
> words were not from God, the prophets permitted
> themselves to lie by saying: "The Eternal said to
> Moses," or, "The Eternal said to me," and *all such
> similar phrases* (emphasis added). As the
> physicians have said: "It is better to amputate one
> infected finger than to let the entire body grow ill
> or die."[20]

Leonard Kravitz, who taught Philosophy at Hebrew Union College-Jewish Institute of Religion, observes that the second statement is completely consistent with Kaspi's overall philosophy. Kaspi, a thorough rationalist, believed that the people whom the Bible calls "prophets" were in reality philosophers. For Kaspi, following Aristotle, God is pure intellect. God is immaterial and never changes. God does not do anything; God just is. Kaspi wrote, "The intellect is God and God is the intellect."[21] If intellect is God, then philosophy *is* divine knowledge. Using that approach today, we might say the prophets were similar to such great minds as Socrates, Buddha, Voltaire, and Baruch (Benedict) Spinoza.

In his commentary on Maimonides, Kaspi cut to the chase: the prophets lied to the populace when they claimed to speak with God, because this was a claim the masses would more willingly accept. The true source of their knowledge was achieved through philosophy, by which the "prophet's knowledge of the future is based on deductive inference, since he or she is well acquainted with the world and with all details of natural causality."[22]

Kaspi similarly lied to his masses by his statement that "all the words of the Torah are to be accepted in their own meaning." He excused the lie by using an analogy of a surgeon inflicting a smaller wound (cutting off an infected finger) in order to save the rest of the body. The finger being the truth, but the body being the whole of the Israelite people. The amputation enabled the patient, the body of Israel, to live. Without prophecy—that is, philosophy—the entire body of Israel would have become ill and died. Kaspi's description of prophetic strategy is in fact a description of his own philosophical strategy.

The details of Kaspi's critique of Zerahiah demonstrate his concerns about the likely reaction of the "masses." Kravitz observes that it was common for medieval scholars to vilify unpopular opinions with which they secretly agreed. By condemning these opinions without refuting their substance, these same scholars would give voice to even more unpopular opinions of their own, and that is just what Kaspi did here. Let us look closely as what Kaspi buried in the core of his criticism of Zerahiah:

> And note that we have written in the Torah:
> "These are the generations of Noah . . . Noah had
> three sons" [Genesis 6:9-10] and the entire story
> of the deluge and the ark.

Kaspi's citation of the Noah tale is completely irrelevant to Zerahiah's reading of Job. Unlike Job, which provides minimal chronological data, the Noah tale is extremely precise. We are given Noah's age when the flood began, the stages of the flood, the day and month on which the ark landed in the mountains of Ararat, and how long Noah waited between sending out birds to find dry land. By referring to "the entire story of the deluge and the ark," Kaspi calls attention to the impossible-seeming events of the tale, which in turn call into question the historicity of the Torah itself—something that Zerahiah had not done at all. Whereas Zerahiah showed only why one biblical selection might be unhistorical, Kaspi provided criteria for regarding the entire Bible as unhistorical. Not only was Job to be read as allegory, but because prophets—the authors of Scripture—permitted themselves to lie, all of Scripture might be philosophical allegory.

For all their differences, the Jews Zerahiah and Kaspi agreed with the Christian Origen that allegory might be the essential nature of a biblical text. But that does not mean that the entire Bible text is unhistorical. There is much in the Bible outside the Torah that has been confirmed.

17. Truth in Myth

*After all, I believe that legends and myths are largely made of "truth,"
and indeed present aspects of it that can only be received in this mode; and
long ago certain truths and modes of this kind were discovered and must
always reappear.* J.R.R. Tolkien (1892–1973), author

To assert the obvious, all ancient myths must be read allegorically
in order to be understood fully, because the gods who populate the
myths never existed. At the same time, the language in which a myth
is related, the institutions and values presented in the myth, and the
depictions of the mythical characters inform us about the historical
human realities that brought myth into being. Often a myth informs
us about the circle in which it was told and the political and social
agenda that it advanced.

The same is true of the fairy tale, which allegorizes in much the
same way as the myth does. Once we have identified a story as a fairy
tale, we abandon certain avenues of historical investigation in favor of
others. The tale of the giant living at the top of the beanstalk, who
smells the blood of an Englishman and wants to grind his bones to
make bread, turns us away from investigating culinary proclivities of
giants and weight-bearing capacities of beanstalks, and instead toward
the possibility of marginalized people rising up against ogre-like
tyrants. Outside myths and fairy tales, the application of historical-
political allegorical study is of obvious value in the study of literary
works in which human traits are assigned to nonhumans. Anatole
France's *Penguin Island* and George Orwell's *Animal Farm* come readily
to mind.

Jewish scholars in the Middle Ages regularly interpreted some
stories in the Hebrew Bible allegorically because the not-found-in-real-
life characters make their historical impossibility as obvious as Greco-
Roman myths and European fairy tales. One such example is the
Garden of Eden story from Genesis 2–3, in which a snake talks and
trees confer wisdom or eternal life on those who eat their fruit.

Although the talking snake and trees place the story in the realm of
myth, there are plenty of aspects to the story that can help us date when
it might have been written. We can start with the historical

circumstance of God's act in planting the pleasure garden in Eden to provide for himself a lovely place to stroll through at the breezy time of day (Genesis 3:8). In the ancient world, it was common to assign the powers and perquisites enjoyed by human royalty to the great gods who populate myths. What this means is that Genesis 2–3, which describes God planting a garden, must reflect a period in which human rulers planted gardens. This indicates an Israel in the shadow of Assyria, as one function of the Assyrian royal gardens was to underline the king's "cosmic role in assuring the fertility and fruitfulness of the land."[23]

As early as the 12th century B.C.E., the Assyrian king Tiglath Pileser I (1115–1077 B.C.E.) showed a strong interest in horticulture, but it was not until the 9th century that the royal garden came into its own. It is then that we begin to see the kings of Assyria speaking eloquently of their luxuriant pleasure garden, the *kirimāhu*.[24] The 8th century B.C.E. king Sargon II of Assyria (not to be confused with the 24th/23rd century B.C.E. Sargon the Great of Akkad) boasts of his own pleasure garden. He also glories in the destruction of the royal tree and fruit gardens of Urartu (modern-day Armenia) because his action proves that his archrival, the king of Urartu, is no longer fit to rule.[25] The linguistic and cultural evidence from Assyria fits perfectly with the biblical information that the first named Israelite king to plant a royal garden was Ahab (1 Kings 21:2), the 9th-century king of northern Israel, who is mentioned in the inscriptions of Shalmaneser III of Assyria.

Because the Garden of Eden tale cannot be true literally, we are free to pursue the story's internal clues to its historical setting, proceeding from the obvious to the arcane. When trying to date the story, scholars note the following clues:

- The language of the Garden story is classical Hebrew of the period around 900–700 B.C.E.

- The only named divinity in the story has the Hebrew name the Eternal-Elohim (Hebrew: Yahweh-Elohim), the name of God found thus far only in Israel. Accordingly, the author was most certainly an Israelite.

- The Israelite author was aware of the sources of riches in other nations: "The gold of that land is good; bdellium (a tree-gum used in incense and medicine) is there, and lapis lazuli" (Genesis 2:12).

- Some contact with the Mesopotamian culture is presupposed because of the use of the term "Kerubim," or cherubs, which are posted to guard the way back into the Garden of Eden after God has banished Adam and Eve (Genesis 3:24). "Kerubim" comes from the ancient Akkadian language of the region that is now modern-day Iraq.

- The four river references are quite telling. The Pishon and the Gihon are given geographic detail, indicating the audience might be less familiar with these two rivers. The Tigris is given the geographic detail that it flows east of Assyria, from which we can surmise that, even if the audience did not know the Tigris specifically, they were aware of the Assyrians. And the fourth river, the Euphrates, is simply listed, indicating common knowledge among the audience (Genesis 2:10–14).

- Another detail is the curse after banishment: that Adam will have to till the ground but only "thorns and thistles shall it sprout for you" (Genesis 3:18). The term "thorns and thistles" is only used one other time in the Bible; in the 8th century B.C.E. book of Hosea (Hosea 10:8). Outside of the Bible, the same phrase can be found in the 8th century B.C.E. Assyrian royal annals of Sargon II.[26]

When it comes to the Garden of Eden story, we follow the leads of Origen, Zerahiah, and Kaspi, who argued that when a biblical text cannot be taken at face value—because like a myth, the story contains an abundance of fantastic elements—it must be read allegorically. Taking the above points into consideration, scholars have concluded that this part of the book of Genesis was written at a time when Assyria was beginning to dominate Israelite political life, but not as early as the Assyrian conquest of the northern kingdom (720 B.C.E.). The audience for the Garden of Eden story was likely one of small farmers and land tillers who were used to the vagaries of farming. What is missing from the story is any sense that rapacious large landholders would drive the farmers off their land. That practice would come later and is something that drew the righteous ire of the prophets Amos and Isaiah (second half of the 8th century B.C.E.)[*], when the successful

---

[*] For examples of their ire, see Amos 9:13-15, which includes the line, "Nevermore to be uprooted from the soil I have given them," and Isaiah 5:7-

seizure of small farms by large landowners was taken for granted. If we accept that this missing element can be used to help us date the Garden of Eden story, we might date the story as being written earlier than mid-8th century B.C.E.

There are other biblical narratives that describe events in which the laws of nature are *not* violated. For example, unlike the Eden story, the tale of Joseph—a tale that we will study later in this book—contains events that could conceivably be historical, with the exception of a few exaggerated life spans. In consequence, numerous attempts have been made to find its setting in 2nd millennium Egypt. But the believability of the characters and a realistic setting of the story do not necessarily amount to authenticity of the tale; they may just as easily indicate allegory.

When examining the historical narratives in the Torah, we must follow the linguistic and cultural clues in order to date the composition of the text. But we should keep allegories like Dryden's "Absalom and Achitophel" in mind and remain cognizant that some narratives are allegories reflecting the historical circumstances and ideological concerns of the writer at the time of composition, rather than being reliable witnesses to their alleged settings.

10, which includes the line, "He hoped for justice, But behold injustice; For equity, But behold iniquity!"

Summary – Part III

- Over the centuries, allegory has been an effective tool in storytelling. It is also often used to convey a hidden meaning, typically a moral or political one.

- Although this book shows that the Torah (Pentateuch) is unhistorical, this does not mean that the Torah is not a source of significant historical information. I believe that the most productive method of interpreting the Torah is to regard it as historical and political allegory.

- The Bible does not specifically state that it is allegorical, but sages as far-removed as Paul the Apostle—the most important figure in early Christianity—and up through the Middle Ages turned to allegory to interpret many biblical passages. However, Jewish and Christian interpreters drew a line at passages that they believed would, or should, be read literally.

- For Bible stories that must be read allegorically, like the Garden of Eden story with magic trees and an upright-walking and talking snake, we can pursue the story's internal clues to help us date the authorship of the work.

- Although some biblical tales belong in the realm of myth, it does not mean that the entire Bible is mythical. There is plenty that has been corroborated by extra-biblical sources. Often a myth informs us about the historical human realities of the audience, in addition to the political and social agenda that the myth advanced.

- Even so, this should not be taken to mean that all believable stories (stories that lack fantastic elements) are historic fact.

- These are topics that philosophers, academics, and clergy, as well as others, continue to debate.

PART IV
CROSS THE JORDAN
(Joshua 1:1)

Overview: The traditions preserved in the Torah were written over a timespan of at least 800 years, and those in the Bible span several hundred years more. Changing circumstances of the Israelites—notably Pre-exilic, Exilic, and Postexilic—required the writers to meet the ever-changing needs of their audiences. Additionally, geographic differences made way for different traditions: specifically, the Foreignness Tradition from the northern region, and the Origin Tradition from the southern region. All of these "traditions" reflect the reality of the Israelites at various stages in their history, culminating in the 6th century B.C.E. belief that the Eternal was the sole god in existence.

18. The Making of Heroes

Show me a hero and I'll write you a tragedy.
F. Scott Fitzgerald (1896–1940), author

John Bright was an American Bible scholar whose book *A History of Israel* was first published in 1959 and updated in four subsequent editions (including a posthumous publication in 2000). Virtually every American Biblicist or seminary graduate of a certain age was required to read his *History*. Bright's book was deservedly popular in circles of religious moderates for its attempt to balance the critical study of Israelite history with respect and reverence for the biblical tradition. Regarding the historical character of a central biblical tradition, Bright wrote:

> There can really be little doubt that ancestors of
> Israel had been slaves in Egypt and had escaped in
> some marvelous way. Almost no one today would
> question it . . . Although there is no direct witness
> in Egyptian record to Israel's presence in Egypt,
> the Biblical tradition a priori demands belief: it is
> not the sort of tradition any people would invent.

Prior to World War I, archaeological expeditions in Israel were backed by parties with an interest in preserving the integrity of the written Bible, for both religious and political reasons. John Bright's contention that the story of Israel's enslavement in Egypt must be historical because no ancient people would have made up such a demeaning tale about themselves fit in well with this narrative.

Excavations continued after World War I and the British, who had assumed control of the land, applied history and scientific method to what the archaeology exposed. This work continued after World War II and the establishment of the State of Israel. But excavations take time and money, and even today only a very small percentage of the archaeological sites from the biblical period have been excavated. In the words of Shakespeare, in the end the "truth will out;" but we are nowhere near the end.

Even so, by 1988 enough archaeological evidence had been unearthed to support conclusions differing from those reached by Bright. For example, in his book *Ancient Israel: A New History of Israelite Society*, Niels Peter Lemche wrote:

> It is generally acknowledged by scholars that the traditions about Israel's sojourn in Egypt and the Exodus of the Israelites are legendary and epic in nature.

Although the archaeology dismantles the deductive (or "a priori") reasoning and concludes that the enslavement and Exodus of the Israelites was not historical, it does not mean that the story of the Exodus is without meaning. A few decades ago in the world of Bible scholarship *literary criticism* was synonymous with *source criticism*. Contemporary Bible scholars have learned that source criticism—the identification of the literary sources or documents from which ancient compliers, redactors, and editors produced our existing Bible—differs from literary criticism. Literary criticism takes into consideration narrative, plot, development of theme, and development of character. Both aspects are instrumental to understanding the story the Bible tells.

The Exodus tradition of the Bible provides us with a compelling narrative; arguably one of the most compelling narratives in the western world. The Egyptian servitude traditions lead naturally to the triumphant conquest traditions. A good example is provided in the following passage in which the humble beginnings of the people Israel serve as a prelude to God's response to their outcries, and as a description of how his saving acts brought about Israel's present happy state:

> My ancestor was a wandering Aramaean who descended to Egypt, sojourning there few in number. But there he became a nation, powerful and numerous. The Egyptians ill treated us, humiliated us, and set hard labor upon us. But we cried out to the Eternal, our ancestral god, who took to heart our humiliation at oppressive labor. The Eternal took us out of Egypt with a hand

mighty and an arm outstretched, accompanied by
great terror and by signs and wonders. He
brought us to the very place. He gave us this land,
a land flowing with milk and honey.
(Deuteronomy 26:5–9, translation by the author)

From a contemporary literary perspective, the biblical accounts of
Israel's journey from servitude to freedom are an example of the
common motif of the hero who—with the aid of divine providence—
rises from less-than-ideal origins. This common motif runs through
multiple stories with which many, if not most, readers will be familiar:
e.g., Romulus and Remus, Jane Eyre, Pip (*Great Expectations*),
Superman, Cinderella, and Harry Potter, to name a few.

Another such tale from the ancient Near East, is the story of Sargon
of Akkad (circa 2334–2279 B.C.E.). According to a legend written
centuries after his time, Sargon was the son of an unknown father and
a priestess who bore the title Entu, whose position carried with it an
obligation of celibacy. Having violated the rule and fearing detection,
Sargon's mother put her son in a basket and abandoned him in the
river.[27] Sargon was rescued from the water and, when he was old
enough, put to work in a garden where he was spotted by Ishtar, the
goddess of love and war. Ishtar granted her love to Sargon, enabling
him to become the founder of the first empire in recorded history:
Akkad (or Agade).

Ancient Near East historian Hayim Tadmor (1923-2005), who
taught at Hebrew University of Jerusalem, designated these stories of
unlikely heroes as "autobiographical apology." Numerous examples of
these types of tales have been found in literary compositions from
Egypt, among the Hittites, in the small Syrian kingdoms, and especially
in Assyria and Babylonia.[28] The hero in the "autobiographies" is a king
who comes to the throne in an irregular fashion. In the Bible the group
has taken the place of the individual, so the role of the hero-king who
rises from obscurity or humble origins is played by the entire people
of Israel. That is, the humble origins of Israel in Egypt are a necessary
prelude to the greatness brought about by divine favor.

19. The Foreignness Tradition:
A "Northern Kingdom" Innovation

I have been a stranger in a foreign land.   Exodus 2:22

Samaria, the capital city of the northern kingdom of Israel, fell to the Assyrians in 720 B.C.E. The Assyrian strategy when they conquered a land was to remove local inhabitants from the land and replace them with other groups.[29] The Assyrian conquest resulted in the popular legend of "the Ten Lost Tribes of Israel."

During this tumultuous time, stories were told, shared, and written down. Through linguistic analysis of the Bible, we know that parts of the book of Judges, as well as the books of Amos, Hosea, 1st Isaiah, Micah, Joshua, Zephaniah, and Samuel date to the 8th century B.C.E. While it is true that these books were subject to editing over the centuries, there is enough linguistic information to make it possible to identify which portions are more ancient than others.

Some of the 8th century B.C.E. lore claims that the Israelites were promised the land of Canaan by God and that they won it as attacking foreigners. This Foreignness Tradition is indisputable in pre-exilic (pre-8th century B.C.E.) texts. One example comes from the detailed prose account of the Exodus and conquest traditions in Joshua 24, set at the northern sanctuary of Shechem.[30] Another example comes from the prophet Micah, who refers by name to the three primary heroes of the Exodus:

> For I brought you up from the land of Egypt and
> redeemed you from the slave house, and I sent
> before you Moses, Aaron, and Miriam. (Micah
> 6:4, translation by the author)

The prophet Amos also knows the Exodus traditions, which he sets in the larger context of migrations. According to Amos, Israel was not the only people whose movements have been directed by God:

> Are you not like the Ethiopians to me, O people
> of Israel? Says God. Did I not bring Israel up

from the land of Egypt and the Philistines from
Captor and the Arameans from Kir? (Amos 9:7,
translation by the author)

Archeological investigations of neighboring peoples show us what
types of evidence to look for in order to determine the veracity of the
Exodus tradition. For example, Israeli archaeologist Trude Dothan
(1922–2016), who taught at Hebrew University of Jerusalem, focused
her study on Philistine settlements in Israel. Dothan's excavations
revealed that the Philistines were undoubtedly foreign settlers who
came to the coast of current day Israel from their home elsewhere in
the Aegean (roughly, modern-day Greece or western Turkey). Dothan
said of one coastal Philistine settlement, "these people introduced by
means of *material culture, cultic practices, and architecture,* a new ethnic
element which reflected their origins in the Aegean"[31] (emphasis
added).

If the Israelites had also come to Canaan as a "new ethnic element,"
we would expect to unearth similar elements of newness. The Kadesh-
Barnea area, located in the modern-day Sinai Peninsula (where Egypt
adjoins Israel), would be a likely area to search for evidence of the
Exodus traditions. According to the Bible, Moses dispatched the spies
from Kadesh-Barnea (Numbers 13), and it was there that Moses
himself was barred from the Promised Land. Also, it was at Kadesh-
Barnea that the prophet Miriam, the sister of Moses, was buried
(Numbers 20). Clearly, Kadesh-Barnea was an area that the biblical
Israelite nation spent some time.

Amihai Mazar (born: 1942), professor at the Institute of
Archaeology of the Hebrew University of Jerusalem, led excavations
of the Kadesh-Barnea area and published the following observation in
The Archaeology of Ancient Israel:

> Not one Late Bronze or (first) Iron Age . . . sherd
> [fragment found by archeologists] was found in
> the survey, which combed the oasis of Kadesh-
> Barnea and its vicinity, or in the systematic
> excavation of the mound. [32]

Although the northern prophets Micah and Amos were familiar with the Exodus traditions, the biblical narrative of Egyptian servitude and the Exodus has simply not been supported by the archaeological findings. Its absence from some biblical texts provides us with an intriguing starting point.

For example, one of our earliest extant biblical records, Deuteronomy 33—a pre-monarchic, southern region of Judah poem (set before 10th century BCE but likely written in the 9th–8th century BCE)—makes no reference whatsoever of the Exodus from Egypt. References to the Exodus are likewise rather sparse in the text of the Prophet Isaiah identified as 8th century writings (chapters 1–39, or First/Proto-Isaiah). In a 1971 publication, University of Glasgow biblical scholar Robert Carroll (1941–2000) discerned that the original "northern tradition of the Exodus" was virtually unknown in the traditions that scholars identify as coming from southern (Judahite) writers.[33]

Understanding the political upheaval in the region can illuminate why there are differences in the narratives of northern and southern writers. In roughly 922 B.C.E. there was an uprising against the united monarchy, which resulted in the land being divided into two separate kingdoms: Judah in the south with its capital at Jerusalem, and Israel in the north with its capital at Samaria. That 200-year separation allowed ample time for divergent histories to evolve. However, the Assyrian invasion of Israel—which led to the 720 B.C.E. fall of Samaria—caused many northern Israelites to journey south and seek refuge in Judah, effecting, at least on some scale, a reunification. The new arrivals from the north brought with them their native literature and traditions, including the traditions of the Exodus, which depicted the people of Israel as foreigners who traveled from Egypt and gained their territory as conquering invaders.

The book of Exodus says that the Israelites were in servitude to Egypt and then the multitudes (roughly two million people) left Egypt and wandered through the desert until, with God's help, they conquered the Promised Land. The lack of discovery at Kadesh-Barnea, and likewise at sites in Jordan where the Bible says Israel traveled after leaving the desert, do not support the Exodus story. This lack of evidence caused Mazar and other archaeologists to conclude that this story is fictitious because:

> There is nothing in the archaeological record to
> suggest that the settlers came from outside the
> land of Israel, as stated in the biblical tradition.[34]

Borrowing Dothan's language from her exploration of Philistine settlements, we conclude that because Israelite material culture, cultic practices, and architecture do not reflect a new ethnic element, Israel's claim to foreignness cannot have originated in a historical reality. Given that these traditions arose in the north, we must now ask why they arose. Israel's outsider status must be considered an ideological statement. In other words, it was not that Israel elevated foreignness to distinctiveness, but rather that Israel asserted its distinctiveness by claiming foreignness.

The ideological underpinnings of the Foreignness Traditions could be classified as either religious or political. Sometimes, however, religious and political objectives share the same goal. The tradition that Israel originated outside Canaan is allegorical for Israelite religious *distinctiveness*. The group was able to latch onto and rally behind a particular notion of distinctiveness that Peter Machinist (born: 1944), professor at Harvard University, named "the making of a counter-identity." We are "them," we are "new," we are "different." We are the group "Israel."

Machinist isolated approximately 433 distinctiveness passages in the Hebrew Bible, held together by a common content:

> [The biblical authors used] this very status as
> newcomer and marginal . . . as the basis for a
> positive picture. In other words, if newcomer and
> marginal had meant, say, for the Egyptians,
> barbarian, immoral and chaotic, in the Bible they
> became proof of the choice of "the almighty
> God"—of new freedom, purity and power . . . All
> speak of Israel or one of its representative groups
> of individuals, including its god, as distinct from
> outsiders, whether humans or gods . . .
> Admittedly, not all of Israel's components were
> from the outside . . . but even in the most radical
> of modern theories about Israelite state formation

in Palestine, the outside component is conceded a
crucial role.[35]
There really is an "us" over against a "them." The
more sharply they (the biblical authors) affirm
the boundary, the more we can be certain that the
reality was muddier and more fragile.[36]

Of course, claims of distinctiveness are not unique to Israel. Analogous claims were made in the cultures of Israel's large neighbors: Egypt and Mesopotamia. But precisely in those older and more populous cultures, distinctiveness is closely connected with notion of, according to Machinist, "autochthonous origins—of a primordial connection between the people and a particular territory."[37] Machinist goes on to say that in Egypt and Mesopotamia, "the tendency was to equate national history [and] the origins of particular cities and urban regions, with cosmogony,"[38] that is, tales about the origin of the universe theory. Myth and ritual articulated the notion that the proper places of the great Egyptian and Mesopotamian cities and their inhabitants had been fixed by the gods at creation.

Machinist observes that, in contrast, Israel's claim that the people come from the outside is itself distinct, if not unique. The northern Israelite ideology of foreignness was based at least in part on some component of Israel originating as a people outside its land. But that "outside" would have been Jordan, itself part of Canaanite culture.

20. Israelites Against the Lawless Lechers

Ethics and equity and the principles of justice do not change with the calendar.   D. H. Lawrence (1885–1930), author

Biblical writers who knew the Foreignness Tradition were trying to create an us-against-them narrative by depicting "Israel" as a self-conscious entity distinct from its surroundings; its foreignness as "proof of the choice of the almighty God."[39] Israel's ideological self-consciousness and religious distinctiveness are expressed by the Torah's repeated denial of Israel's Canaanite heritage. According to the Torah, the priesthood, the sacrificial cult, the tabernacle, the festivals, most of the covenant traditions to serve God exclusively and the laws governing most of life's activities, originated outside the Promised Land.[40] By claiming that Israel's most important religious institutions had originated in the desert—the "no-man's land" (Jeremiah 2:6) where God found the people (Deuteronomy 32:10)—the writers of the Torah strengthened the claims they wished to make for Israelite distinctiveness. Particularly illustrative is Leviticus 18:

> The Eternal spoke to Moses, saying, "Speak to the
> Israelite people and say to them: I am the Eternal
> your god. You shall not emulate the practices of
> the land of Egypt where you dwelt, nor shall you
> emulate the practices of the land of Canaan where
> I am taking you. Not their statutes shall you
> follow but *my* norms you shall observe and you
> shall take care to follow *my* statutes. I am the
> Eternal, your god." (Leviticus 18:1–4, translation
> by the author, emphasis added)

The phrases "practices of Egypt" and "practices of Canaan" are used pejoratively here and are another way that the Israelites emphasized their distinctiveness: by claiming that their god expected superior behavior from his followers. The chapters of Leviticus that follow this selection list the "abominations"—sexual, cultic, and moral—allegedly favored by Canaanites. Indeed, Leviticus 18:27–28 asserts that these abominations had polluted Canaan so thoroughly that the land itself revolted and "vomited" out the Canaanites. Not content to let the members of the audience draw the inference themselves, the writer of the chapter informs the Israelites that they too will be regurgitated if they persist in Canaanite practices.

The Bible depicts the Canaanites as a bunch of lawless lechers who delighted in abominable practices. The generally accepted picture of debased Canaanites was so pervasive that even scholars who studied and admired much of Canaanite culture, like William F. Albright, felt no misgivings about referring to Canaanites as "low level" and "relatively primitive." However, recent research has required contemporary scholarship to retreat from its uncritical acceptance of this belief. Donald B. Redford (born: 1934), of Pennsylvania State University, once commented that, "In the historical pastiche that ancient Israel fabricated to justify its ingress, all the iniquity of the ages is heaped upon the Canaanites, who thereby became the most maligned race in history."[41]

Biblical narrative claims that God required his followers to act to a standard of ethics and morals unknown in their neighbors, and that a fear of God incentivized the Israelites toward obedience to these divine commands. However, research has shown that people in neighboring communities also worshipped gods who promoted the cause of justice in their societies. The execution of justice was usually left to rulers whom the gods had designated. These same rulers provided the gods with temples where they might be properly served, just as Israelite kings did for their god, the Eternal.

The fictional Ugaritic King Daniel (the hero in a 14th century B.C.E. text) was praised for "getting justice for the widow, and adjudicating the case of the fatherless." King Yehimilk of Byblos in Phoenicia (present-day Lebanon) prided himself on being "a king of justice and a king of righteousness before the holy gods."[42] In Egypt, justice was embodied in the great goddess Ma'at. In Mesopotamia, law was often personified by the gods Kittu (Justice) and Misharu (Equity); and Shamash, the all-seeing sun god, was hymned as "judge of gods and humans" and as "Lord of Law."[43] Kings Lipit-Ishtar (Sumer, circa 1870–1860 B.C.E.) and Hammurabi (Babylonia, circa 1810–1750 B.C.E.) explicitly told their audiences that they had compiled "law codes" because the gods had designated them to promote law and justice.[44]

Rituals in ancient Mesopotamia included the incantation series Shurpu, likely dating from the 14th century B.C.E. but possibly even earlier, which cataloged the sins that people committed—or were likely to commit—such as cheating on weights and measures, marking boundaries falsely, having intercourse with the wife of a neighbor, omitting the name of a god from an incense offering, disarranging an altar, and eating the taboo food of a city.[45] Similar codes of conduct prevailed in Egypt. The Middle Egyptian work *Going Forth by Day* was a set of instructions that people should take with them when they died, so that they would know what to tell the divine judge who examined them before they passed into the next life. Buried in tombs, this composition—also known as *The Book of the Dead*—directed its readers to proclaim their innocence of blaspheming the gods, doing violence to a poor man, killing, depriving cattle of fodder, damaging the bread of a god, having sexual relations with a boy, and disregarding the time of sacrifice.[46] Naturally, "ethics and morals" varied from one society to the next. For example, marrying one's sister's daughter might be viewed as a meritorious act in one culture but as incest in another.

Some of the prohibitions regarding customs ascribed to other cultures—like blaspheming God, having intercourse with the wife of a neighbor, or eating taboo foods—were present in early Israelite law and remain well-known prohibitions today. Even if the other cultures did not actually participate in these objectionable practices, the fact is that it is human nature for people to believe lies about people they consider "other."

Now that we know that Israel was not correct in its claim that only their god dictated ethics and morals, we have to ask the purpose of the biblical passages that make this claim. The assertion that Israel practiced superior norms and statutes helped to foster Israelite religious, social, and political solidarity. Israel was encouraged to maintain its solidarity by asserting its distinctiveness from its neighbors, a distinctiveness that—according to the Torah—was closely related to Israel's foreign origins. As long as Israelites were conscious of their foreignness, they would be able to maintain their alleged religious and moral superiority. As foreigners with no roots in Canaan or Egypt, they would find it easier to heed the admonitions of the authors of the Torah to reject Canaanite and Egyptian practices.

21. The Origin (Indigenous) Tradition

God appeared to Abram and said, "I will assign this land to your offspring." Genesis 12:7

Genesis chapter 2 describes God's creation of just two people: Adam and Eve. The entire population of the world is said to spring from them. Complicating their procreation effort is a murder in just the second generation, when Cain kills his brother Abel in Genesis 4. Nevertheless, the human population soldiers on and expands.

Unfortunately, because of the wickedness of man in the time of Noah, God had second thoughts about his creation:

> . . . the Eternal regretted that he had made man on
> earth, and his heart was saddened. The Eternal
> said, "I will blot out from the earth this human
> race whom I created." (Genesis 6:6–7)

Noah and his family survive the flood and, generations later, a man named Terah is born who goes on to have three sons of his own. God changes the name of Terah's son Abram to Abraham. Terah and his offspring, including his son Abraham, journey from the city of Ur in southern Babylonia toward the land of Canaan in the 18th century B.C.E. (if we translate biblical chronology into our own dating system). Although the stories of Terah and his offspring appear at the beginning of the Bible we should not assume that they were written first. It is generally agreed by scholars that these traditions are among the later stories in the Torah.

To understand how these stories might have arisen, we need to look at the next political upheaval that resulted from invasion. Roughly 130 years after the Assyrian invasion of Israel, Babylonian king Nebuchadnezzar II (reign 605–562 B.C.E.) attacked Judah in 597 B.C.E. and then again in 587 B.C.E. The culminating attack in 586 B.C.E. resulted in the devastation of the city of Jerusalem, including the destruction of the Temple where the Israelites worshipped their god. Both attacks are recorded in the Bible, in 2 Kings chapters 24 and 25—and the first was also recorded in a Babylonian chronicle—

providing evidence to scholars that these attacks (though not necessarily the recorded details) were actual occurrences.

The Babylonians forced those leaders of Judah who would not willingly submit to Babylonian rule into captivity in their capital city of Babylon or in other Babylonian cities. The Babylonians allowed Israelites who were not among the elites to remain in place. Even so, because Jerusalem was devastated by war, some of those Israelites who might have been allowed to stay chose to leave the city. There was safety in numbers and people might have sought out communities where there were other Jews. If they had looked to Egypt, they would have found Israelite/Jewish communities, but these communities should not be conflated with the fictional body of Israelites who, tradition claims, were slaves in Egypt.

One such Israelite community was located on the island of Elephantine, located at the first cataract of the Nile River in the south of Egypt. It is likely that around 650 B.C.E. there was a military agreement between Judah and Egypt, resulting in the installation of Jewish troops in an outpost on Elephantine in order to check aggression from the neighboring Nubians. A discovery of as many as 175 letters and business documents written in Aramaic—some as early as the 5th century B.C.E.—attest to the existence of a thriving Jewish community in Egypt at Elephantine. Also, the prophet Jeremiah, who prophesied from 626 B.C.E. (according to the book of Jeremiah) until after the Babylonian invasion, makes reference to "all the Judeans living in the land of Egypt" (Jeremiah 44:1). Although there is no record of Jeremiah's death, scholars believe he lived his final years in Egypt. Yes, there were communities—but they were not the *600,000 men allegedly enslaved in Egypt* a millennium earlier.

Thomas L. Thompson (born: 1939), who taught at the University of Copenhagen, provides an important starting point for our investigation to date the biblical tales that do not know the northern, Foreignness Tradition. These southern traditions belong to what Thompson terms "The Toledoth of Terah: The Story of Abraham," and they claim that the Israelites had been in Canaan for centuries.[47] "Toledoth" is Hebrew for offspring, and Terah, as we said, is the name of Abraham's father. Evidence from the language used—along with geographical and historical references—indicates that "The Toledoth of Terah" tales originated after 539 B.C.E., when the Persian Empire had granted Jews living abroad the right to return to their ancient homeland. The Toledoth of Terah tradition belongs to the Priestly source which has clear indications that—at least in its final form— dates to the 6th century B.C.E. Persian period.

For example, when God instructs Moses in detail about the attire to be worn by the priests when entering the holy place, he says:

> You shall also make for them linen breeches to
> cover their nakedness; they shall extend from the
> hips to the thighs. (Exodus 28:42)

Apparently, it was a concern that as the priest entered the holy place, or Tent of Meeting, his tunic would fly open and he would flash God. The punishment for flashing God, according to Exodus 28:43, was death. Breeches would have provided the necessary modesty, but breeches were not known in Judah at the time in question. According to biblical dating, the Exodus would have taken place in the 14th/13th century B.C.E. Scholars trace the creation of breeches to China, where the innovation would have aided in the comfort of horse riding. The oldest discovered trousers have been radiocarbon dated to between the 13th and 10th century B.C.E. However, the use of breeches did not travel west into Persia until centuries later, as documented by art historians who find no evidence of the arrival of breeches in the region prior to their appearance in Persian reliefs of the 6th century B.C.E. The Persians, who mastered the effective use of calvary in war, conquered Babylonia in the second half of the 6th century B.C.E. and assumed control of Judah. It was they who introduced breeches to the Israelites.[48] Thus, breeches for Israelite priests in the 14th/13th century B.C.E. are anachronistic.

The 539 B.C.E. Persian defeat of the Babylonians brought more than just pants to Judah. The Persians were responsible for the spread of the Aramaic language, which was becoming the lingua franca of the region (as Akkadian had been a millennium earlier). Eventually, Aramaic would replace Hebrew as the language of the Jews. This change explains why certain books of the Hebrew Bible, such as Daniel and Ezra, were originally written in Aramaic. Persian rule also allowed some of the Jews who had been exiled by the Babylonians, roughly 48 years earlier, to return to Judah by granting permission for those people to return to their ancient homeland.

The Jews returning to their ancestral land did not want to be perceived as foreigners. Their former land "Judah"—Hebrew: *Yehudah*—had become a Persian province called, in Aramaic, Yehud. Through the Toledoth traditions, they created a new origin story that, as Thompson points out, conveyed a strong ideological message that Israel is not a foreigner in Canaan but was formed in place and is "indigenous." The Jews were fulfilling a divine plan put in place by God immediately after Noah's flood. Any opposition to Jewish claims to the land was a challenge to that divine plan. The land had been clearly marked for the Israelites by God when he said to Abraham, "I will assign this land to your offspring." In biblical chronology, that promise was made in the 18th century B.C.E.! However, critical scholarship of the "Toledoth of Terah" tales reveals that—based on their language, geographical and historical references—they must have originated after 539 B.C.E. That is, after the exiled Jews were able to return.

Similarly, the book of Chronicles, a biblical book composed in the 4th to 3rd century B.C.E and preserved in the section of the Hebrew Bible called the "Writings," shares the "indigenous" ideology of the Toledoth traditions in the Torah. Israeli Biblicists Yairah Amit and Sara Japhet contend that the Exodus tradition in the book of Chronicles is muted and underplayed to the point of virtual absence, creating the impression that Israel had always been in the land before the exile.

These are the two traditions at work in the Bible: First, and centuries older, we have the Foreignness Tradition that served to distance Israel from its Canaanite relatives by creating a new identity for itself, as a conqueror bringing a new and superior culture. Second, we have the Origin (Indigenous) Tradition that claimed the Jews had always been in Israel and were just coming back to what had always been their homeland. The Jews who returned from exile (post-539 B.C.E.) did not want to be identified as outsiders. For them, and subsequently for their descendants, exile from the land of Israel had to be presented as an abnormality, an aberration. This new "history" necessitated the conscious and deliberate devaluation of the Foreignness Tradition.

Every year at Passover, the Exodus of the Israelites out of bondage, through the desert, and into the Promised Land of Canaan is celebrated—demonstrating the lasting impact of the stories from the Foreignness Tradition. Even so, both traditions are preserved in the Bible.

22. Pre-Exilic, Exilic, and Postexilic

I know how men in exile feed on dreams.
Aeschylus (525–456 B.C.E.), poet

Before we can once again discuss the Egyptian servitude and the Exodus narrative, let's review what scholars have generally agreed upon regarding the movement of the Jews during and after the exile. Judah fell to the Babylonians early in the 6th century B.C.E., and by 586 B.C.E. the Israelite leaders who were not accommodating of Babylonian rule were forced into exile in Babylonia (in modern-day southern Iraq). Babylonia was more advanced militarily, economically, scientifically, and culturally than Judah.

One outstanding cultural contribution of the Babylonians was King Hammurabi's (circa 1810–1750 B.C.E.) collection of laws concerning aspects of religion, agriculture, administration, and business. This collection, popularly known as the Code of Hammurabi, was carved on a stone slab, referred to as a stela. After the original was produced, copies were made during the next thousand years and displayed all over the middle east. In 1901, the original stela was recovered in present-day Iran, and it can be seen on display today at the Louvre Museum in Paris, France. The impact of this collection of laws on human history has been so significant that modern-day replicas of the stela can be found in museums in Belgium, Iran, and Russia (among others), and there are several replicas throughout the United States.[49]

The Babylonian's scientific advances included the recording of the movement of the stars and planets, the division of each month into 30 days, and the use of the sexagesimal system (base 60)—which they inherited from the Sumerians—to give us the 60-minute hour, and the 60-second minute. Culturally, what many scholars consider the oldest surviving great work of literature, the *Epic of Gilgamesh*, began with Sumerian myths that the Babylonians expanded and transformed into one epic story in their own Akkadian language.

It was in this culture that former residents of Judah found themselves in the exilic and postexilic periods. *Exilic* and *postexilic* are primarily theological constructs. *Exilic* means the time of the Babylonian exile. *Postexilic* indicates the time after the Babylonian empire fell to Cyrus II (600–530 B.C.E.) of Persia in 539 B.C.E. Conquerors before Cyrus were brutal in their treatment of the conquered people. As we know, nonconforming leaders were exiled. Conquerors would sometimes impose their own religion and culture on the newly conquered people. If you were a successful attacker, your god was clearly better! He would surely be pleased to have a wealth of new subjects worshipping him and helping to ensure success in future battles.

Cyrus II, commonly known as Cyrus the Great, was more accepting of people's differences. He believed there were advantages to be gained if he allowed people to maintain the customs and religions they already had in place. Cyrus created a 6th century B.C.E. "melting pot," which became the largest empire the world had yet seen. Cyrus also encouraged the exiled Israelites to come home, to rebuild their temple, and to worship their god (Ezra 1:2–4).

After the destruction of Jerusalem by the Babylonians (roughly 586 B.C.E.) the people would have yearned for a savior. King Cyrus of Persia would have looked pretty good to them. The writings of the prophet referred to by scholars as Second Isaiah, or Deutero-Isaiah, proclaim Cyrus, a non-Jew, as the "anointed one" (Isaiah 45:1):

> It was I, the Eternal, who roused him for victory
> And who level all roads for him.
> He shall rebuild my city
> And let my exiled people go
> Without price and without payment. (Isaiah 45:13)

The final passage in the Hebrew Bible is from 2 Chronicles and it reads as follows:

> Thus said King Cyrus of Persia: The Eternal, the
> god of Heaven has given me all the kingdoms of
> the earth, and has charged me with building him a
> house in Jerusalem, which is in Judah. Any one of
> you of all his people, the Eternal his god being
> with him, and let him go up." (2 Chronicles 36:23)

Although this sounds like an idyllic time for dispersed Jews to come home to Jerusalem, the reality is that the majority of descendants of deported former Judahites remained in the diaspora. The formerly exiled elites of Judah had been living in the thriving metropolis of Babylon—as well as in other cities and towns in Babylonia—for almost 50 years, establishing families and adopting new customs. But there were some who did return from Babylon. These Jews produced an abundance of literature when compared with the paucity of literary and archaeological findings from other Jewish communities. And we must not forget the many descendants of Israelites who had never been deported and remained in the home country throughout the Neo-Babylonian period.

There were Jews in Babylon, Jews in Jerusalem, Jews in Egypt, and Jews living elsewhere. Each group learned different word usage, adopted different accents in their speech, and were exposed to languages of other cultures. Biblically, Genesis 11 explains why these same people, springing forth from the same ancestors, speak different languages. At the beginning of the Tower of Babel story, "Everyone on earth had the same language and the same words" (Genesis 11:1). As the population expanded, in an effort *not* to be "scattered all over the world" (Genesis 11:4), the people built a city with a very tall tower that reached to the sky. God, looking at this construction, in a fit of indignation over their innovation, said:

> Nothing that they may propose to do will be out
> of their reach. Let us, then, go down and
> confound their speech there, so that they shall not
> understand one another." . . . That is why it is
> called Babel, because there the Eternal
> confounded the speech of the whole earth; and
> from there the Eternal scattered them over the
> face of the whole earth. (Genesis 11:6–9)

Thomas L. Thompson explains that Genesis 10–11 must be postexilic because its narrative serves to remind the people that Israel is "indigenous" to the land. The story reveals (allegorically):

> [T]he spread of mankind . . . and their languages
> that is the heart of the causation narrative found
> in Genesis 10:1–11:9. As all nations spread abroad
> to take their proper place in the world after [the
> scattering from] Babel, so too did Israel . . .
> According to the origin (Indigenous) tradition . . .
> Israel [was formed in place, a people] indigenous
> to Palestine."[50]

In other words, the Tower of Babel story makes the claim that the Israelites had always been in Palestine. Thompson demonstrated convincingly that the Origin Traditions came after the end of the 6th century B.C.E., the period often labeled *postexilic*. Precisely during that period, the returning Jews needed to defend their claim to the land against all other claimants.

23. One God for All

O Eternal, there is none like you, and there is no other god but you,
as we have always heard.   I Chronicles 17:20

The early Israelites, like their neighbors around them, believed that
there were different gods for different people.

> "For all the peoples shall walk each in the name of
> its own god. But we will walk in the name of the
> Eternal our god forever and ever." (Micah 4:5,
> translation by the author)

And:

> "And when you look up to the sky and behold the
> sun and the moon and the stars, the whole
> heavenly host, you must not be lured into bowing
> down to them or serving them. These the Eternal
> your god allotted to other peoples everywhere
> under heaven." (Deuteronomy 4:19)

When it came to early Israelite practices, one person who was
instrumental in specifying the rules was King Josiah. There are no
direct extra-biblical references to Josiah, but in as much as royal
predecessors and successors of his as well as foreign contemporaries—
including his assassin, Pharaoh Necho (II Kings 23:29)—are attested,
there is no reason to doubt his historicity. According to the book of II
Kings, Josiah's father, Amon, was assassinated when Josiah was eight
years old, at which time Josiah became king and ruled for 31 years.
Scholars date the reign of Josiah from circa 640–609 B.C.E.

II Kings 22 tells us that during a renovation at the temple a High
Priest reported, "I have found a scroll of the Teaching (*sefer ha-torah*) in
the House of the Eternal" (II Kings 22:8). Although the particular
scroll is not named, scholars believe it was the book of Deuteronomy,
which provides a set of codes regarding religious observances and
rituals, as well as codes for military, criminal and civil law.

In the story, Josiah despaired when he realized that the Israelites were not following the codes detailed in the scroll. Josiah asked his counselors to go to the female prophet Huldah and confirm that the scroll was indeed the word of God, and that the instructions should be followed. Huldah confirmed that God had intended to "bring disaster upon this place and its inhabitants . . . because they have forsaken me and made offering to other gods and vexed me with their deeds" (II Kings 22:16–17). Upon getting this confirmation, the distressed Josiah went to the temple where "he read to them the entire text of the covenant scroll which had been found at the House of the Eternal . . . [and he solemnized] that they would follow the Eternal and observe his commandments, his injunctions, and his laws with all their heart and soul" (II Kings 23:2–3). After that, Josiah removed and burned all objects having to do with any other gods, and demolished shrines to other gods, mandating strict adherence to Israelite worship and the end of illicit forms of worship throughout Judah.

Just as we questioned the claims of lawlessness of neighboring societies, we may ask the same question about the claim of fundamental difference between the Israelites' religion and other religions of the Near East. Did different cultures worship their god(s) differently? Was the worship of the Eternal in pre-exilic Israel different from the worship by Israel's neighbors of quite similar gods?

For all their diversity of opinion, the many writers of the individual compositions that became the Bible agree on one thing: it was never legitimate for an Israelite to worship a god other than the Eternal (Hebrew: *Yahweh*). In other words, although some writers accept the existence of other divinities and others deny it, the consensus demanded of all Israelites is that they worship their god to the exclusion of all others. Historians of religion refer to the form of worship in which only one god is served as *monolatry*.

Jeremiah, who prophesied during the period of King Josiah's reforms, tells us that not all Israelites were onboard with abandoning the worship of other gods. According to Jeremiah, Israelite husbands knew that their wives would, "make offerings to the Queen of Heaven and to pour libations to her, as we used to do, we and our fathers, our kings and our officials, in the towns of Judah and the streets of Jerusalem" (Jeremiah 44:17).

Yahwistic monotheism, or even monolatry, had not been the

dominant stream in the Israelite religion before the exile, but this is not
to say that monolatry was unknown in the ancient Near East. In the
14th century B.C.E., Akhenaten, king of Egypt, inaugurated a solar
monolatry in which the royal family worshiped the Aten—the disk
representing the sun—and prohibited the worship of Egypt's
traditional gods. Mesopotamian mythology describes the temporary
worship of a single god in an emergency.[51] In addition, ancient Near
East prayer literature regularly employed monolatrous language. That
is, a worshipper might approach various gods in succession, declaring
that each one was the only divinity worthy of worship.

Even though monolatry was not unique to Israel—a fact that makes
the biblical demands more credible—monolatry seems to have been
much more significant in Israel than elsewhere. Specifically, if Israelite
history begins at the time that a segment of the population of Palestine
begins to think of itself as Israelite, then we should think of the
worship of God (*Yahweh*) alone as part of the formation of an Israelite
identity.

The eminent historian Morton Smith (1915–1991), of Columbia
University, drew attention to the political aspects of Israelite monolatry
in his 1971 book, *Palestinian Parties and Politics that Shaped the Old
Testament*. Although part of his argument accepted the biblical picture
of Israelites as invaders, which has been disproved by archaeology, his
thesis was essentially correct. In brief, Smith saw Israelite religious
history as a centuries-long struggle between the "Yahweh Alone" party
and—what for convenience might be called—the "Yahweh-Plus"
party.[52] The approach adopted here takes up Smith's hypothesis, but
attempts to account for the religious ideologies of the Yahweh Alone
monolaters and their opponents by using economist and sociologist
Max Weber's (1864–1920) notion of covenant union—a form of
association determined by bonds of shared society or circumstance.

Contemporary scholarship is virtually unanimous in viewing Israel
as an ethnically diverse group that arose within Canaan. Archaeology
has revealed a sharp increase in the number of small, unwalled
settlements in the central Palestinian hills that date to the 12th–11th
century B.C.E.—just the timeframe indicated for the establishment of
a people called "Israel." It is plausible that dissident elements of a
Bronze Age (circa 1570–1150 B.C.E.) society in Canaan, along with
some Transjordanian elements, colonized new areas in the hinterland

and coalesced into this new group.

The notion of a covenant with a god was not unknown outside of Israel, but the notion that the ancient Israelite people held their land due to a covenant with their god was particularly tenacious. Political upheaval in the region forced people to rethink their concepts of God. Israelite victims of the Assyrian or the Babylonian exile, those who had formed a covenant with the Israelite god, would not want him to think they had left him, or—even worse—to come to believe that he had abandoned them! A new way of thinking emerged. Maybe their god traveled with them. Or maybe there was just one god.

In the late 6th century B.C.E. a new and distinct characterization of the Israelite religion began to form: the belief that the god of Israel, Yahweh—or in English, "the Eternal"—was the sole god in existence. Indeed, it was this monotheistic ideology that motivated the later prophets, like 3rd Isaiah (Trito-Isaiah), to call for all the peoples of the earth, not just the Israelites, to worship the Eternal.

> As for the foreigners
> Who attach themselves to the Eternal,
> To minister to him,
> . . .
> Their burnt offerings and sacrifices
> Shall be welcome on my altar;
> For my House shall be called
> A house of prayer for all peoples. (Isaiah 56:6–7)

And:

> [The time] has come to gather all the nations and
> tongues; they shall come and behold my glory.
> (Isaiah 66:18)

But not only will they worship the Hebrew god, they also will be given significant roles!

> And from them likewise I will take some to be
> levitical priests, said the Eternal. (Isaiah 66:21)

Israel was not the only land invaded and occupied by enemies, and to have its leaders exiled. And with many gods protecting many specific peoples, the fall of Jerusalem to invading forces should have attested to its god's inadequacy. After all, Jerusalem fell. Other cults of the eastern Mediterranean have disappeared. But the Israelite religion, with its god who seemed to be an inadequate defender, survived.

Summary – Part IV

- From a contemporary literary perspective, the biblical accounts of Israel's journey from servitude to freedom are an example of the common motif of the hero who rises from humble origins with the aid of divine providence. Typically, the hero in ancient tales is a king who comes to the throne in an irregular fashion. In the Bible, the group has taken the place of the individual, so the role of the hero-king who rises from obscurity or humble origins is played by the entire people of Israel. That is, the humble origins of Israel in Egypt are a necessary prelude to the greatness brought about by divine favor.

- Although only a very small percentage of the archaeological sites from the biblical period have been excavated, the fact is that the narrative of the Israelite Exodus out of slavery in Egypt has simply not been supported by the archaeological findings and therefore must be reevaluated.

- The first five books of the Bible—the Torah (Pentateuch)—appear at the beginning of the Bible, but we should not assume that they were written first. It is generally agreed by scholars that the traditions concerning how the Israelites came to live in the land of Canaan are among the later stories in the Torah.

- Some of the 8th century B.C.E. lore claims the Israelites were promised the land of Canaan by God and they won it as attacking foreigners. This "Foreignness Tradition" is indisputable in pre-exilic (8th century B.C.E.) texts.

- The traditions that came in the postexilic time, after 539 B.C.E., convey a strong ideological message, that Israel is not a foreigner in Canaan but was formed in place and is "indigenous."

- Within the Hebrew Bible are two distinctly different traditions: the Origin (Indigenous) Tradition and the Foreignness Tradition. Passages from Micah, Amos, and Joshua can be dated to the 8th century B.C.E. and take the Exodus tradition for granted. However, some passages from Deuteronomy and Isaiah make almost no mention of the Exodus.

- Israel's outsider status must be considered an ideological statement. The claim is distinct, if not unique.

- The biblical assertion that Israel practiced superior norms and statutes helped to foster Israelite religious, social and political solidarity. Israel was encouraged to maintain its solidarity by asserting its distinctiveness from its neighbors.
- In the late 6th century B.C.E. a new and distinct characterization of the Israelite religion began to form: the belief that Israel's god was the sole god in existence.

PART V
THE LAND WHERE YOU ARE SOJOURNING
(Genesis 28:4)

Overview: Archaeological evidence and extra-biblical accounts reveal that the Israelites inhabiting Canaan were not slaves *in* Egypt, but they were slaves *to* Egypt through a system of corvée, or forced labor, until about the middle of the 12th century B.C.E. At that time Egypt was invaded, forcing it to withdraw from vassal territories in order to protect its home front. The tribes in Canaan were left to patrol themselves. Being somewhat rootless, these tribes began to create their own "foundation" stories, using examples from neighboring communities as their guide (e.g., *The Epic of Gilgamesh*).

24. Forced Labor

When Israel was in Egypt's land
Let my people go
Oppressed so hard they could not stand
Let my people go
        lyrics from the African American Spiritual
        "Go Down Moses"

The original lyricist for the song "Go Down Moses" is unknown, but the inspiration comes straight out of the Bible. Unlike the African slaves who were taken from their home countries and forced to work in a new land, according to the book of Genesis the Israelites went to Egypt voluntarily to escape a famine in their own region (Genesis 42:5–7). The book of Exodus tells us that, generations later, the Israelites had become so numerous that Pharaoh became concerned about their growing numbers. In order to keep the Israelites in line, Pharaoh "set taskmasters over them to oppress them with forced labor" (Exodus 1:11).

The institution of forced labor goes back to the earliest recorded history, and most certainly before. Forced labor was used as a form of tax, which was especially practical when no cash monetary system had been established. For example, if your land had been conquered, you owed some sort of "tribute," to the conqueror—an early form of extortion. One way to pay that tribute was to perform labor for the conqueror, sometimes for long periods. The conqueror sets the terms. Military conscription was another form of forced labor used by rulers and conquerors. It should be noted that forced laborers—despite often being subjected to cruel and harsh treatment—were higher in status than slaves, who could be bought and sold. (However, Leviticus 26:13 and Deuteronomy 15:15, as well as other passages, describe the Israelites in Egypt as outright slaves.)

In less agrarian societies, forced labor was used for public works projects. We see both ancient and more recent examples of this in China (Great Wall), Egypt (pyramids, Suez Canal), France (roads), Japan (coal mines), Philippines (structures, including churches), and the United States (convict farming and road maintenance).

Forced labor is often referred to as corvée, a term which derives from the Latin word *corrogare*, or requisition. In Bhutan, people are encouraged to perform corvée work to get a discount on their tax obligation. In Rwanda, citizens are required to give one Saturday a month as corvée. In Vietnam, people between the ages of 18–35 must perform corvée 10 days a year.[53] In 2016, President Nicolás Maduro of Venezuela signed a decree that able-bodied people must work 60 days of corvée, but the resulting uproar forced him to quickly walk the decree back.[*]

The Egyptian empire claimed Canaan as its own from circa 1560– 1080 B.C.E. (the 18th through 20th dynasties). The Egyptian system of corvée is evidenced in the Amarna letters, the 14th century B.C.E. preserved correspondence discovered in 1888 (and mentioned in Part II of this book). The close to 400 letters, preserved on clay tablets, record diplomatic correspondence between the ruling Egyptians and their representatives in subjugated lands. One such letter from an Egyptian loyalist, Rib-Addi, reports of the discovery of a revolutionary proposal put forth to rise up against the king of Egypt:

> We shall drive the city-state rulers out of the land
> so that all the land will become *hāpiru*-land, and
> so justice will be done in all the lands. [Our] sons
> and daughters will be undisturbed forever. If then
> the king [of Egypt] ventures forth, with all the
> lands in opposition to him, what can he do to us?
> (translation by the author)

The *hāpiru* were a social class whose presence was found all over the Near East throughout the 2nd millennium B.C.E. The word means, roughly, "fugitive," and in the Amarna letters has the connotation of "brigand" or "outlaw." There has been some speculation that it may be more than just coincidence that *hāpiru* is so close to the word "Hebrew," although this is now considered unlikely. Rib-Addi, loyal to

---

[*] Fun Fact: the term for forced labor in Czech is "robota." Czech playwright Karel Čapek introduced the word "robot" for his 1920 play R.U.R. (Rossum's Universal Robots) to refer to the automatons that worked for their human owners.

the king of Egypt, adds: "To this end they have sworn an oath [or "covenant"] among themselves" (El Amarna, 74).

Biridiya, another Egyptian loyalist, was the ruler of the city of Megiddo, in the north of present-day Israel. Biridiya reported to the Egyptian king that he was able to bring in forced labor—which he calls *"mas"* people—to work the royal fields (El Amarna 365). He also points out that he is "the only one" of the city rulers to bring in these people.[54] Clearly, Biridiya wanted recognition from the pharaoh that he had successfully fulfilled his obligation by requiring people to work.

Under Biridiya, those workers who did not come from Megiddo itself were required to travel from the communities of Jaffa and Nuribta. Those forced to travel could not attend to their own land so, in addition to having to travel and to work for free, they experienced the indignity of having their own crops suffer from lack of care. Workers could also be moved from one area to another, which meant that those forced to travel could not even count on a predictable commute.

It is unlikely that this ancient institution of forced labor by *"mas"* people was any more popular in Biridiya's, or Rib-Addi's, time than it would be four centuries later when:

> King Rehoboam [son of Solomon] sent Adoram,
> who was in charge of the forced labor, but all
> Israel pelted him to death with stones. (I Kings
> 12:18)

Exodus 1:11 reads, "They set taskmasters over them to oppress them with forced labor." In light of the Amarna letters, we should translate the verse, "Over them they appointed corvée-overseers in order to humble them with their forced labor projects." The Israelites living in Canaan were not literally enslaved in Egypt, but they were subject to forced labor by their Egyptian oppressors.

25. Collapse of the Late Bronze Age

Empires dissolve and peoples disappear:
Song passes not away.
> from "Lachrymae Musarum"
> by Sir William Watson (1858–1935), poet

Although we do not have literary sources like the Amarna letters for the succeeding centuries, it is clear that Canaan of the 13th and 12th centuries B.C.E. witnessed considerable turmoil as part of the general disruption of the western Mediterranean. One disruptive group, called Israel, is mentioned in a stela (stone slab) dating from the fifth year of reign of Pharaoh Merneptah (circa 1220 B.C.E.). The text contains the only mention of Israel in an Egyptian source:

> Canaan is captive with all woe
> Ashkelon is captured, Gezer seized
> Yanoam made non-existent
> Israel is wasted, bare of seed.[55]

The mention of Israel has given the text the modern name "Israel stela," even though most of it is dedicated to Merneptah's account of his victory over the people of what is now Libya. Only the final twelve lines speak of Syria-Palestine, probably to convey the impression that the pharaoh was victorious throughout those lands. Although many scholars have studied the text, there has been disagreement on many points. The general consensus is that by the 13th century B.C.E., a group designated as Israel had a political identity. Unfortunately, we have a gap of a century or more between the Israel of the stela and any relevant archaeological data on the Israel of the Bible.

Despite the sparse documentation of Israel in Egyptian sources, the biblical number of 430 years of servitude in Egypt (Exodus 12:40) fits remarkably well with known chronology of the region. Ahmose I (reign: circa 1570–1546 B.C.E.), pharaoh of the of the 18th Egyptian dynasty, successfully drove out the Hyksos—an Egyptian term meaning "rulers from foreign lands" (probably Western Asia)—from Egypt in about 1560 B.C.E. Shortly thereafter, extensive Egyptian military campaigning in Syria-Palestine laid the foundation for the Egyptian empire in Asia. Ahmose's successors continued his military policy, attempting to expand beyond the Euphrates at the expense of the rival imperialist powers in the area. At the battle of Megiddo, Thutmose III (reign: circa 1504–1450 B.C.E.) won a decisive victory, after which he established an administrative system in Canaan that survived until the collapse of the Late Bronze Age (circa 1150 B.C.E.).

Let's take a closer look at that collapse: Sometime around 1200–1150 B.C.E. there was a seismic shift in control. Archaeological evidence from that period points to the destruction of coastal cities around this time. In a preserved letter, a ruler of the ancient coastal city-state of Ugarit pleads with his neighbor to help against "ships of the enemy." Scholars cannot identify exactly who attacked from the sea, so they have been dubbed the "Sea Peoples." With the invasion of these Sea People, the old order began to break down.[56]

An analysis of records from the Near East of the 13th and 12th centuries B.C.E. shows that:

> The destruction of the Canaanite urban culture
> and the withdrawal of Egypt from Canaan during
> the second third of the twelfth century were part
> of a "worldwide" historical process that extended
> over the entire eastern Mediterranean region.[57]

Against this international background of turbulence, we see populations caught between the fighting of rival city-states, traders whose livelihood was disturbed by unstable conditions, and debtors and peasants who felt themselves overtaxed or overburdened by corvée. Then there were the ever-present, nomadic pastoralists who witnessed the strife around them. The Bible, the Amarna letters, and other sources show how talented leaders could mobilize different groups of opportunists and malcontents. In the passages below, we see entire tribes joining forces to defeat a common enemy (Judges), and large groups of desperate individuals hoping for a better life by uniting under one leader (I Samuel):

> Judah then said to their brother-tribe Simeon,
> "Come up with us to our allotted territory and let

us attack the Canaanites, and then we will go
with you to your allotted territory. So Simeon
joined them. (Judges 1:3)
Everyone who was in straits and everyone who
was in debt and everyone who was desperate
joined [David], and he became their leader; there
were about four hundred men with him. (I
Samuel 22:2)

The new group, "Israel," consisted of locals who no longer had a place in the social order. Its members gave themselves a new "national" identity. They began to depict themselves as an invading group from outside the land—a group that had withdrawn from Egypt. This was a phenomenon for which they had more than one model. The following passage from Amos shows that the prophet's listeners were aware that some of the neighbors were immigrants:

Are you not like the Ethiopians [or Nubians;
Hebrew: *Cushites*] to me, O people of Israel? says
the Eternal. Did I not bring Israel up from the
land of Egypt and the Philistines from Caphtor
and the Arameans from Kir? (Amos 9:7,
translation by the author)

The Philistines were one of the original Sea Peoples who came from Caphtor (either Crete or Cyprus)[58] to invade the Egyptian-controlled Canaan. Ramses III (reign: circa 1198–1166 B.C.E.) arrived at an agreement that the Philistines would man garrisons in coastal areas of Canaan to protect Egypt against newer invaders. This system worked as long as it served the interests of both groups: the Egyptians, who no longer needed to deploy their own native troops on the coast of Canaan, and the Philistine immigrants from the Aegean who needed a place to live. But once the Egyptian government became too weak to exercise close control, the Philistines broke free of Egyptian rule and were able to organize themselves into a five-city consortium—a "pentapolis." As for the Arameans, also mentioned in the passage above, they came to Aram (present-day Syria) from a place called Kir.

The Israelites had another example in the Sikil—another of the Sea

Peoples mentioned in Egyptian sources. In the manner of the Philistines, the Sikil originated in the Aegean and settled on the Mediterranean coast at Dor, south of Mount Carmel, after being repulsed by the Egyptians.[59] The Aramaeans, the Sikil, and the Philistines provided inspiration to the Israelite ideologues. If these peoples could come from abroad and establish their own polities, it was not a big leap to weave a story in which the Israelites had done the same.

26. Inspired Selfhood

*Here is where our real selfhood is rooted, in the divine spark or seed,
in the image of God imprinted on the human soul.*
Sue Monk Kidd (born: 1948), author

By the middle of the 12th century B.C.E., Egypt's rule over Canaan
had ceased. It is then that we see the rise of local groups struggling for
control, often against one another, over former Egyptian territory. At
this point, the presence of Israelites in the hill country and Philistines
on the coastal plains becomes increasingly visible in the archaeological
record. Archaeologist William G. Dever (born: 1933), of both the
University of Arizona (Tucson) and Lycoming College, identified
material culture—or objects—in excavations of Iron Age I (roughly
1200–1000 B.C.E.) hill-country villages, indicating that the people
inhabiting the land had originated as Canaanite peasant farmers of the
Late Bronze Age (the period immediately prior).[60] Scholars surmise
that Egyptian rule of Canaan had become economically and politically
burdensome to these farmers, causing them to withdraw from the
more stratified social order to which they objected. Given that the
Amarna letters demonstrate local consciousness and strong opposition
to the collusion between the Canaanite rulers and Egypt, we must
interpret the Hebrew traditions of servitude *in* Egypt as allegories of
servitude *to* Egypt.

The 430 years that the Bible allots for Israel's subjugation in Egypt
(Exodus 12:40) reflect the duration of Egypt's empire in Western Asia
from a Canaanite perspective. The group that became 1st millennium
Israel had indeed been subjugated by kings of Egypt, but in its native
land. We can interpret the "Foreignness Traditions" as evolving from
that group's desire to establish themselves as a separate people. In
addition, they serve a specific political agenda of justifying the northern
Israelite claims in Jordan.

The traditions regarding Israel's encounter with Moab after leaving
Egypt may serve as a good example: Moab was located to the east of
the Dead Sea and its chief city was Madaba, about 30 km south of
present-day Amman, Jordan. Among other towns in the areas were
Heshbon, Jahaz and Elealah. Both the Israelites and the Moabites

claimed the territory as their own, and their writings assert their proof of ownership. However, their writings are in opposition to each other. In 1868, an Anglican missionary working in Jordan discovered a basalt stela. Known as the Moabite Stone—or the Mesha Stela, named for its author, King Mesha of Moab—the stela dates to around 840 B.C.E. The Moabite Stone provides us with synchronisms between rulers of Israel and kings of Moab at that time.

The inscription tells the story of how King Mesha defeated the Israelites living in Ataroth, a town in northern Moab. The author of the inscription relates that Israelites controlled the area and had built walls, cities, and forts. He also notes that members of the Israelite tribe of Gad had dwelled in the land of Ataroth "forever" (Moabite: *m'lm*), and that the king of Israel, Omri (reign: 884–873 B.C.E.) had built the town specifically for the Gadites. The Moabite Stone goes on to describe how, with the help of the Moabite god Chemosh, the Moabites defeated the Israelites in many cities, including Hesbon, Jahaz, and Eleaheh.

Lines 4 through 9 of the Moabite Stone are translated below. They give King Mesha's account of his defeat of the Israelite King Omri and, subsequently, Omri's son. The reference to "Madaba-land" is to the large Moabite city of Madaba:

> As for Omri, king of Israel, he humbled Moab
> many days, for [the god] Chemosh was angry
> with his land. His (Omri's) son succeeded him.
> He too said, "I shall humble Moab." In my days
> said he thus. But I saw [my triumph] over him
> and his dynasty, and Israel perished utterly and
> forever. For Omri had taken possession of
> Madaba-Land and dwelled there throughout his
> days and half his son's days, forty years. But
> Chemosh returned it in my days. (translation by
> the author)

The fact that the Moabite Stone dates from the period it is recording lends weight to its historicity. However, like contemporary rulers, Mesha would not be innocent of exaggeration. The statement that "Israel perished utterly and forever" is—obviously—not factual.

Indeed, every story has at least two sides to it. The Hebrew Bible gives an entirely different take. Numbers 21:21–31 tells us that, while en route to Canaan from Egypt during the Exodus, the Israelites attempt to pass peacefully through territory held by an Amorite king, Sihon—who had himself already taken this land from the Moabites. The Israelites, with the help of God, defeat the Amorites and became the rightful occupants of the land:

> Israel now sent messengers to Sihon king of the
> Amorites . . . Let me pass through your country . .
> . we will follow the king's highway . . . But Sihon
> would not let Israel pass . . . and went out against
> Israel in the wilderness. He came to Jahaz and
> engaged Israel . . . But Israel put him to the sword
> and took possession of their land, from the Arnon
> to the Jabbok . . . Israel took possession of all
> those towns . . . of the Amorites, in Heshbon and
> all its dependencies. Now Heshbon was the city
> of Sihon, king of the Amorites, who had fought
> against the first king of Moab and taken all his
> land from him as far as the Arnon. Therefore the
> bards recite, "Come to Heshbon . . . Sihon's city.
> Fire went forth from Heshbon, flame from
> Sihon's city, consuming Ar of Moab. You are
> undone people of Chemosh. His sons are made
> fugitive and his daughters captive by the Amorite
> king Sihon." So Israel occupied the land of the
> Amorites. (Numbers 21:21-31, translation by the
> author)

In other words, during the Exodus, Israel asked Sihon for permission to pass peacefully through his Amorite land; Sihon refused permission and battles ensued. The Israelites won, fair and square.

Translated into political propaganda, the biblical traditions vindicate Israelite claims to northern Moab against counterclaims made by the Moabites. According to the Torah, Moab was not entitled to the land because no Moabite king had been able to hold onto it.

Furthermore, the story goes, Israelites never took the land from
Moab—it was already under the domain of King Sihon, who lived in
the city of Heshbon.

We might be tempted to credit the biblical story with some
historical authenticity, especially because King Mesha himself says that
the Gadites had dwelled in Ataroth "forever." But, once again, the
archaeological evidence points in another direction. Extensive
excavation at Tell Hesban—the site of Heshbon—shows only flimsy
architectural remains until the 9th–8th centuries B.C.E., making it highly
unlikely that Heshbon was a royal city at the time of the supposed
Exodus.

There is, however, evidence for the construction of a nearly two-
million-liter-capacity reservoir sometime in the 9th-8th century B.C.E.,
the same timeframe as the reign of King Omri of Israel, and his son.
The archaeologist Lawrence Geraty (born: 1940), of La Sierra
University, theorized that the reservoir might have been part of King
Mesha's attempt to fortify his northern border with Israel.[61] It appears,
then, that the account of Numbers 21 is allegorical. Behind the tale of
an Israelite conquest of Amorite territory during the Exodus is a
historical, 9th century B.C.E. military push into Transjordan during the
reigns of both King Omri and his son, Ahab.

The Amorites in this verse were migratory people who came into
Canaan and made a meaningful impact on the area from about 2000–
1600 B.C.E. They left a legacy in the region that lasted for generations.
The prophet Amos, active in the mid-8th century B.C.E.—roughly a
century after the Moabite Stone was inscribed—formulated a clear
connection between the Exodus and the Transjordanian conquests:

> For I brought you up out of Egypt and led you
> through the wilderness for forty years* so that
> you would conquer the land of the Amorites.
> (Amos 2:10, translation by the author)

The implication from Amos is that, because God enabled the Israelites

---

* The time period of "forty years," used in both the Moabite Stone
inscription and in the biblical verse from the prophet Amos, is understood
to indicate the timespan of a generation.

to defeat the legendary Amorites—who were "as tall as cedars and as stout as oaks" (Amos 2:9)—surely he would aid his people against the historical Moabites.

The turmoil depicted by the Moabite Stone inscription and in the Bible describes a time when the Egyptian subjugation of the people living in Canaan came to an end. Some scholars have posited that there was a *peasant revolt*, but that term is much too limited—it was a time when a political vacuum was created, and several peoples attempted to fill that vacuum with their own claims to ownership. Each writer told the story as they wanted it preserved, and those stories were useful in fortifying a sense of community and defining a destiny.

27. Foundation Stories

Those who have a 'why' to live, can bear almost any 'how.'
from *Man's Search for Meaning* by Viktor Frankl (1905–1997),
neurologist, philosopher, and Holocaust survivor

Why? How? People have long sought to understand: What is the meaning of life? How did we get here? What is it all about? Before we had evidence-based science, people relied on "foundation stories"—imaginary tales about how places and institutions originated and the personalities behind their origin. To better understand the impact of foundation stories on the societies for which they were written, let us turn to more recent foundation stories and work our way back.

Americans know the story of young George Washington chopping down the cherry tree, and when asked by his father if he did it answering, "I cannot tell a lie. I did cut it with my hatchet." The myth was created by Mason L. Weems (1759–1825) just after the death of George Washington in 1799 and quickly became entrenched in American culture. One of the Founding Fathers of America is presented as a virtuous and moral child and therefore, by correlation, a virtuous and moral man who went on to lead the nation. This story presents, according to Weems, of the ideal of what it meant to be an American.

Aeneas is the hero of Virgil's *Aeneid* (written circa 29–19 B.C.E.) and a veteran of the Trojan War, where he fought for Troy. After the fall of Troy, Aeneas and his company of survivors boarded ships and went on many adventures, including a trip to the underworld and a long stay in Carthage that ended with broken hearts and hostility between Aeneas and Carthage's Queen Dido. Led by omens and prophecies about the future greatness of Rome, Aeneas and his men finally land in Italy to establish their new homeland. The *Aeneid* reflects ideals of Roman virtue by presenting the brave and dutiful warrior Aeneas as founder. In addition, it offers a mythic origin story (love vs. duty) for the historical Punic Wars. Throughout, the epic looks forward to a future golden age when the city will be ruled by Caesar Augustus.

Gilgamesh was a king of the Sumerian city-state of Uruk sometime between 2800 and 2500 B.C.E. By 2100 B.C.E., people immortalized the legendary exploits of Gilgamesh in poems, five of which survive on clay tablets. Sometime between 1600–1155 B.C.E. the surviving poems were expanded and woven together to create the Babylonian *Epic of Gilgamesh*, which is currently the oldest foundation story known. Samuel Kramer (1897–1990), who taught at the University of Pennsylvania, noted that "Gilgamesh became the hero par excellence of the ancient world—an adventurous, brave, but tragic figure symbolizing man's vain but endless drive for fame, glory, and immortality."[62]

The stories of George Washington, Aeneas, and Gilgamesh are just three examples, separated by about 2000 years each, of hundreds of foundation stories that can be found world-wide, and that serve their people by instilling a sense of pride and a story to rally behind. Trade and war throughout the Mediterranean and Sinai regions created cross cultural pollination. And all people love a good story. The stories of Gilgamesh were clearly known in some form to the Greek poet Homer (circa 1200 to 800 B.C.E.). Homer's hero Odysseus experiences some of the same travails as Gilgamesh: a battle with a monster, the death of a beloved, and a journey to the end of the world. And Virgil's Aeneas was a minor character in Homer's *Odyssey* and *Iliad*, around whom Virgil built an epic.

The earliest Israelites were also aware of the early stories—specifically, the *Epic of Gilgamesh*. Both the *Epic* and the Bible contain stories about a great flood, where the main character of the flood narrative is instructed by his god to construct a vessel for himself and his family. After the destruction of the earth, these people will be left to start over and repopulate the earth. In both stories, a dove is sent out in search of dry land. Adopting themes or characters from older traditions has a benefit over and above not having to create a new story: the benefit of familiarity. If an audience heard stories that they felt they already knew, they'd assume these stories to be true—or at least be worth preserving and transmitting for the wisdom and value they exemplified.

The story of the Exodus is the foundation story for the Jewish people.

Summary – Part V

- Forced labor has been utilized by rulers and conquerors for millennia as a way to tax their subjects.
- The 18th dynasty of Egypt was founded by Ahmose 1 around 1570 B.C.E. Through successful military campaigns over the next 120 years, the Egyptian empire expanded into Syria-Palestine and beyond the Euphrates River.
- The 14th century Amarna letters demonstrate that Egypt had conquered the area of Canaan and required forced labor, which some people tried to subvert.
- The collapse of the Late Bronze Age, circa 1150 B.C.E., saw the Egyptians pull back to protect their homeland, leaving a vacuum in that region.
- Talented and opportunistic leaders mobilized different groups of malcontents to fill the vacuum. Among these groups who created a new "national" identity for themselves was "Israel."
- The Egyptian dominance of the region that started with the empire of Ahmose I and continued until the collapse of the Bronze Age, an age spanning the years, roughly, from 1570–1150 B.C.E., fits nicely with the biblical assertion of 430 years of slavery to Egypt. The group that became 1st millennium Israel had indeed been subjugated by kings of Egypt, but in its native land.
- When the Egyptians withdrew from Canaan, rival groups made a push to control land. For example, Numbers 21 provides the justification for the northern Israelite claim to land in modern-day Jordan. Alternatively, the Moabite Stone, carbon-dated to 840 B.C.E., tells the Moabite version of why they claim the land.
- Evidence proves that some of the biblical tales are untrue. We might wonder why the stories were written, but when we understand the politics of the time we can also understand a desire to mobilize people around a common cause. One way to do that is through foundation stories that serve their people by instilling a sense of pride and a story to rally behind, which helped to unite the people as a group.
- The story of the Exodus is the foundation story for the Jewish people.

PART VI
GRACIOUS COVENANT
(1 Kings 8:23)

Overview: Early in the 1ˢᵗ millennium B.C.E., the Israelite people were monolatrous; believing that, even if there were many gods in existence, only a single god should be worshipped. A pact, or covenant, between the Israelites and their god, the Eternal, was established using legalistic language in terms drawn from politics or government. The covenant stipulated that the Eternal would provide protection to the Israelites in return for their singular worship. A covenant between the Eternal and the Davidic dynasty (descendants of King David) was developed soon after. After the Babylonian invasion (587 B.C.E.) there was no longer a Davidic king on the throne, which necessitated a new contract between the Eternal and the Israelite people.

28. A Force of Nature

In all things of nature there is something of the marvelous.
Aristotle (384–322 B.C.E.) philosopher

A trove of approximately 1,500 cuneiform texts and fragments dating from the 13th and 12th centuries B.C.E. has been unearthed in Syria at the ancient city of Ugarit. The Ugaritic texts include descriptions of Ugaritic cult and ritual practices, as well as an epic poem about the Canaanite god, Baal. Part of the poem recounts the people celebrating the victory of Baal, the land god, over Yamm, the sea god.[63]

If the comparative method has taught us anything about the realities of the biblical period, it is that ancient Israel was not fundamentally innovative—if by "innovation" we mean creation *ex nihilo*, out of nothing. The genius of the Israelites' innovation was their remarkable ability to draw out the creative potential of concepts and institutions that Israel shared with its neighbors in order to achieve new syntheses. The Hebrews borrowed their earliest script from the Phoenicians and their later script from the Arameans. They borrowed poetic forms from the larger Syro-Palestinian culture, and laws from Mesopotamia. They borrowed the story of the great flood from Mesopotamia and the figure of Balaam from Transjordan.

Although there was a great deal of overlap among the cultures, a common misconception holds that the ancient Israelites believed their god acted only in human (historical) affairs—e.g. delivering a victory in battle—while the people of neighboring Near East cultures believed that their god(s) acted only in the realm of what we call "nature"— mythical tales of gods battling one another explained the occurrence of thunder, storms, drought, etc. This generalization often holds true, but not always. The literature of the ancient Near East often depicts the gods of the nations involved in human affairs; the Assyrian kings, for example, regularly describe how their gods overwhelmed their enemies and brought about Assyrian victory. The Bible, for its part, often depicts God in mythic terms, as the following biblical passages demonstrate:[64]

it was you who pulverized the sea monster with
your might,
who smashed the heads of the monsters in the
waters;
it was you who crushed the heads of Leviathan,
who left him as food for the denizens of the
desert;
it was you who released springs and torrents,
who made mighty rivers run dry;
the day is yours, the night also;
it was you who set in place the orb of the sun;
you fixed all the boundaries of the earth;
summer and winter – you made them. (Psalms
74:13–17)

And:

With his strength he stilled the sea,
with his skill he smote Rahab,
with his wind he put the sea monster in a net,
his hand slew the elusive serpent. (Job 26:12–13,
translation by the author)

The difference between Israel and the other near eastern cultures
was the greater role of "history" in the Israelite cult. In contrast to
the cultic celebrations of Egypt, Mesopotamia and non-Israelite
Palestine, the religious celebrations of the worshippers of the Eternal
emphasized the acts of their god that had brought his people political
triumph. The holiday of Sukkot offers a good example of an early
Israelite celebration of God's ability to control nature. Sukkot, also
known as the Feast of Booths, was originally an agrarian holiday that
celebrated the completed harvest and included prayers for a
successful season to come. In biblical times, and still today, part of
the celebration calls for people to bundle a branch each of palm
(lulav), willow (aravot), and myrtle (hadassim). These three bundled
items are held in the hands of worshippers along with a fragrant
citrus called an etrog, and then shaken joyfully, creating a sound

quite close to the sound of the patter of rain. Rain is especially important in the arid climate of Israel and the shaking of the lulav and etrog, most certainly, was part of an ancient rain dance. But the Bible instead maintains that the festival commemorates God's providing of booths—a temporary shelter—to house the Israelites when they left Egypt (Leviticus 23:43). Similarly, Mazzot, the Festival of Unleavened Bread, initially an agricultural celebration, harks back to the hurried departure of the Israelites from Egypt which left no time for their bread dough to rise (Exodus 12:39; Deuteronomy 16:3).

In ancient times, each community had its own god, or gods. The Israelites worshipped their god, the Eternal, and understood that each neighboring community worshipped its own distinctly different god(s). With each community having at least one god, there were many gods in the heavens, the earth, and the netherworld, and this was perfectly acceptable. In fact, biblical statements in support of this polytheistic system are evidenced by passages such as, "God said, 'Now that the man has become like one of _us_, . . .'" (Genesis 3:22).

According to the pioneering German Bible scholar Julius Wellhausen, the early Israelite religion was rooted in the "natural" needs of Israel's agrarian society. But as the teachings of the prophets Amos, Isaiah, and Jeremiah gained traction—teachings which denied the existence of other gods—the power of Israel's god expanded beyond the natural world, and the Israelite religion moved away from its natural roots. Instead, Israelite religious leaders increasingly taught that humans could please God though their punctilious observance of the Torah's ritual laws, e.g. observing the Sabbath and dietary restrictions, and upholding the sacrificial system. Wellhausen viewed these ritual laws as post-exilic inventions of the priesthood, which led him to conclude that the legalistic covenant, or contract (Hebrew: _berît_)[*], between the Israelites and their god was also a late development. However, the next chapter will show that the _berît_ metaphor goes back to the earliest times.

---

[*] See Exodus 19:3-8, 24:3-11; Deuteronomy 29; Joshua 24; Hosea 8:1, etc.

29. Sacred Marriage

May these vows and this marriage be blessed.
Rumi (1207–1273), poet, scholar, and theologian

Sacred marriage between humans and their god(s) was a ritual whose language the Israelites borrowed and metaphorically incorporated into their religious imagery.[65] Thorkild Jacobsen (1904–1993), a Harvard University scholar of the ancient Sumerian language and culture, showed in his article "Religious Drama in Ancient Mesopotamia" that the ritual imagery of sacred marriage among Sumerian gods was quite graphic. There is evidence of the sacred marriage—actual or literary—from the third millennium B.C.E. to the first millennium B.C.E., when it would have influenced the author(s) of the Song of Songs (a.k.a. Song of Solomon).

A Sumerian ritual recorded circa 2100–1800 B.C.E. reads:

> Milady bathes her holy loins in water, bathes
> them in water for the loins of the king, bathes
> them in water for the loins of [King] Iddin-
> Dagan. Holy [goddess] Inanna rubs with soap,
> sprinkles the floor with cedar perfume. The king
> goes with lifted head [euphemistic for "erection"]
> to her holy loins, goes with lifted head to the loins
> of Inanna, Amaushumgalanna goes to bed with
> her. In her holy loins he can but truly praise the
> woman: "O my one of holy loins! O my holy
> Inanna!" After he on the bed, in the holy loins,
> has made the queen rejoice, after he on the bed, in
> the holy loins, has made holy Inanna rejoice, she
> in return soothes the heart for him there on her
> bed: "Verily, I am the constant prolonger of
> [King] Iddin-Dagan's days of life."[66]

The fertility of the gods boded well for the fertility of the land—which, of course, was critical to the survival of the agrarian people. Thus, when the gods got busy, the people had cause for celebration.

When it came to divine sex, early Israelites were surely also familiar with the Ugaritic stories of the Syro-Palestinian god, Baal. Baal was known to be a vigorous deity whose relationships encompassed not only anthropomorphic deities but beasts as well:

> Baal loved a heifer in the pasture, a cow in the
> fields by the shore . . . He lay with her times
> seventy and seven. She let him mount times
> eighty and eight.[67]

Hosea was an 8th century B.C.E. prophet from the northern region of Israel who, aware of sexual imagery relating to gods, took the bold step of elevating the Israelite people to the status of bride of God. Just as there is only one groom per bride, so is there just one god for Israel. But Hosea's imagery does not rule out the potential availability of other grooms. In other words, Hosea himself makes no claim that the Eternal is the sole god in existence; only that fidelity is part of the conditional covenant under which God will give protection to his bride, Israel. This is monolatry, a stop along the way to monotheism. All that Hosea does here is restate the demand that the Eternal alone be worshiped, using a metaphor that had the potential to appeal to his contemporaries. In one striking passage, Hosea is told by God:

> Go love a woman . . . love her as I, the Eternal,
> love the Israelites, although they resort to other
> gods. (Hosea 3:1, translation by the author)

In a classic case of misery loves company, God, knowing that the Israelites will be unfaithful to him, instructs Hosea to marry a promiscuous woman who, by definition, will be similarly unfaithful. Having experienced the heartbreak of unfaithfulness, Hosea calls on the people of Israel to chasten the rulers of Israel for faithlessness to God, and he refers allegorically to God as the wronged husband; to the rulers of Israel as the faithless wife and mother; and to the common people of Israel as the children of the union. In Hosea 2, the prophet parodies the imagery of marriage. He uses the image of an outraged husband accusing his wife of infidelity, and does so in the most graphic language:

> Call your mother to account, for she is not my
> wife, nor am I her husband. Let her get her
> whoring out of my sight, along with her
> adulterous breasts! Or else I shall strip her bare,
> parade her naked as the day she was born . . . She
> has been promiscuous, their mother has. She who
> bore them has been shameless. (Hosea 2:4–7,
> translation by the author)

The prophets Jeremiah and Ezekiel, who succeeded Hosea, elaborated the bridal image which had become increasingly popular as the movement toward monotheism expanded in the Israelite religion. In the following passage from Ezekiel, God speaks to Israel:

> I tended you like an evergreen plant growing in
> the woods; you thrived and grew. You came to
> full womanhood; your breasts became firm and
> your hair grew, but you were still bare and
> naked. I came by and saw that you were ripe for
> love. I spread the skirt of my robe over you and
> covered your body. I plighted my troth and
> entered in covenant [berît] with you, says the
> Eternal, and you became mine. (Ezekiel 16:7–8,
> translation by the author)

Julius Wellhausen considered Hosea's image of Israel as God's bride to be an expression of Hosea's pioneering monotheistic tendencies. However, when Hosea says, "although they resort to other gods" (Hosea 3:1), he verges on acknowledging the existence of other gods. So Wellhausen's theory cannot be correct. Hosea did not originate the marriage allegory in a movement toward monotheistic thinking. On the contrary, Hosea used the marriage allegory despite its polytheistic associations, because the stories were tantalizing, exciting and provocative! The Israelite god was no less virile than

Baal and, in words attributed to Reverend George Whitefield (1714–1770),"Why should the devil have all the best tunes?"

30. Divine-Human Covenant

He who is protected by God cannot be harmed by anyone.
Abu Bakr (573–634 C.E.)
father-in-law and companion to the prophet Muhammad

Berît, which means "covenant," can also be translated as "pact" or "contract." Simply put, it is a formal agreement between two parties. The Israelites were not unique in having a binding covenant between divinities and human beings; this was yet another practice that the Israelites borrowed from their neighbors.[68] But the covenant of the Israelite religion was unique in one aspect: it assumed far greater significance in biblical writings than in other extant ancient Near Eastern literatures. A central, political image in the Bible is of Israel allegorically having made itself subject to God the king through *berît* (Judges 8:23; I Samuel 8:7). Perhaps this is so because the Israelites' story demands monolatry—that Israel must serve God and no other gods.

The covenant between the Israelites and God fits the theological definition of a contractual agreement establishing the commitment between God and his people. From earliest times, Israel saw itself united to God in a conditional *berît*. In his magisterial book, *Egypt, Canaan and Israel in Ancient Times*, Donald B. Redford refers to the "notion of a contract between Yahweh the god of the group and the human community" as one of the "primitive concepts of the community."[69] This contract carried rewards for obedience and penalties for disobedience.

The allegory in this case is that God and Israel were linked in a *conditional covenant* under terms requiring Israel to pledge exclusive loyalty to God. Adherence to the terms of this covenant would ensure God's continuing support of Israel and its continued control of the land of Israel. Disobedience, however, would provoke God's wrath. He would punish his disloyal subjects by destroying their nation and expelling them from the land. Some of the best-known texts in the Torah allege that the covenant between God and Israel had been mediated by Moses in the desert, after the Exodus from Egypt:

So Moses ascended to God (Hebrew: *Elohim*), the
Eternal (Hebrew: *Yahweh*) who called to him from
the mountain, saying, "Speak thus to the house of
Jacob, and tell the children of Israel [that] you
have seen what I did to Egypt, how I carried you
on wings of eagles and brought you to me. Now if
you heed my voice closely and observe my
covenant (Hebrew: *berît*), then you shall be my
personal possession more than any other people,
for the earth is mine, and you shall be to me a
kingdom of priests and a holy nation. These are
the words you are to speak to the children of
Israel." So Moses came and gathered the elders
of the people and set before them all these words
kol ha-debarim ha-eleh that the Eternal
commanded him. The people spoke up all
together, saying, "Whatever the Eternal has said,
we will perform." Moses brought the people's
words back to the Eternal. (Exodus 19:3–8,
translation by the author)

Worshipers of God emphasized the acts of salvation that had
brought his people political triumph. This made the new Israelite
religion political on a fundamental level. If God embodied Israelite
nationhood, it made perfect sense for God's representatives to claim for
him total allegiance. This required that he alone be worshiped. The
language that they used for this total allegiance was allegorical imagery
drawn from the political language of *berît*.

The crucial element of devotion to only one god, and the
admonition to never identify this god with false gods, is front-and-
center in the Ten Commandments:

God spoke all these words *kol ha-debarim ha-eleh*
saying, I am the Eternal, your god, who took you
out of the land of Egypt—the slave barracks. You
shall have no other gods in my presence. You
shall not bow before them or serve them, for I,

the Eternal, your god, am a jealous god, requiting
ancestral sin on children, on the third, and on the
fourth generation to my foes but maintaining
loyalty *hesed* to those who love me and observe
my commandments. You shall not pronounce
the [proper] name "the Eternal," your god, to
that which is false [that is, a false god], for the
Eternal will not acquit one who pronounces his
[God's] name to that which is false. (Exodus
20:2–7, translation by the author)

The more traditional translation of the phrase "slave barracks" is "house of bondage," but that translation does not fully convey the writers' intended image. The institution of slavery was well-known to the Israelite people, as is evidenced by how the Israelites are instructed to recognize the slaves in their midst. For example, the Sabbath commandment states, "you shall not do any work—you, your son or daughter, your male or female slave, or your cattle, or the stranger who is within your settlements" (Exodus 20:10). And the commandment against coveting states, "You shall not covet your neighbor's house: you shall not covet your neighbor's wife, or his male or female slave, or his ox or his ass, or anything that is your neighbor's" (Exodus 20:14). Clearly, the Israelite audience knew how slaves lived. Calling Egypt one big "slave barracks" would make the audience appreciate God's generosity in getting his people out.

Another text in Exodus provides a detailed and graphic account of how Moses mediated a covenant between God and the people:

Moses came and related to the people all the words
and norms of the Eternal. Then the people spoke
up with one voice, saying, "All the words *kol ha-
debarim* that the Eternal spoke, we will perform."
So Moses wrote down all the Eternal's words.
Upon rising in the morning, he built an altar at
the bottom of the mountain, as well as twelve
stelae for the twelve tribes of Israel. He then sent
Israelite lads who offered bulls as whole burned-

offerings and as sacrifices of well-being to the
Eternal. Moses took half the blood and put it in
bowls, and half he dashed on the altar. He took
the book of the covenant *sefer ha-berît* and read it
in the people's hearing. They said, "Everything
the Eternal has said, we will perform
obediently." So Moses took the blood [in the
bowls], dashed it on the people, and said, "This is
the blood, of the covenant *dam ha-berît* that the
Eternal concluded with you regarding all these
words *kol ha-debarim ha-eleh*. Then ascended Moses
and Aaron and Nadab and Abihu and seventy of
the elders of Israel. They saw the god of Israel,
the soles of whose feet were like worked white
sapphire, as pure as heaven itself. But he did not
harm the representatives of Israel, who saw the
god but ate and drank. (Exodus 24:3–11,
translation by the author)

More often than not, when the eyes of an ordinary human behold
a god, there are harmful, or even deadly, consequences for the human.*
An important detail from the passage above is that the Israelites were
spared this time. The making of the covenant was a critical component
of the ongoing relationship between God and the Israelites. Not only
did the Israelite representatives see the divine and live, but they also
had the opportunity to enjoy a meal.

---

* See Leviticus 16:2; Judges 3; Judges 6:22–23; Judges 13:22.

31. A Promise of Political Victory

Political campaigns offer [people] an opportunity to adjust direction, reaffirm values, and recommit to the covenant that binds them together.
Stanley A. McChrystal (born: 1954), U.S. Army four-star general, retired

A properly functioning community requires that the majority of people adhere to its laws. Murder, enslavement (illegal globally, but not criminalized worldwide), and failure to worship God are all punishable offenses. The first by both government and God, the second by government only, and the third by God only. The concept of the separation of church and state dates to antiquity. The Christian theologian Augustine (354–430 C.E.)—aware of the plurality of religious observance in his own time—advocated for peace between different religious groups because he believed that discord would create angst on earth and not be beneficial to one's own salvation.[70]

However, in biblical times, and still in many countries today, religion was a driving force in political affairs. In contrast to other cults of the 1st millennium B.C.E.—e.g., Egypt, Mesopotamia, and non-Israelite Syria-Palestine—which emphasized their gods' acts within the realm of nature, Israelite worship emphasized acts of salvation their god delivered through victories over their enemies, leading to the expansion of territory.[71] (As we have already learned, this emphasis was not to the point of exclusivity.) Good examples of these political triumphs can be found in the book of Joshua.

Joshua 24 is a much-studied chapter that describes the Israelites' binding covenant with God. The setting of Joshua 24 is Shechem, where, after finally crossing into the Promised Land, Joshua summons all the tribes of Israel to stand before God and learn what they must do to remain in the Promised Land. Addressing the assembly, Joshua summarizes Israel's "history," beginning with the ancestors who lived beyond the river and served other gods. Among other tales, Joshua relates the story of Moses parting the Red Sea, the crossing of the Jordan, and finally God's gift of the land to the Israelites.

After completing his narration, Joshua turns to the people, admonishing them to remove the "foreign gods" and to serve God (the Eternal) exclusively:

> And now, fear the Eternal and serve him fully
> and faithfully. Remove the gods your ancestors
> served on the other side of the [Euphrates] river
> and in Egypt, and serve the Eternal. But if it
> displeases you to serve the Eternal, choose now
> whom you will serve, either the gods your
> ancestors served on the other side of the river or
> the gods of the Amorite in whose land you dwell.
> But I and my household shall serve the Eternal.
> (Joshua 24:14–15, translation by the author)

The people then affirm that they too will serve God. Joshua warns
them that God's service is impossible:

> You will not be able to serve the Eternal, for he is
> [a veritable pantheon of] holy gods. He is a
> jealous god. He will not bear rebellious sinfulness.
> If you abandon the Eternal and serve foreign gods
> after the good he did for you, he will turn and
> harm you and destroy you. (Joshua 24:19–20,
> translation by the author)

The people protest that they are prepared to serve God, and to
bear witness for the decision of the entire community. Once the
people have agreed to abandon all the "foreign gods," Joshua makes
a covenant on their behalf. Marking the occasion, Joshua creates a
document of the divine instruction *(sefer torat elohim)* and, to memorialize
the event, he places a large stone at the foot of an oak tree in the sacred
courtyard at Shechem. The stone is designated to serve as the witness to
God's word to the people.

The making of a covenant at the city of Shechem, a place
unconnected with the conquest traditions detailed elsewhere in Joshua,
would be puzzling to readers familiar with another biblical tale that
shares the setting of Shechem—that of Judges 8–9.[72] Judges 8–9 tells
the story of Abimelech, a man who killed his seventy half-brothers so
that he could have sole claim to the kingdom of Shechem. After being

ruled by Abimelech for three years, the citizens of Shechem turned on their power-hungry leader. In return, Abimelech massacred all the citizens of Shechem and, as part of the massacre, caused about 1000 men and women to perish when he set fire to a tunnel where they sought refuge from the rampage.

The tunnel in question led to a temple dedicated to the worship of a divinity variously known as *El Berît*, "El of the Covenant/ God of the Covenant" (Judges 9:46) and *Baal Berît*, "Baal of the Covenant/Lord of the Covenant" (Judges 9:4). The writer clearly distinguishes this divinity as separate from the Eternal:

> [T]he Israelites again went astray after the Baalim, and they adopted Baal-berith as a god. The Israelites gave no thought to the Eternal their god, who saved them from all the enemies around them." (Judges 8:33–34)

I would argue that Abimelech probably didn't object to the citizens' worshipping of Baal; the tunnel simply offered a convenient way to kill many people in one blow.

The passages of Joshua 24 describe the Israelites making a covenant with the Eternal at the city of Shechem, while the passages of Judges 8–9 describe the murderous rampage of a despotic ruler of the city of Shechem—a city where Baal was worshipped. It's not hard to wonder at the incongruity of these two stories. Extra-biblical finds from archaeologists have shown that Shechem, located on the west bank of the Jordan River, was a vital city located on active trades routes. It was the site of ancient religious traditions reaching well back into the 2nd millennium B.C.E.[73] Eventually, Shechem would become the first capital city of the northern kingdom of Israel.

Unfortunately, because of its location in the West Bank and the current precarious political situation there, more excavation of Shechem is not possible at this time. But given what we have learned, it was indisputably known as a place where covenants were made. The authenticity of the Judges tradition is given credence by the archaeological finding of the name *il brt*—that is, *El Berît*—in a document from the late 2nd millennium B.C.E. Theodore Lewis, professor of Near East Studies at Johns Hopkins University, has even speculated that the divinity worshipped at Shechem was a god that guaranteed treaties.[74]

The only way to understand these unharmonious stories, which were likely written at approximately the same time, is to acknowledge that the stories come from two different traditions. Recall that in roughly 922 B.C.E., the united tribes living in Israel separated into the northern kingdom of Israel and the southern kingdom of Judah. Early in the 1st millennium B.C.E., the people of the northern kingdom of Israel reinterpreted the making of a covenant in light of their own historical, mythical, and religious needs. Those needs included a divinity that bound the people together and represented a force to carry them forward. Whatever the original significance of the name of the non-Israelite god *El Berit*, he fit nicely into the Israelite allegory of God, who had made a covenant with his people.

For the writer of Joshua 24, who came from the northern kingdom, the temple at Shechem was a sacred site where it was natural that such a consequential promise to the divine would take place. The writer of Judges 8–9, in contrast, was from the southern kingdom, for whom Shechem was not sacred at all.

Biblical scholar George Mendenhall (1916–2016), who taught at the University of Michigan, contends that the writer of Joshua 24 was inspired by the language of international treaties to employ the language of political covenant to get his theological message across. Mendenhall points to significant parallels between the biblical accounts of *berit* and the international Hittite "suzerainty treaties" of the latter half of the 2nd millennium B.C.E. In these treaties, one state controls another state, and one king becomes subordinate to the other. These treaties are essentially elaborate fidelity oaths with two fundamental components: obligations to the great king that must be met, and divine punishment for failing to meet the obligations. Only the inferior king is bound by the stipulations of the treaty, and only he takes an oath of obedience.[75]

In the biblical scheme, God is the great king and the people, Israel, play the part assigned in the political treaties to the minor (or inferior) king. Like the minor king, Israel will be blessed and maintain its land and wellbeing if it fulfills detailed obligations and serves exclusively the great king, the Eternal. If Israel proves to be unfaithful and turns to other gods, it will suffer the same accursed fate as the minor king who is duplicitous and aligns with kings other than the great king with whom they made the treaty—e.g., the destruction of their nation and the expulsion from the land. Like the marriage oath, this is a conditional covenant.

Joshua 24 cannot be contemporary with the 14th/13th century B.C.E. events it describes. For one thing, the chapter accepts the historical authenticity of the Exodus from Egypt and the successful conquest of both sides of the Jordan by a united army of Israelite invaders. These are useful allegories when trying to unite disparate people, but as has been noted earlier in this book, archaeological evidence disputes their historicity. According to Joshua 24, God instructs Joshua to remind the people:

> Then you crossed the Jordan and you came to
> Jericho. The citizens of Jericho . . . fought you,
> but I delivered them into your hands. I sent a
> plague ahead of you, and it drove them out before
> you. (Joshua 24: 11–12)

The plague is, indeed, a miraculous intervention by God. But the biblical account in Joshua 6, retold in a 19th century African American Spiritual (Joshua fit the battle of Jericho, Jericho, Jericho, Joshua fit the battle of Jericho and the walls came tumbling down) is even more fabulous!

> Now Jericho was shut up tight because of the
> Israelites; no one could leave or enter.
> The Eternal said to Joshua, "See I will deliver
> Jericho and her king [and her] warriors into your
> hands. Let all your troops march around the city
> and complete one circuit of the city. Do this for
> six days, with seven priests carrying seven ram's
> horns preceding the Ark [of the Eternal's
> Covenant]. On the seventh day, march around
> the city seven times, with the priests blowing the
> horns. And when a long blast is sounded on the
> horn—as soon as you hear that sound of the
> horn—all the people shall give a mighty shout.

Thereupon the city wall will collapse, and the
people shall advance, every man straight ahead."
(Joshua 6:1–5)

These two very different stories about the conquest of Jericho have no
archaeological support, and neither is useful for dating the respective
chapters. However, by studying the language of Joshua 24, its date of
composition can be placed, with a good deal of confidence, in the 9th/8th
century B.C.E. The audience addressed lived in a time of peace and
comfort, and there is no reference to external enemies or looming
exile. To narrow it down even further, I believe Joshua 24 dates from
the reign of King Jeroboam II who ruled circa 789–748 B.C.E.—a
long and prosperous period in Israelite history.

32. Which Came First: Marriage or Politics?

The chicken came first—God would look silly sitting on an egg.
Abraham Maslow (1908–1970), psychologist

Selections from the Torah relating to covenant allegory have not been dated with certainty. Therefore, modern scholars have differed widely in their assessment of the antiquity of the covenant allegory. Julius Wellhausen believed the less "natural" a biblical concept or institution seemed to be, the later it had been adopted by the Israelites. "Natural" refers to concepts that are connected to the needs of an agrarian society where cultivation of the land is the primary source of wealth. Wellhausen's theory (which is closely aligned, theologically, with the 1st century C.E. writings of Paul the Apostle) claims that the "human affairs," such as the closely regulated hierarchical priesthood and the punctilious observance of complicated rituals, were obviously not "natural" and therefore were a late development. By the same criterion, the covenant notion was not "natural" but "legalistic" and, accordingly, a latecomer to Israelite ideology.

The move to a more "legalistic" religion regulating "human affairs" is a move toward what we would today call politics or government. This political emphasis is seen in the gradual transformation of long-standing, traditional agricultural festivals into rituals focused on the themes of Exodus and a promise of land.

For example, the holiday of Sukkot, also known as Tabernacles and as the Feast of Booths, is described in Deuteronomy 16 as a harvest festival:

> Celebrate the Festival of Sukkot for seven days
> after you have gathered the produce of your
> threshing floor and your winepress. Be joyful at
> your festival—you, your sons and daughters, your
> male and female servants, and the Levites, the
> foreigners, the fatherless and the widows who live
> in your towns. For seven days celebrate the
> festival to the Eternal your god at the place the
> Eternal will choose. For the Eternal your god will

bless you in all your harvest and in all the work of
your hands, and your joy will be complete.
(Deuteronomy 16:13-15, translation by the author)

At harvest time it was necessary to spend as much time as possible
in the fields to reap the crops. Temporary field shelters, or *sukkot*
(plural of *sukkah*), made that possible and provided the festival with
its name.

The holiday is celebrated in modern times with participants
enjoying festive meals served in a temporary structure, a *sukkah*, that
people have built at their home and/or synagogue. Coming on the
heels of Rosh Hashanah and Yom Kippur, Sukkot today has less
prominence among non-Orthodox Jews. But in biblical times Sukkot
was the major holiday, celebrated joyously for a full week by every
man, woman, and child—free or slave—with copious amounts of
food and libations.

The older, agrarian rituals would not be easily cast aside. Instead,
they were modified, rebranded, and incorporated into the Exodus
narrative—thereby reinforcing the new political mythology.
According to the book of Leviticus, during the festival of Sukkot a
priest is required to hold up a sampling from the first harvest, give
thanks to God, and then make a ritual burnt offering (Leviticus
23:10-11). And then:

> . . . all citizens in Israel shall live in booths
> (Hebrew: *sukkot*), in order that future generations
> may know that I made the Israelite people live in
> booths when I brought them out of the land of
> Egypt. (Leviticus 23:42–43)

Other ancient rituals underwent a similar transformation from
their agrarian roots to a celebration that would reinforce the new
political mythology through a rebranding. In Deuteronomy the same
priestly ritual is performed, but it commences with a recitation
reminding the Israelites that their people had been transformed from
a "wandering Aramean" to a people whom "The Eternal freed us
from Egypt by a mighty hand . . . [and] brought us to this place and
gave us this land" (Deuteronomy 26:5–9).

Another ritual practiced by the earliest Israelites—and in neighboring communities—was child sacrifice. A plain reading of the text of Exodus 22:28–29 demands that the first-born son be sacrificed to God. Text from the book of Jeremiah, in contrast, claims that child sacrifice was never the action intended (Jeremiah 7:30–31). Text from the book of Ezekiel derides the people for sacrificing their children to other gods (Ezekiel 16:20–21). However, the same prophet later laments that God, as a form of punishment for Israelite faithlessness, demanded child sacrifice and imposed other laws, which God himself acknowledges "were not good and rules by which they could not live" (Ezekiel 20:25–26).

The numerous mentions of child sacrifice in the Hebrew Bible demonstrate that this atrocious practice actually occurred.[76] Although we do not have any direct evidence (yet) of child sacrifice in Syria-Palestine in the 8th century B.C.E. evidence of a highly probable child sacrifice site was unearthed by archaeologists in the Phoenician city-state of Carthage (present day Tunisia). The ancient thinking behind this atrocity was likely that if you gave up your first born as an offering the deity would bless you with even more in the future.

The book of Deuteronomy specifically forbids child sacrifice, and the Israelites are warned that it is an "abhorrent" practice (Deuteronomy 12:30–31 and 18:10). The rebranding of the ritual of child sacrifice is found in Exodus 13:11–16, which claims that the first-born son belongs to God as repayment for freeing the Israelites from Egypt:

> It was with a mighty hand that the Eternal
> brought us out from Egypt, from the slave
> barracks. When Pharaoh stubbornly refused to let
> us go, the Eternal slew every first-born in the land
> of Egypt . . . Therefore I sacrifice to the Eternal
> every first male issue of the womb, but redeem
> every first-born among my sons. (Exodus 13:11–15,
> translation by the author)

Mercifully, the passage provides an alternative to child sacrifice. Parents still had the obligation of giving their first-born son to God— which may have meant the child became a worker in the Temple (see the example of the prophet Samuel who, as a child, went to work at a temple: 1 Samuel 1:24–28). However, financially solvent parents could circumvent the obligation by paying a fee of five shekels to the Temple priests (Numbers 18:15).* A biblical shekel was a unit of measure, so five measures of silver.

There was another way in which Israelites gave their sons to God which also may have originated in a longstanding agrarian ritual. As members of an agrarian society, the early Israelites understood the benefit of pruning their crops to encourage more, and studier, growth. It is possible that the ritual of circumcision was a fertility ritual that began with a belief that, like pruning the crop, pruning the penis would produce more and studier offspring. In the course of biblical rebranding, the practice of circumcision, too, was reinterpreted to support the new narrative. It became a covenant associated with God's promise of Canaanite land after the Exodus:

> I assign the land you sojourn in to you and your
> offspring to come, all the land of Canaan as an
> everlasting holding . . . You shall circumcise the
> flesh of your foreskin, and that shall be the sign of
> the covenant between me and you. (Genesis 17:7–
> 14)

Even the Sabbath, whatever its origin, became a reminder of servitude in Egypt:

> Remember that you were a slave in the land of
> Egypt and the Eternal your god freed you from
> there with a mighty hand and an outstretched
> arm; therefore the Eternal your god has
> commanded you to observe the Sabbath day.
> (Deuteronomy 5:15)

Wellhausen believed that the transformation from an agrarian

---

* Orthodox Jews still "redeem" their first-born son (*pidyon ha-ben*) by paying five silver dollars to someone claiming descent from the ancient priesthood.

religion to a legalistic religion was accelerated when the leaders of the
Israelites were forced to leave Jerusalem and relocate to Babylon. At
the time of the exile, 586 B.C.E., the Babylonians had a significantly
more advanced society with a developed series of contracts that could
be called upon as needed. Covenants and political alliances with
multiple gods have been found in ancient prayer literature written in
Akkadian, the ancient Semitic language used by the Babylonians. For
example, a 12th century B.C.E. prophecy attributed to the Akkadian
god Marduk indicates, "that prince shall rule all the countries, for I
alone, all you gods, have a covenant with him." Another example
found in the Akkadian texts states that, "the gods will be his allies."[77]

Wellhausen believed that the imagery of God and Israel as bride
and groom in the prophetic writings was evidence of an early nascent
movement toward monotheism. In contrast to the earlier, sexual
marriage imagery used in the 8th century B.C.E. writings of Hosea, he
believed the unromantic legalese of *berît* (or "covenant") used to
describe Israel's relation to its god must have been a later development.
Wellhausen believed the final form of the Torah (Pentateuch, post 539
B.C.E.) fixated on observance of ritual law by emphasizing its
contractual elements.

But Wellhausen had it backwards. The early Israelites did not view
marriage as a contract. In undisputed *pre*-exilic biblical writings, *berît* is
used to describe political and social relations of various kinds, but not
the relation of marriage. The early Israelites were already aware of
the use of covenants and/or alliances with both the divine world
and the human world. This was not a concept developed after the
exile.

The writings of the prophets Ezekiel and Malachi—which date
from the exilic or postexilic period (586 B.C.E. or later)—are the only
biblical writings to use the term *berît* to describe a marriage. In Ezekiel
16:8 the prophet has God the husband say to his wife, Israel, "I
plighted my troth and entered into a covenant [*berît*] with you." In
Malachi 2:14 the prophet denounces every man who has divorced
the woman who was "your covenanted spouse [*'ešet berîteka*]." This
is evidence that, in keeping with what regularly happens when
speakers of one language come in contact with speakers of a
different language, the Hebrew language expanded. The Akkadian
language of Judah's Babylonian conquerors included the word *riksu*

to refer to a wide range of contracts—including marriage. Under the influence of Akkadian *riksu*, the semantic range of Hebrew covenant [*berît*] was expanded to include marriage.[78]

In the previous chapter, we saw that biblical scholar George Mendenhall believed the conditional covenant between God and Israel mirrored the political covenants made by ancient kings. In his view, the covenant with God was the religious expression of the mundane cultic and military union of the different groups that had merged to form the people of Israel. In other words, the covenant with God was an allegorical way of expressing an emergent national unity. God, who was viewed as the force responsible for the emergence of the new group, thus became a partner in the confederation, and accordingly the guarantor of the Israelite social order and its material prosperity.

The allegory of a covenant modeled on international treaties also makes the most sense at the earliest stages of Israel's political development. As we have seen, contemporary scholarship is virtually unanimous in viewing Israel as an ethnically diverse group that arose within Canaan. Their covenants with their god solidified both cultic and military unity within the group.

33. Monotheism

Monotheism makes me grouchy. I don't trust any religion that makes God look like one of the ruling class.
Gloria Steinem (born: 1934), feminist, journalist and activist

Religious communities in biblical times borrowed liberally from their neighbors. But unlike their polytheistic neighbors, the Israelites were to worship just one god—and, according to them, their god was the best! We see evidence of this in Psalms:

> There is none like you among the gods, O
> Eternal,
> and there are no deeds like yours.
> All the nations that you have made
> will come to bow down before you, O Lord
> (Hebrew: *Adonai*).
> (Psalms 86:8-9)

And in the clarion call still repeated daily at Jewish services:

> Hear, O Israel! The Eternal is our God, the
> Eternal alone. (Deuteronomy 6:4)

George Mendenhall believed that the formal similarities of political treaties to the biblical language used in the underlying traditions of the Ten Commandments (referred to often as "The Decalogue") and Joshua 24 justified dating the passage to the period when Israel first arose as a political entity:

> This covenant type is even more important as a
> starting point for the study of Israelite traditions
> because it cannot be proven to have survived the
> downfall of the great empires of the late second
> millennium B.C. When empires arose again,
> notably Assyria, the structure of the covenant by

which they bound their vassals is entirely
different.[79]

Although there are studies by other scholars who claim that
Mendenhall overstated his case, the consensus is that he was generally
correct, and other theories have not gained traction. The Ten
Commandments are listed in Exodus 20:1-14 and Deuteronomy 5:6-
18, and in both places state, "You shall have no other gods besides
me." Joshua 24:23 insists that the Israelites "put away the alien gods
that you have among you and direct your hearts to the Eternal, the god
of Israel." These texts stand in contrast to later monotheistic passages
in the Bible because they do not claim that the Eternal is the sole god
in existence and so make no corollary demand that gentiles, too, must
worship the Eternal. Mendenhall, however, viewed the covenant
notion as monotheistic, saying:

> The population of the twelve tribes were
> predominantly native Palestinians who had
> *converted to monotheism* under the covenant with
> Yahweh (emphasis added).[80]

Other scholars—such as Moshe Weinfeld—agreed with
Mendenhall's assessment, claiming that the covenant was a "perfect
metaphor" for loyalty in a monotheistic religion and that the notion
of divine-human covenant was unique to Israel.[81]

But there is no necessary connection between divine covenant
and monotheism. And in studying cultures, especially ancient
cultures, one should never make the mistake of assuming
uniqueness. In the 9th century B.C.E., the Assyrians conquered a
kingdom in present-day Syria, not far from the Euphrates River.
Archaeological excavations started in 1928 revealed colossal lion
statues, giving the site the name Arslan Tash (Turkish for "Lion
Stone"). According to UNESCO, the stone lions were bulldozed by the
Islamic State in 2015. Fortunately for scholars, however, some of the
more culturally significant finds were protected in museums. One of
the Phoenician inscriptions from Arslan Tash guarantees divine
protection from demonic stranglers, claiming, "They made eternal
covenants with us. Asshur made them with us as did every divinity

and great one—the council of all our holy beings" (translation by the author). Needless to say, this same text shows that it is incorrect to view the notion of covenant with divinity as necessarily monotheistic.

It is at the monolatrous stage that the allegorical narrative of covenant modeled on the international treaty form makes the most sense. The great kings bound the lesser kings by treaty because they acknowledged the very real possibility that the lesser king could serve another master. Both the Ten Commandments and Joshua 24 acknowledge the possibility that Israelites could serve other gods. This is why it was necessary for the Eternal to bind them by covenant. It is striking that in the exilic and postexilic period, when the Israelite religion became consistently monotheistic, the concept of a conditional national covenant between the Eternal and the people of Israel became a dead letter—meaning a law still on the books but now irrelevant. (I have explored these concepts in depth in my articles "Rethinking Covenant in Late Biblical Books" (*Biblica*, 1989), and "An Arslan Tash Incantation: Interpretations and Implications" (*Hebrew Union College Annual*, 1982).)[82]

The 6th century B.C.E. was a momentous time for the Israelites. It was likely during this century that the Israelites began their shift from monolatry to monotheism. Readers may recall that in ancient times people worshipped the gods who, they believed, had dominion over their lands. The Babylonian exile (beginning roughly 586 B.C.E.) would have caused the Israelites to rethink this immobile conception of the Eternal: if the Eternal was tied to the land, how could they take him with them when they left? Once the Israelites began to see their god as "being everywhere," the transition to monotheism was not far behind.

34. The Mosaic Covenant:
God's Conditional Covenant with Israel

[T]he story was really about love in all its possible forms—how and why we decide to bestow it, or withdraw it; how we decide what is more worthy of being loved, and what is less. We are masters of conditional love.
Kenneth Oppel (born: 1967), author, regarding his novel *Half Brother*

As I have observed, the ethnically diverse group that coalesced in Canaan and became "Israel" solidified its unity through the establishment of a covenant with God. However, geopolitical upheaval necessitated that the group adapt and change in order to remain in existence. Over the centuries, as the Israelites adapted so did their concept of covenant.

Exodus 19–24 relates the parameters of the covenant between God and the Israelites, as relayed through Moses. Referred to as the Mosaic Covenant, this covenant is a conditional promise that God will provide protection to the Israelites in return for their singular worship of him:

> Now if you heed my voice closely and observe
> my covenant then you shall be my personal
> possession more than any other people. (Exodus
> 19:5, translation by the author)

Moses, in Deuteronomy 4:1–2, reminds the people to adhere to God's rules and laws—the Ten Commandments—to earn God's promise of land:

> And now, O Israel, give heed to the laws and
> rules that I am instructing you to observe, so that
> you may live to enter and occupy the land that the
> Eternal, the god of your fathers, is giving you.
> You shall not add anything to what I command
> you or take anything away from it, but keep the

commandments of the Eternal your god that I
enjoin upon you.

Abundance is the focus of Deuteronomy 28:10–12, which promises
abundance of offspring, livestock, crops and wealth:

> All the peoples of the earth shall see that the
> Eternal's name is proclaimed over you, and they
> shall stand in fear of you. The Eternal will give
> you abounding prosperity in the issue of your
> womb, the offspring of your cattle, and the
> produce of your soil . . . The Eternal will open for
> you his bounteous store, the heavens, to provide
> rain for your land in season and to bless all your
> undertakings. You will be creditor to many
> nations, but debtor to none.

In some cases, the covenants were based on a pure legalistic
understanding of a contract, similar to what a conquering king might
agree to with the conquered leader of another people. In other cases,
the covenant was based upon the legally binding marriage contract.
The treaty language makes it clear that God can rescind his promise of
protection from a wide variety of misfortunes—including, but not
limited to, natural disasters, enemy incursions, or a state of
childlessness. Moses relates in Deuteronomy 28:20–41 what will
befall the Israelites if they disobey God's laws:

> The Eternal will let loose against you calamity,
> panic, and frustration in all the enterprises you
> undertake . . . You shall not prosper in your
> ventures, but shall be constantly abused and
> robbed, with none to give help. If you pay the
> bride-price for a wife, another man shall enjoy her
> . . . Your sons and daughters shall be delivered to
> another people, while you look on; and your eyes
> shall strain for them constantly . . . [but] they

will not remain with you, for they shall go into
captivity.

As if all this was not bad enough, disobeyers will also be stricken
with hemorrhoids!* (Deuteronomy 28:27)

National covenants were often sealed by sacrifices, or cultic
procedures that resembled sacrifices, which were administered by the
priesthood and established a relationship of loyalty between the parties.
The following pre-exilic (pre-8th century B.C.E.) passage from Psalms
is an example:

> Gather to me my loyalists [ḥasiday]. Those who
> make a covenant with me by sacrifice [zebaḥ].
> (Psalms 50:5, translation by the author)

The literary prophets of the 8th century B.C.E. were aware of the
covenant allegory, but they ignored or criticized covenant [berît] when
they considered the popular perception to be misguided. There are
several examples of this:

> What need have I of all your sacrifices?" Says the
> Eternal.
> I am sated with burnt offerings of rams,
> And suet of fatlings,
> And blood of bulls. (Isaiah 1:11)

And:

---

* Fun Fact: As part of typical Jewish worship services, sections of the
Torah, known as the "Torah portion," are read on an annual cycle (a minority
of congregations read it on a 3-year cycle). Typically, the portion is chanted
out loud by the reader. However, from medieval times up to and including
the present, some Jewish leaders worried that the chanting of these
horrendous curses in Deuteronomy—or their parallel in Leviticus 26—
would cause the curses to come about. To avoid incautiously reminding God
of the curses, some communities, even today, read the curses in a rapid
whisper.

If you offer me burnt offerings—or your meal
offerings—
I will not accept them;
I will pay no heed
To your gifts of fatlings. (Amos 5:22)

A passage from Hosea (also an 8th century B.C.E. prophet), whose
full significance has not always been appreciated, asserts that going
through the motions is not enough. Hosea's audience had participated
in the ritual of covenant making (the sacrifice) but had shown their
disloyalty by violating the covenant itself. God, proclaims Hosea,
delights not in the ritual of covenant but in the loyalty in which the
relationship of covenant is supposed to be expressed:[83]

For I delight in loyalty [hesed], not sacrifice [zebaḥ],
acknowledgment of God rather than whole burnt
offerings. But they, to a man, violated the covenant.
This [Gilead] is where they betrayed me. (Hosea
6:6–7, translation by the author)

The allegory of conditional covenant was a strong component of
the early Israelite writings but, as the preceding passages indicate, in
some prophetic circles had fallen into relative unimportance in the 8th
century B.C.E.

In other circles, however, the allegory of conditional covenant
experienced a brief revival. Throughout the ancient Near East,
historians have documented a widespread nostalgia for an old world.
In Babylonia, for example, at the very time that the ancient native
Akkadian language was being heavily Aramaicized, the Neo-Babylonian
kings—themselves more at home in Aramaic than in Akkadian—were
sponsoring searches for ancient inscriptions and attempting to revive the
revered Old Babylonian script. The royal inscriptions of these same
Neo-Babylonian kings ignored the proper grammatical case endings
but regularly used archaisms of the "yea-verily" kind. Likewise, in
Egypt, the Saite dynasty (reign: 664–525 B.C.E.) encouraged a cult of
antiquity, which included the restoration to prominence of forgotten
divinities and the reuse of Old and Middle Kingdom titles.[84]

King Josiah of Judah (reign: circa 640-609 B.C.E.) played a pivotal role in the revival of the allegory of conditional covenant in Israel. As has been noted in this book, scholars believe that the book of Deuteronomy was the "Teaching" (*torah*) that was "found" in approximately 622 B.C.E. In keeping with the zeitgeist of the region, passages in the 7th century B.C.E. book of Deuteronomy hark back to times long since passed, providing evidence of the antiquarian interest of the authors of Deuteronomy (e.g., Deuteronomy 2:10–12, 20–23; 3:9–11; and 32:8–15). The reforms instituted by Josiah included a set of laws attributed to the figure of Moses who, if historical, would have lived in the 14th/13th century B.C.E.

However, the book of Deuteronomy—using supposed ancient characters and rituals—contains significant revisions to ancient Israelite worship. The Bible contains passages that attest to the onetime importance of temples at Shiloh and Bethel. For example:

> This man used to go up from his town every year to worship and to offer sacrifice to the Eternal of Hosts at Shiloh.—Hophni and Phinehas, the two sons of Eli, were priests of the Eternal there. (I Samuel 1:3)

And:

> Then all the Israelites, all the army, went up and came to Bethel and they sat there, weeping before the Eternal. They fasted that day until evening, and presented burnt offerings and offerings of well-being to the Eternal. The Israelites inquired of the Eternal (for the Ark of God's Covenant was there in those days, and Phinehas son of Eleazar son of Aaron the priest ministered before him in those days), "Shall we again take the field against our kinsmen the Benjaminites, or shall we not?" The Eternal answered, "Go up, for tomorrow I will deliver them into your hands." (Judges 20:26–28)

King Josiah also played a pivotal role in consolidating worship of the Israelite people by destroying places of worship outside of Jerusalem—such as Shiloh and Bethel (see 2 Kings 23). The destruction of the sites that had previously been acceptable as places of worship forced the Israelites to journey to the Temple in Jerusalem:

> . . . look only to the site that the Eternal your God
> will choose amidst all your tribes as his
> habitation, to establish his name there. There you
> are to go, and there you are to bring your burnt
> offerings and other sacrifices, your tithes and
> contributions, your votive and freewill offerings,
> and the firstlings of your herds and flocks.
> Together with your households, you shall feast
> there before the Eternal your God, happy in all
> the undertakings in which the Eternal your God
> has blessed you. (Deuteronomy 12:5–7)

The changes instituted by King Josiah may have been done in a genuine effort to save his people, or it may have been a self-serving power play. From the passage above we can imagine the power, riches and prestige that became centralized in Jerusalem.

35. The Davidic Covenant:
God's Unconditional Covenant with King David

Everybody pulls for David; nobody roots for Goliath.
Wilt Chamberlain (1936–1999), professional basketball player

King Josiah played an instrumental role in ensuring that the ritual worship required by the conditional covenant between God and the Israelites was followed. As a descendant of King David, Josiah was the beneficiary of another covenant with God—and this one was unconditional. A. D. H. Mayes (born: 1943), who taught at Trinity College in Dublin, explains that in a tradition "current in the time of David or very shortly afterwards, [God] had chosen David and his dynasty and made a covenant promise that the Davidic line should always occupy the throne in Jerusalem."[85]

To understand the origin of this covenant, let's look at the books of Samuel. Scholars believe the books of Samuel are a collection of traditions hundreds of years old which were reworked into the text that became the books of Samuel mostly in the late 7th century B.C.E., with more added during the 6th century B.C.E. Babylonian exile. The books continued to be reworked for at least another hundred years. (As an aside: There are not actually two different parts to Samuel—1 Samuel and 2 Samuel. Scrolls with a lot of text could become unwieldy and needed to be divided simply because of the size. 2 Samuel is a continuation of 1 Samuel, but on a second scroll. The same is true regarding 1 Kings and 2 Kings, and 1 Chronicles and 2 Chronicles.)

1 Samuel 10 tells us that David was chosen by God to be king (1 Samuel 10:24). Although there is no evidence of an actual King David, in 1993 there was an exciting discovery at location in northern Israel of a 9th century B.C.E. artifact that refers to the "House of David." It is possible that stories told over generations started with an actual King David, who in legend grew from a lyre-playing shepherd to the vanquisher of Goliath and a military hero. With King David, the Davidic dynasty begins:

The Eternal declares to you that he, the Eternal,
will establish a house for you. When your days
are done and you lie with your fathers (die), I will
raise up your offspring after you, one of your own
issue, and I will establish his kingship. He shall
build a house for my name, and I will establish
his royal throne forever ... Your house and your
kingship shall ever be secure before you; your
throne shall be established forever. (2 Samuel 7:11–
16)

And, from Psalms:

I have sworn by my holiness, once and for all;
I will not be false to David.
His line shall continue forever,
his throne, as the sun before me,
as the moon, established forever,
an enduring witness in the sky. (Psalms 89:36–38)

In the book of Jeremiah there is a prophecy that the messiah, or the
promised deliverer of the people, will be descended from King David.

See, a time is coming—declares the Eternal—
when I will raise up a true branch of David's line.
He shall reign as king and shall prosper, and he
shall do what is just and right in the land. In his
days Judah shall be delivered and Israel shall
dwell secure. And this is the name by which he
shall be called: "The Eternal is our Vindicator."
(Jeremiah 23:5–6)

These biblical statements have had a lasting influence. Assuming
King David actually lived 3000 years ago, people who can claim
descent from him are multitudinous. Following is a list of just a few
people who rose to prominence who claim, or their followers claim on

their behalf, their descent from the Davidic line:

- Jesus Christ
- The Jewish sage Hillel (circa 110 B.C.E. – 10 C.E.), an older contemporary of Jesus
- The medieval French rabbi Rashi (1040–1105)
- Judah Loew ben Bezalel (1520?–1609), Talmudic scholar and Jewish mystic in Prague (said to the be creator of the Golem of Prague)
- The Baal Shem Tov (1698–1760), the founder of Hasidic Judaism
- Menachem Mendel Schneersohn (1902–1994), the last rebbe of the Lubavitcher Hasidic dynasty

After the defeat of Jerusalem by the Babylonians in 586 B.C.E., the Babylonians selected a loyalist to put on the throne. Their hand-picked successor was not from the line of David, which meant that God's unconditional covenant with the Davidic dynasty had come to an end.

36. The Abrahamic Covenant:
God's Unconditional Covenant with Israel

See, a time is coming—declares the Eternal—when I will make a new covenant with the House of Israel and the House of Judah.
Jeremiah 31:31

Readers of the Bible should not be lulled into thinking that the books in the Bible appear in the order they were written. As we know, certain clues help scholars identify the likely time of authorship. And scholars have used these clues to date the tales of the biblical patriarch Abraham to the postexilic period, or post-539 B.C.E.

Beginning in late pre-exilic times and continuing through the. exile and finally the 539 B.C.E. return to Judah, God's covenant with the Israelite people was adapted and further developed to fit the needs of the community. Jews returning to Judah needed a new origin story, and a new covenant. Building on the love of nostalgia—which was used to great effect by King Josiah—the author of Genesis 12 tells of the unconditional covenant between God and Abraham (named "Abram" at this point in the biblical narrative):

> The Eternal said to Abram, "Go forth from your
> native land and from your father's house to the
> land that I will show you.
> I will make of you a great nation,
> And I will bless you;
> I will make your name great,
> And you shall be a blessing.
> I will bless those who bless you
> And curse him that curses you;
> And all the families of the earth
> Shall bless themselves by you." (Genesis 12:1–3)

Unlike the conditional covenant described earlier, there is no "If" in this covenant. In these few lines, God has promised Abraham land, offspring and blessings. There is never a consideration that Abraham might do wrong or prove himself to be unworthy. This promise is passed down to the descendants of Abraham—that is, all Israelites. And Abraham is told that his descendants will be "as numerous as the star of heaven and the sands on the seashore" (Genesis 22:17).

In the previous three chapters, we examined how the allegory of covenant was adapted and developed to fit the needs of the Israelite community. Following is a theory of what might have happened in history to necessitate these adaptations to covenant. This list is not definitive but offers a rough idea of what *could* have been. Storylines and dates are open to adjustment:

- The concept of a covenant with the divine goes back at least 3000 years.
- Reign of King David, king of Israel and Judah, is estimated at about the year 1000 B.C.E. (the "kingdom" originated with Saul banding tribes together, and the unification strengthened over time).
- Borrowing language from neighboring communities, the Israelites developed a concept of a conditional covenant between God and the people. The people will worship only the Eternal—the god who will provide protection from political rivals and natural elements. Sacrificial rituals were a common way to worship God.
- During the reign of King David, or very soon after, the allegory of covenant between God and the Davidic dynasty became known. This covenant promised that a descendent of the Davidic line would reign over Jerusalem forever.
- While not all prophetic writings were in agreement, some 8th century B.C.E. writings—those of prophets such as Isaiah, Amos and Hosea—questioned the need of sacrificial rituals. Today we might describe this approach as liberal, or reformist.
- In the 7th century B.C.E. there was widespread nostalgia for older customs, which lead to the religious reforms of King Josiah. Today we might describe these reforms as conservative.
- As a result of the Babylonian exile of 586 B.C.E., there was no longer a king of the Davidic dynasty leading the Israelite people.
- Post 539 B.C.E.: In an effort to keep the community of Israelites together, new stories were told. Beginning in late pre-exilic times and continuing through the exile and return, God's unconditional

covenant with the Davidic dynasty was replaced by God's unconditional covenant with Israel.

Summary – Part VI

- The Israelite god, the Eternal, is worshipped for his control over the forces of nature and for his ability to bring political victory to his people. Over time, the Israelite religion emphasized God's ability to influence human affairs.

- God is worshipped in the role of husband to his bride: the Israelites. Or, as a great king ruling over another king, through a pact, or covenant [*berît*], where homage is paid to the great king.

- Once the covenant is made, monolatry—the worship of only one god, while allowing that other gods may exist—becomes obligatory. And with it, sacrificial practices common to a temple and its priests.

- The Davidic covenant promises that a descendant of King David would reign on the throne of Jerusalem forever. The Davidic covenant may be as ancient as the reign of King David, and could have co-existed with the monolatrous covenant between God and the Israelites.

- In the 8th century, some of the prophets began to teach that the sacrifices were not what mattered to God.

- Nostalgia for the old world was widespread across the Near East in the 7th century. The 622 B.C.E. religious reforms of King Josiah mandated the revival of earlier practices.

- In 586 B.C.E., the Babylonian invasion devastated Jerusalem and there was no longer a Davidic king on the throne. The intellectuals of the time collected Jewish traditions in an effort to preserve the culture.

- Ancient allegories were used as a familiar base of stories, but then edited to create a new allegory of the Israelite people. In these new allegories the unconditional covenant with David and his descendants was transferred to the entire Israelite people.

PART VII
ABRAHAM & DAVID

Overview: The character of Abraham is central to the Israelite religion. The archaeological and historical evidence, combined with critical reading of the text, however, throws doubt on the existence of Abraham as a specific person. The parallels between the Abraham traditions and what was happening with both the Israelite people and with the progenitor of the Davidic line of Israel, King David, demonstrate that the Abraham traditions are allegorical stand-ins for the Israelite experience. These parallel tales served to give ancient Israelites assurance that the religious and political actions they were experiencing had already been approved by God because they had already happened to Abraham.

37. Abraham

What then are we to say about Abraham, our forefather according to the flesh?   Romans 4:1

Using the biblical text, and assuming that the biblical figure Abraham actually existed, he would have lived in roughly 1800 B.C.E. To Jews worldwide, Abraham is the founding father of the Jewish religion. The New Testament Gospel according to John claims descent from Abraham for Christian people (John 8:33). Muslims recognize Abraham as "a man of truth and a prophet" (Quran 19:41).

The first mention of Abraham in the Bible is in Genesis 11:26, when it says that Abraham (then known as Abram) was born to his father, Terah. By verse 29, just three verses later, Abraham is married to Sarah (then known as Sarai). The Bible tells us nothing about Abraham's formative years, so rabbis filled in the blanks with what is called in Hebrew, "midrash"—stories created post-biblically to help answer any lingering questions not already covered by the text. The oldest preserved midrash comes from Jewish scholars who lived during the first seven centuries C.E. and, while not an officially organized group, they are collectively known as "The Rabbis."

Rabbi Hiyya (circa 180–230 C.E.) is credited with a midrash about Abraham's father, Terah, a shop owner who was in the business of making and selling idols. One day Abraham was left to tend the shop:

> A man walked in and wished to buy an idol.
> Abraham asked him how old he was and the man
> responded, "50 years old." Abraham then said,
> "You are 50 years old and would worship a day-
> old statue?!" At this point the man left, ashamed.
> Later, a woman walked into the store and wanted
> to make an offering to the idols. So Abraham took
> a stick, smashed the idols and placed the stick in
> the hand of the largest idol. When Terah
> returned, he asked Abraham what happened to all
> the idols. Abraham told him that a woman came

in to make an offering to the idol. The idols
argued about which one should eat the offering
first, then the largest idol took the stick and
smashed all the other idols. Terah responded by
saying, "Why are you sporting with me? Do they
(the statues) have any awareness?" Whereupon
Abraham responded by saying, "Can't your ears
hear what your mouth is saying?" (Genesis
Rabbah 38.13)[86]

For more than a century, modern Bible scholars have argued
whether Abraham (as well as the other men and women around
whom the tales of Genesis revolve) was a real, historical character.
Fundamentalists read the Bible as being a historically accurate
document that gives an inerrant account of the journey—both
physical and metaphysical—of the character Abraham. Ironically,
Abraham, who some rabbinic literature identifies as the smasher of
idols and the first practitioner of monolatry, was once thought to
have been worshipped as a god himself! During the first two
decades of the 20th century, there was a widespread current of
opinion that the mothers and fathers of Israel had originated as
divinities in prebiblical times, and that only in the course of time had
they been "humanized."

According to this analysis, the tombs of Abraham, Sarah, Isaac,
Rebecca, Jacob, and Leah in Hebron originated as cult sites of
Canaanite gods and goddesses. Abraham was a particularly good
subject for mythic interpretation because biblical traditions
associated him with the cities of Ur (in present-day Iraq) and Harran
(in present-day Turkey); both known to have been centers of the
ancient Mesopotamian moon cult.[87] In addition, his father's name,
Terah, could be related to Yerah, the moon. Abraham even had a
relative named Laban, "the white one," a transparent reference to
the moon.

The 20th century was a time of consequential archaeological
discovery in the Middle East. By the end of World War I, it appeared
that the historicity of the Bible was being corroborated by "parallel"
findings dated to the second millennium B.C.E. In fact, the scholarly
consensus in favor of historical authenticity had become so

overwhelming in the early 1970s that Thomas L. Thompson could safely write the following in his doctoral thesis (published in 1974):

> Even literary critical studies of individual
> traditions within Genesis now accept the basic
> historicity of Abraham, Isaac and Jacob.[88]

Shortly thereafter, however, this consensus collapsed. Detailed studies by Thompson and independent research by John van Seters (born: 1935), who taught at the University of North Carolina (see especially van Seters's book *Abraham in History and Tradition*[89]), as well as research by other scholars, combined to demonstrate that many of the "parallels" validating the biblical stories of the patriarchs and where they fit into the history and institutions of the 2nd millennium B.C.E. could not sustain close examination.

38. Closer Examination

The proper route to an understanding of the world is an examination of our errors about it.
Errol Morris (born: 1948) documentary film director

In contrast to fundamentalists, religious moderates may have wanted to believe the Bible was true, but as the old Russian proverb (popularized in America by President Ronald Reagan in the 1980s) says, they sought to "trust, but verify." The period from 1930 to 1970 was a particularly fruitful time for biblical archaeology. There were groundbreaking extra-biblical finds of corroborating evidence, validating the general accuracy of some of the Bible stories. The findings generated immense excitement and more researchers wanted to jump on the bandwagon. But in their enthusiasm, their research, either intentionally or not, was flawed. As was noted earlier, biblical archaeologists of this period sometimes were careless or misleading in their attempts to demonstrate the general accuracy of the Bible.

The relationship between husbands and wives in the Torah is one of the areas where faulty research is evident. In Genesis 11 we are introduced to Abraham and Sarah. In Genesis 12 they set out for the land of Canaan, where God "will make of you a great nation." Twice during their journey to Canaan, Abraham is concerned that the ruler of the land they pass through will find Sarah so beautiful that the ruler will kill Abraham in order to have Sarah to himself (Genesis 12 and 20). To protect himself, Abraham asks Sarah to say she is his sister. This scenario is repeated in Genesis 26 by the next generation of patriarchs/matriarchs when Isaac, the son of Abraham and Sarah, has the same fear and makes the same request of his wife, Rebekah.

These stories were disturbing to early readers of the Bible, as they are today to readers of the 21st century! The patriarch traveling abroad with his wife attempts to conceal their marital status by claiming that his traveling companion is his sister. Because the wife is very beautiful, the wife is coveted by a foreign ruler. As a sister and not a wife, the woman has the potential to become sexually available to the ruler. Although that potential is only realized in the first story—Genesis 12, where Pharaoh beds Sarah—it would be fair to say that our patriarch offered up his wife in order to protect, and incidentally enrich, himself. The resulting complications from these stories call into question the moral and ethical character of the ancestors of Israel.

Trying to address this quandary, E. A. Speiser (1902–1965), who taught at the University of Pennsylvania, claimed that such wife-sister marriages were a privilege of the mid-2nd millennium upper classes. Speiser based his theory on his understanding of a trove of tablets discovered at Nuzi, an ancient Mesopotamian city located in modern-day Iraq. According to Speiser, legal contracts found at Nuzi showed that a man might marry a woman and simultaneously adopt her as his legal sister in order to give their marriage greater prestige. Speiser believed that the patriarchs followed this Nuzi practice and also took their wives as legal "sisters." In between the time these traditions about the patriarchs originated and the time they were written down, the ancient practice was forgotten. Because none of the authors of the Torah had access to the original social setting of the stories, each writer provided his own version. Speiser's reading of the wife-sister stories was an ingenious attempt to demonstrate the compatibility of archaeology, source criticism, and biblical veracity. Criticism demonstrated how the sources diverged with respect to detail, and archaeology showed "what really happened." According to Speiser, the fact that the writers of the Torah preserved traditions they no longer completely understood was a testimony to their trustworthiness and the "general accuracy" of the preserved traditions.[90]

Speiser's theory was once paraded as a sterling example of how archaeology proved the authenticity of the Bible. But scholars later demonstrated that Speiser's analysis was hopelessly misguided.[91] As it turned out, there was no evidence from the documents he cited that a woman could be simultaneously a wife and a sister. Instead, what these documents showed was a case in which a woman had been contracted for a marriage, but the man changed his mind and the marriage did not occur. The same woman was then adopted as a "sister" by the man who no longer wished to take her as a wife. Especially damaging to Speiser's reading was the discovery that women adopted as sisters came from the lower classes, not from the upper class, as he maintained. By adopting these lower-class women, their "brothers" gained the right to sell them as slaves or to derive financial profit from arranging their marriages to other parties. Thus, Speiser had rewritten not only the biblical account but also the extrabiblical documents as well. In attempting to interpret the wife-sister stories of Genesis in light of the 2nd millennium document, he did justice to neither.[92]

Even though Speiser's attempt was a failure, archaeology was able to show that some of the elements presented in the Bible about the period of the patriarchs were unquestionably reflective of the 2nd millennium B.C.E. But these elements were not *exclusive* to the 2nd millennium B.C.E. For example, some scholars attempted to date the text based upon the belief that certain names indicated antiquity. But the fact that some of the names of characters in the patriarchal narrative corresponded to names found in 2nd millennium sources proved only that certain names were tenacious. Yes, there are some names that pass out of style, but there are many, like David, that were used 3000 years ago and are still popular today. Similarly, some scholars asserted that the rights and obligations of surrogate mothers outlined in the Bible (Genesis 16, 21) were strictly 2nd millennium conventions. But further research showed that what the Bible says about the rights and obligations of surrogates is irrelevant to dating the text because the same practices continued well after the 2nd millennium.

More troublesome were the 1st millennium elements that were used in supposedly 2nd millennium stories. In Genesis 12 we are told that Abraham acquired slaves and livestock, including camels. And camels figure importantly in the Genesis 24 story of how Rebekah is selected to become the wife for the patriarch Isaac. That the patriarchs Abraham and Isaac owned camels is a sign of their wealth and adds heft to the story. But archaeology "dates the arrival of the domesticated camel in the eastern Mediterranean region to the 10th century B.C.E. at the earliest, based on radioactive-carbon techniques."[93] Also anachronistically out of place, is the fact that Rebekah is identified as being an Aramean (Genesis 25:20). Archaeology shows that the Arameans came to the Levant during the Bronze Age (circa 1570–1150 B.C.E.), well after the setting of the story. Similarly, Abraham and Isaac are both said to have dealt with the Philistines; Abraham even, "resided in the land of the Philistines a long time" (Genesis 21:34). But research shows that the Philistines were one of the original Sea Peoples who first appeared in the eastern Mediterranean at the end of the 13th century B.C.E., centuries after the setting of the Abraham stories.

Now that the veneer of historical authenticity had been stripped away scholars had to, once again, confront the fact that "the Bible is largely a tissue of miracle stories."[94]

39. What's in a Name?

There stands the shadow of a glorious name.
Lucan (39–65 C.E.), poet

Not all scholars were happy with the conclusion that some of the biblical figures dearest to believers were fictional. In his decidedly conservative 1992 opinion, A. R. Millard (born: 1937), who taught at the University of Liverpool, argued that a date for a historical Abraham at the beginning of the 2nd millennium B.C.E. was necessary because his being so is:

> ... important for all who take biblical teaching about faith seriously ... Without Abraham, a major block in the foundations of both Christianity and Judaism is lost; a fictional Abraham might incorporate and illustrate communal beliefs, but could supply no rational evidence. Inasmuch as the Bible claims uniqueness, and the absolute of divine revelation, the Abraham narratives deserve a positive, respectful approach.[95]

In other words, Abraham has to be a historical figure because "biblical teaching about faith" requires a historical figure. Needless to say, this is hardly a historical argument.

When studying the Bible for historical information, we must bear in mind that the writers regularly attempted to explain phenomena that were well known to their audiences (if not to us) but whose origins were remote or obscure. Some of these explanations are less credible than others. For an example, we can look to an early chapter in Genesis. At the beginning of the Bible, Adam and Eve are created and have the sons Cain and Abel. After Cain kills Abel, God banishes Cain from the Garden of Eden, and Cain resettles east of Eden (Genesis 4:8–16). Somehow, Cain—the lone surviving offspring of the first people on earth—finds a wife out of nowhere and they have children, who have children, etc. The fifth generation after Cain produces the man Lamech who marries Zillah, and:

> Zillah . . . bore Tubal-Cain, the father of all who
> forge implements of bronze and iron. (Genesis
> 4:22)

The implication of Genesis 4:22 is that specialized metalwork is well-known to the author's audience, who would want to know the name of the inventor, or "father," of the necessary technology. For this ancient audience, the name Tubal-Cain was an obvious choice, because Tubal means "metalworker" and Cain means "smith"[96] According to Genesis 5:28, Lamech was also the father of Noah and, according to Genesis 11, the eleventh generation after Lamech produced our patriarch, Abraham. Knowing that biblical dating places Abraham around 1800 B.C.E., Tubal-Cain, the father of metalwork, must have been born a long, long time ago. However, Syria-Palestine did not enter the Iron Age until roughly 1200 B.C.E., therefore the passage about Tubal-Cain cannot be dated earlier than 1200 B.C.E. Needless to say, a historian of technology would not accept the biblical explanation and would look elsewhere.

This same analysis is precisely what we must do with regard to the name Abraham. Genesis 17 states that the first Hebrew patriarch was known as Abram until God changes his name, saying:

> As for me, this is my covenant with you. You
> shall be the father of a multitude of nations. And
> you shall no longer be called Abram, but your
> name shall be Abraham. (Genesis 17:3–5)

Let's analyze why here, too, "Abraham" was an obvious choice of name by the author. While the author's explanation that the name was given by God may have served the audience in biblical times, this explanation is by definition not historical and so we, the contemporary audience, must look elsewhere.

Recall that many scholars agree that before there was an "Israelite" people there were loosely banded tribes of people living in current day Israel. In 1901, the scholar Hermann Gunkel (1862–1932), who taught at the University of Giessen, suggested one productive avenue of inquiry which continues to be convincing today:

> [W]hen we regard [Israelite] heroes, Ishmael,
> Jacob, Esau, and others, as tribes and try to
> interpret the stories about them as tribal events;
> we are simply getting at their meaning as it was
> understood in primitive times in Israel.[97]

We cannot be as certain as Gunkel is about "the meaning as it was understood in primitive times." However, scholarship and archaeology lend credence to the possibility that the figure of Abraham probably originated in such a "tribal event." In 1921 an account of a major victory written in Egyptian on a stela was discovered at Beth-Shean, near the present-day border between Israel and Jordan. The stela, erected to honor Seti I, king of Egypt from 1290–1279 B.C.E., commemorates the victory of a battle that the Egyptians joined with a group called the "Raham."[98] At present, we have no further information about the subsequent fortunes of the Raham group. If the Rahamites became part of the new coalition Israel, it would have been natural for a Hebrew writer to provide them with an ancestor, just as was done for all the other Israelite tribes (as well as for the Ammonites and Moabites). In Semitic languages, "ab" can mean either "father" or "chieftain." Therefore, the name Ab-Raham, or Abraham, would have indicated the "father of the Raham tribe." Over time, this original sense would have been forgotten and the name reinterpreted as "father of a multitude of nations" (Genesis 17:4–5).

Personification of ideas or things (such as animals, human attributes, the elements, or objects), or of groups of people, is not new. In ancient times, when people questioned the causes—or source of power—of natural phenomena, answers were provided in the stories about human-like figures who eventually acquired distinctive personalities. Think for example of Poseidon, the Greek god of the sea, and his Roman counterpart, Neptune. Or Aphrodite, the Greek goddess of love and beauty, and her Roman counterpart, Venus. These personifications helped ancient cultures to understand the world around them.

Similarly, human nature would impel the ancient Israelites to attempt to answer the age-old questions of, "Why am I here? What is it all about?" It is conceivable that the united Israelite tribes invented characters who originated as the embodiments of tribes, and over time these characters acquired more sharply defined human characteristics. Because the biblical characters belonged to the larger community, accounts of their lives were circumscribed by both communal needs and political and social realities, while still being creative and entertaining. Against this background, we may best comprehend the biblical Abraham as a shifting allegory, sometimes symbolizing events both real and imagined in the life of the entire people and at other times standing for historical characters of different periods.[99]

40. Abraham as Allegory of Israel

I will make of you a great nation.   Genesis 12:2

Let's revisit the wife-sister stories of two chapters ago: A patriarch traveling abroad with his wife attempts to conceal the couple's marital status by claiming that the woman in question is his sister. In Genesis 12:10, Abraham and his wife Sarah (known as Abram and Sarai at this point) move to Egypt to reside there temporarily because of the severe famine in Canaan. Approaching the Egyptian border, Abraham fears that Sarah's great beauty will tempt the Egyptians to kill him and abduct his wife. In Genesis 12 Abraham asks of Sarah:

> Please say that you are my sister, that it may go
> well with me because of you, and that I may
> remain alive thanks to you. (Genesis 12:13)

The fact that Abraham encourages Sarah to become sexually available to Pharaoh may be offensive to readers. But the phrase "that it may go well with me," is an even more troubling complication, the meaning of which is illuminated just a few sentences later:

> And because of her, it went well with [Abraham];
> he acquired sheep, oxen, asses, male and female
> slaves, she-asses, and camels. (Genesis 12:16)

Abraham prostitutes his wife and is paid handsomely for this deception. Pharaoh, in contrast, acts honorably! Pharaoh wants Sarah as his wife. As was customary in the ancient Near East, a prospective groom was expected to pay a bride-price to the bride's father or brother, and so Pharaoh pays Abraham, her "brother," a substantial bride-price to seal the deal. God enters the story at this point and afflicts "Pharaoh and his household with mighty plagues on account of [Sarah]" (Genesis 12:17). Pharaoh, correctly interpreting the plagues as a sign that he has been deceived, summons Abraham and rebukes him for having misrepresented Sarah's marital status. He then sends Abraham and Sarah out of Egypt—with their newly acquired, ill-gotten gains.

About two thousand years ago, a Jewish reader decided to clean-up the story, but his sanitized version remained unknown until after World War II. In 1946, Bedouin shepherds discovered ancient writings that would come to be known as the Dead Sea Scrolls. One of original scrolls, known as the Genesis Apocryphon, is an embellished retelling of the stories of the patriarchs. Carbon-dated to the 3rd–1st century B.C.E., the writer of the Genesis Apocryphon attributes the deception of Pharaoh to Sarah, who suggests it to her husband in order to save his life.[100] The scroll's author adds the detail that, although Sarah was abducted, Pharaoh did not have sex with Sarah. This early text is only one in a long line of commentaries asserting that Sarah remained virtuous, such as those by the Jewish historian Josephus (37–100 C.E.), the medieval Jewish commentator Nahmanides (1194–1270 C.E.), and, more recently, the modern Bible scholar Nahum Sarna (1923–2005) who taught at Brandeis University.

On the level of narrative, the story is about the (mis)adventures of Abraham and Sarah in Egypt. But the rabbis of late antiquity noted that the story also operates at a second level as a symbolic prefiguration of what would later happen in Egypt to the descendants of Abraham and Sarah. Rabbi Phineas (2nd century C.E.), citing his teacher Rabbi Hoshaya, made the following observation: "The Holy, Be He blessed, said to Abraham our father, 'Go pave the way for your children.' So you find that everything written of Abraham our father, is written of his children." Similarly, a 3rd century teaching by Rabbi Levi states: "The Holy, be He blessed, gave Abraham a sign, so that whatever happened to him happened to his children." These rabbinic teachings note the parallels in the stories as follows:[101]

Of Abraham it is written: (Genesis 12:10–13:2)	Of Israel it is written:
There was famine in the land	for these two years, famine Genesis 45:6
[Abraham] went down to Egypt	Our ancestors went down to Egypt Numbers 20:15
to sojourn there	to sojourn in the land we came Genesis 47:4
for the famine was severe in the land	For the famine was severe in the land Genesis 43:1
They will kill me but keep you alive	Every male born you shall cast in the Nile but keep every female alive Exodus 1:22
Pharaoh put men in charge of him and sent him off	The Egyptians pressed the people to send them off quickly Exodus 12:33
[Abraham] was rich in cattle, silver and gold	He brought them out with silver and gold Psalms 105:37

Rabbis Hoshaya, Phineas and Levi express no doubt that the events of both the earlier "Abraham" and the later "Israel" had actually transpired. Because God was the cause of all events, he could shape the contours of an early event to symbolize and prefigure a later event, of which he was also the cause. On this point, the rabbis were in full agreement with Paul, who some two centuries earlier had observed the following of his biblical ancestors:

> All these things happened to them as symbolic
> types [*typikos*] but were written for us as warning.
> (1 Corinthians 10:11, translation by the author)

To understand the critical point of the Abraham-Sarah-Pharaoh text we need only substitute the symbolic reading with an allegorical reading. That is, Abraham's descent into Egypt is an allegory of Israel's descent into Egypt. God's plagues on Pharaoh and his household in Genesis 12 are allegories of the plagues God will later inflict on Pharaoh and Egypt in Exodus 13. The language of Pharaoh's expulsion of Abraham is precisely the language of expulsion of the Israelites. Just like Abraham, the Israelites leave with riches of silver and gold, as we see in Exodus 12:

> The Israelites had asked the Egyptians for silver
> and gold jewelry . . . Because God had made the
> Egyptians well disposed toward them, they let
> Israelites have whatever they asked. (Exodus
> 12:35–36, translation by the author)

What the rabbis of late antiquity did not observe is that, because the tradition of Israelite servitude in Egypt seems itself allegorical, the Abraham-Sarah-Pharaoh episode is an allegory of an allegory.

41. Wicked Cities

God bears with the wicked, but not forever.
Miguel de Cervantes (1547–1616), author

With the support of God and of his wife, "From Egypt, [Abraham] went up into the Negeb, with his wife and all that he possessed, together with Lot" (Genesis 13:1). Lot, Abraham's nephew whose father died earlier in the telling, had been traveling with the group since they set out on this journey. At this point, "all that he possessed" had grown into a considerable fortune of livestock, slaves, and precious objects. In fact, the abundance had become an overabundance and Abraham and Lot saw that "their possessions were so great that they could not remain together" (Genesis 13:6) because their herdsmen were quarreling. Abraham and Lot agree to part ways within the region of Canaan. Although the inhabitants of Sodom were known to be "very wicked sinners against the Eternal" (Genesis 13:13), Lot saw that the plain of the Jordan River near the city of Sodom was fertile, so he went north-east and pitched his tent there. Abraham went south-west and pitched his tent in Hebron.

Genesis 14, the next chapter in the Abraham story, is one of the most debated chapters in contemporary scholarship.[102] The chapter begins by specifically naming eight kings who reigned simultaneously, plus one more king who is not named. This unusual list of multiple kings has led some scholars to view the chapter as a precious historical record, possibly from the 2nd millennium B.C.E. If some, or any, of the kings could be identified with certainty, then a date might be confidently assigned for the historical Abraham. Other scholars however have interpreted this chapter as a kind of midrash written in the Persian period between the 6th and 4th centuries B.C.E. or, even later, in the Hasmonean period between the 2nd and 1st century B.C.E.

The first eleven verses of the story make no mention of Abraham or his family. Instead, this section describes a war between two sets of allies: four kings from outside the area of Canaan who have formed a coalition to subdue five kings reigning within Canaan, in the same fertile plain in which Lot had settled. The "four kings against those five" (Genesis 14:9) demand regular payments of tribute from the conquered, eventually leading the five to revolt. The four ruling kings march to squelch the uprising, subduing other territories along the way, including Amorite territory, and maintain the upper hand. It is at this juncture that the events become relevant to Abraham:

> So the enemy took all the goods of Sodom and
> Gomorrah and all their provisions and went their
> way; they also took Lot, the son of [Abraham's]
> brother, who dwelled in Sodom, and his goods
> and departed. (Genesis 14:11-12, translation by the
> author)

A refugee from the battles brings news of the capture of Lot and his possessions to "Abram the Hebrew" (Genesis 14:13), who is living in Hebron and has become allied to three Amorite brothers. Abraham thus has a personal and military obligation to enter the war, even though this puts him on the same side militarily as the wicked cities of Sodom, Gomorrah, and the others. Mustering his 318 troops, Abraham:

> went in pursuit as far as Dan . . . [Abraham] and
> his servants deployed against them and defeated
> them; and he pursued them as far as Hobah,
> which is north of Damascus. He brought back all
> the possessions; he also brought back his kinsman
> Lot and his possessions, and the women and the
> rest of the people. (Genesis 14:14-16)

Upon Abraham's victory, the king of Sodom greets him and as a reward offers Abraham the opportunity to keep any captured goods for himself, but Abraham refuses. Abraham does not want to be too closely associated with the king of the wicked city of Sodom, or to appear to be acting as a mercenary. However, Abraham does allow the men working under him to take their share of the hoard. During the same kingly greeting, Melchi-zedek, king of Salem and a priest as well, brings bread and wine for Abraham and offers a blessing. Abraham, apparently appreciating the acknowledgment of the glory of God, gives to Melchi-zedek "a tenth of everything" (Genesis 14:20).

There are a few reasons to question the historical authenticity of the Genesis 14 story. First, we are told that Abraham went in pursuit as far as the town of Dan. According to Judges 18, during the time of Joshua, four generations *after* the time of Abraham, the members of the tribe of Dan were "seeking a territory in which to settle" (Judges 18:1). They found a town, Laish, where the people were "tranquil and unsuspecting, and they put them to the sword and burned down the town . . . They rebuilt the town and settled there, and they named the town Dan, after their ancestor" (Judges 18:27–29). Scholars believe the narrative in the book of Judges is more closely aligned with history, so it is unlikely that a town named Dan existed at the time of Abraham.

The second reason we know these passages cannot be historical lies within the moralistic tale of the cities of Sodom and Gomorrah. Recall that Abraham allied himself with the five kingdoms that had been oppressed. Although the kingdoms of Sodom and Gomorrah were the most notorious of the five, all five kingdoms were said to have been populated by "wicked sinners against the Eternal." The king of Sodom is named "Bera," which can be translated from Hebrew to "In-Evil," and the king of Gomorrah is named "Birsha" which can be translated to "In-Wickedness." These names would not be out of place in a fictional, morality play.

A third reason to question the authenticity of the passages is that, although the names of the invaders have a more authentic ring, those that can be identified were not contemporaneous with each other. Needless to say, an international alliance of this scope would almost certainly have left more traces than Genesis 14.

It is worth reviewing the Sodom and Gomorrah story for readers who may not recall the details or be familiar with its place in modern discourse. In Genesis 13 we are told that the people of Sodom are "wicked," but are given no specifics. Then, in Genesis 18, God says to Abraham, "The outrage of Sodom and Gomorrah is so great and their sin so grave!" God decides to send two angels to inspect Sodom and report whether the atrocities that have reached God's ears are correct. At this point, Abraham begins to bargain with God on behalf of the cities and their inhabitants. Abraham asks God, "What if there should be fifty within the city who are innocent; will you then wipe out the place and not forgive it for the sake of the innocent fifty who are in it? . . . And the Eternal answered, 'If I find within the city of Sodom fifty innocent ones, I will forgive the whole place for their sake'" (Genesis 18:24–26). Abraham continues to bargain by lowering the number of innocents to forty-five, then forty, then thirty, then twenty, and finally, ten innocent people.

The reader might be forgiven for imagining that there would be at least ten innocents and the city would be saved. The writer of Genesis 19 precludes that possibility by graphically illustrating the depth of Sodom's depravity. The two angels sent by God arrive at the entrance to Sodom in the guise of travelers and prepare to go into the town. Abraham's nephew, Lot, sees the men at the entrance and presses them to avail themselves of his hospitality. Lot provides food and accommodation to the traveling men. But that very night, all the men of Sodom, young and old:

> . . . gathered about the house. And they shouted to
> Lot and said to him, "Where are the men who
> came to you tonight? Bring them out to us, that
> we may be intimate with them." [Lot countered]
> "I beg you, my friends, do not commit such a
> wrong. Look, I have two daughters who have not
> known a man. Let me bring them out to you, and
> you may do to them as you please; but do not do
> anything to these men, because they have come
> under the shelter of my roof." (Genesis 19:4–8)

Undeterred, the wicked mob attempts to break down the door to Lot's house and seize him. A blinding light makes it impossible for the mob to pursue Lot and his family. The angels lead Lot, Lot's wife, and his two unmarried daughters out of Sodom, warning them not to look back at the divine demolition that was about to befall the city. Then:

> . . . the Eternal rained upon Sodom and Gomorrah
> sulfurous fire from the Eternal out of heaven. He
> annihilated those cities and the entire Plain, and
> all the inhabitants of the cities and the vegetation
> of the ground. Lot's wife looked back, and

thereupon turned into a pillar of salt." (Genesis 19:24-26)*

---

* Fun Fact: In popular culture, references to Lot's wife turning into a pillar of salt were used in Kurt Vonnegut's *Slaughterhouse Five*, and in a line uttered by Robert De Niro in the movie "Once Upon A Time In America." Also, because the men in this story wanted to be "intimate," or have sexual intercourse with the visiting men, this story provides the origin of the words sodomy and sodomite.

42. Abraham as Allegory of David

Behold, the lion of the tribe of Judah, the root of David.
Revelation 5:5

In a 1982 *Journal of Jewish Studies* article, biblical scholar Yohanan Muffs (1932–2009), who taught at the Jewish Theological Seminary, shows how Genesis 14 depicts Abraham as a paradigmatic noble warrior:

> Each element of Genesis 14 has its exact
> counterpart in the laws of war and in the etiquette
> of booty restoration found sporadically in the
> international treaties of Boghazköi and Ugarit.
> The Israelite narrator brings together all these
> ancient laws of war and peace in his depiction of
> Abraham as the most noble of warriors.[103]

King David is a similar exemplar. David does not seek out the position of king, it is thrust upon him by God through the prophet Samuel (I Samuel 16:12). The Bible tells us that David was the eighth son of Jesse and lived in Bethlehem, a town near Jerusalem located in the southern part of the united Hebrew kingdom. David is said to be "skilled in music; he is a stalwart fellow and a warrior, sensible in speech, and handsome in appearance, and the Eternal is with him" (I Samuel 16:18). And when the Philistine Goliath provokes the Israelites, David announces that, as a shepherd:

> ". . . if a lion or bear came and carried off an
> animal from the flock, I would go after it and
> fight and rescue it from its mouth. And if it
> attacked me, I would seize it by the beard and
> strike it down and kill it. Your servant has killed
> both lion and bear; and that uncircumcised
> Philistine shall end up like one of them, for he has

defied the ranks of the living God." (I Samuel
17:34–36)

Although a full set of armor is offered to David, David realizes he
cannot move properly in the armor and opts to face Goliath in his own
shepherd's clothing, armed with a slingshot, stones, and the support of
the Eternal. David uses his slingshot to strike Goliath in the head,
causing Goliath to fall to the ground, dead. Having no sword of his
own, David runs to Goliath, stands over him and uses Goliath's own
sword to behead him (I Samuel 17:38–51).

The David and Goliath story has had a lasting impact on western
culture. David's defeat of Goliath inspired artists such as Donatello,
Michelangelo, and Caravaggio to create artistic masterpieces. The trope
of an underdog defeating a mightier opponent continues to be a
compelling storyline—think of Star Wars' Luke Skywalker vs. Darth
Vader, or the Hunger Games' Katniss Everdeen vs. President Snow.
And, in real life, the 1980 US Olympic men's hockey team vs. the
Russian hockey team, and Malala Yousafzai vs. those who would deny
females an education.

But what do we know about the actual King David of Israel?
Historians agree that a King David probably existed around 1000
B.C.E., but none of the biblical tales can be verified. As of this writing,
the only evidence we have of a David is from a stela found during a
1993–1994 excavation at Tel Dan in northern Israel and dated to about
870 B.C.E. Although the stela is broken, a line on it refers to "the
House of David."[104]

The biblical text has noteworthy parallels between the tales of
David and the tales of Abraham. The medieval French Jewish scholar
Joseph Bekhor Shor (12th century) compared the scene in Genesis 14
where Melchi-zedek brings bread and wine to Abraham with a scene
in 2 Samuel 17 where David's supporters bring provisions to him and
his troops during Absalom's rebellion.[105] (We will take a closer look at
details of this particular parallel in chapter 44. *Note: The character
Abraham is named Abram at this point in the story. We refer to him as Abraham
for clarity.*)

The scholars Benjamin Mazar (1906–1995) and Moshe Weinfeld
(1925–2009), both of whom taught at Hebrew University of Jerusalem,
as well as other scholars, note that Genesis 14 goes into geographic

detail about where Abraham's campaign occurs. The named locales were known to the original audience of the text, who would have positively responded to this justification of Israel's possession of the land on both sides of the Jordan River in the Davidic period. And they would have nodded affirmatively at the end of Genesis 13, immediately preceding the account of Abraham's battles, when told that Abraham dwelled in Hebron, the city that every Israelite knew had served as David's capital for seven years.

Anachronistic inconsistencies in the text are another flag for us. As mentioned in the prior chapter, we know that the town of Dan, where Abraham is said to have pursued an enemy, had not yet been named "Dan" at the time of the patriarch. Significantly, according to 2 Samuel 17:11, Dan is the northern border of David's Israelite kingdom. In a similar vein, Genesis 14 specifies Abraham's campaign stop at Tamar which, according to 1 Kings 9:18, was built during the period of David's successor, his son Solomon (hundreds of years after the time of the biblical Abraham). Another stop on the campaign was Kadesh, located at Ein Qudeirat near the junction of a road leading from Suez to Beersheba and Hebron. Archaeology of the site shows three superimposed fortresses, the earliest dating from the 10th century B.C.E.—that is, also from the time of King Solomon.[106]

In short, we have strong indications that Genesis 14 was composed for the aggrandizement of David and Solomon. Abraham the noble warrior is allegorical for David the noble warrior. A good example is provided by biblical scholar Yohanan Muffs who demonstrates that Genesis 14 corresponds very closely to 1 Samuel 30. Following is a side-by-side analysis of the similarities:

Abraham's campaign in Genesis 14:	David's campaign in I Samuel 30:
Four kings commence a campaign of seizure and occupation while Abraham had traveled away.	The city of Ziklag, where David and his troops lived, is attacked by Amalekites while they had been battling elsewhere.
"The invaders seized all the wealth of Sodom and Gomorrah and all their possessions . . . They also took Lot" [Abraham's nephew].	"David and his men came [back to Ziklag] and found it burned down, and their wives and sons and daughters taken captive."
Abraham defeated the enemy and "brought back all the possessions; he also brought back his kinsman Lot and his possession, and the women and the rest of the people."	"David rescued all that the Amalekites had taken away; He rescued his two wives. Nothing of all of theirs was missing, young or old, large or small, sons or daughters or possessions, whatever has been taken all of it David brought back."
Abraham refuses the spoils of war for himself, but gives a tenth of everything to the king/priest who blesses Abraham in the name of God.	David, "sent some of the spoil to the elders of Judah and to his friends, saying, 'This is a present for you from our spoil of the enemies of the Eternal.'"

Another interesting parallel is provided in Genesis 14:15, which relates how Abraham the noble warrior engaged in battle "north of Damascus." That point would not have been lost on an audience familiar with the information provided in 2 Samuel 8:

> When the Arameans of Damascus came to help
> King Hadadezer of Zobah, David killed 22,000
> men of the Arameans. Then David put garrisons
> among the Arameans of Damascus, and the
> Arameans became servants to David and brought
> tribute. God gave victory to David wherever he
> went. David took the gold shields that were
> carried by the servants of Hadadezer and brought
> them to Jerusalem. From Betah and from
> Berothai, towns of Hadadezer, King David took a
> great amount of bronze. (2 Samuel 8:5–8,
> translation by the author)

The scholars Hayim Tadmor and Peter Machinist, among others, observed that David and his successor, Solomon, had made radical changes in Israelite society. [107] One of the most radical of David's policies was military expansionism, which brought glory and wealth to the throne but at the same time risked unacceptable losses to the Israelite populace. A success like the one referred to above might not necessarily compensate for collateral damage. In fact, I Samuel 30:6 tells us that David was met with an insurrection among his troops after the Amalekites burned down Ziklag, a city under David's protection, and they carried off the women and children living there:

> David was in great danger, for the people spoke of
> stoning him, because all the people were bitter in
> spirit on account of their sons and daughters. (1
> Samuel 30:6, translation by the author)

A story that Abraham reluctantly, but nobly, fought his enemies could justify David's military adventures. If father Abraham had made war and put lives at risk, so could David.

Also questionable was David's choice of the company he kept. David's Israelite contemporaries might have wondered why David associated with their long-time foes the Philistines. According to I Samuel 27, David fled to the land of the Philistines and lived in Philistine territory for 16 months, where he and his men served in a Philistine army.

Abraham too had some questionable alliances, but his heroism and nobility went a long way in overcoming that embarrassing fact. In Genesis 14, Abraham fought on the same side as the wicked kings; the kings of the cities of Sodom and Gomorrah that were, later, justly destroyed by God because of their unmitigated wickedness. We are also told that Abraham had been living among the Amorites, who are the enemies of the Israelites in other parts of the Bible. (For example, in Deuteronomy 31:4 we are told that, "The Eternal will do to them as he did to Sihon and Og, kings of the Amorites, and to their countries, when he wiped them out." And in Joshua 10:12, "the Eternal routed the Amorites.")

But alliances change. And in the Bible sometimes terms change, too. The term "Amorite" is not always used for the same specific ethnic group.[108] In fact, when reading I Samuel 7 we can see where the term "Amorite" was interchanged with the term "Philistine."

> The cities that the Philistines had taken from
> Israel returned to Israel . . . these cities Israel got
> back from the Philistines, there being a pact
> [šalom] between Israel and these Amorites. (I
> Samuel 7:14, translation by the author)

Again, if Abraham could practice *realpolitik* and enter into questionable alliances, so could David. The allegory of Abraham is a piece of political propaganda, composed during the reign of Solomon (circa 970–931 B.C.E.), David's son and successor, to answer criticisms of the monarchy.

43. Water Rights & Loyalty

. . . a parched and thirsty land that has no water.   Psalms 63:2

During their travels to Canaan, Abraham and Sarah journey through the land of the Philistine king, Abimelech of Gerar. Abraham is invited to settle on Abimelech's land (Genesis 20:15). After Abraham has lived there for some time, and Abimelech sees that Abraham has prospered, he says to Abraham:

> "God is with you in all you do. Now swear to me
> by these gods that you will not betray me or my
> future descendants but that you will be as loyal to
> me and to the land where you have sojourned as I
> have been to you." Abraham responded, "I will
> swear." (Genesis 21:22–24, translation by the
> author)

Abraham agrees to swear, but first needs to resolve a condition precedent:[109] During his sojourn on Abimelech's land, Abraham had dug a well at Beersheba—a well which was later seized by Abimelech's underlings. Although Abimelech denies any knowledge of the seizure, Abraham insists upon making it clear that he owns the rights to the well. To formalize this, Abraham gives Abimelech seven ewes and says:

> "You are to accept these seven ewes from me to
> attest that I dug this well." This is why that place
> was named Beersheba, for there the two of them
> swore an oath . . . Then [Abraham] planted a
> tamarisk* at Beersheba and invoked there the
> name of the Eternal, God Everlasting. And
> Abraham resided in the land of the Philistines a
> long time. (Genesis 21:30–34, translation by the
> author)

---

* A type of tree. Because trees are so long-lived, they often served as a lasting memorial to an oath.

Water rights in this arid part of the world would have been of prime importance. Bible scholar Hermann Gunkel (1862–1932), who taught at the University of Giessen, believed that the disputes between the characters Abraham and Abimelech were in fact literary representations of conflict among larger constituencies:

> Once in ancient times, so we may assume, there
> were conflicts over wells between the citizens of
> Gerar and the neighboring bedouin, ending in a
> compromise at Beer-sheba. The legend depicts
> these affairs as a war and a treaty between
> Abimelech, king of Gerar, and the patriarchs
> called in the legend Abraham or Isaac.[110]

Biblical dating of the patriarch Abraham places him around the year 1800 B.C.E. which would indeed be "ancient times," as Gunkel describes them. But how "ancient" could they really be? Let's start with Abraham's treaty with the Philistine king. We know that the earliest reference to the Philistines comes from Pharaoh Ramses III (circa 1198–1166 B.C.E.), who identified them among a group of "sea peoples" arriving from the area of the Aegean Sea to the Levant in the 12th century B.C.E., well after the time of the biblical Abraham.

Inasmuch as the digging of the well is central to the biblical story, establishing the date of its construction would be relevant. Archaeology at the site of the biblical Beersheba has thrown doubt on the veracity of the tale. Tel Beersheba is located in southern Israel, just a few miles from modern-day Beersheba. By carbon-dating a ceramics collection, including shards of Philistine pottery, archaeologists established that the earliest occupation of the site is from sometime around the end of the 12th century or beginning of the 11th century B.C.E.[111] Evidence of substantial building increases from the mid to late 11th century B.C.E., with an organized site plan that is dated to the late 11th or early 10th century B.C.E. Once again archaeology proves that the details of this story could not have happened at the time of the biblical Abraham.

Finally, the oath, which is couched in treaty terminology, specifies that Abraham will demonstrate continuing loyalty (ḥesed) to Abimelech, just as Abimelech had to Abraham. The oath is binding upon the descendants of the original parties as well as the parties themselves, meaning that Abraham is not to be disloyal to Abimelech himself or to his child or grandchild or to the land in which he has lived. The language of disloyalty to the future generations is couched in treaty terminology that would not be out of place in the 10th century B.C.E.[112]

We have ascertained that in 1800 B.C.E. the Philistines were not in Canaan, Beersheba was not inhabited, and the treaty language in the biblical tale is anachronistic for 1800 B.C.E. However, a 10th century date for this Abraham tale fits perfectly with the events of King David's life. According to the narrative of 1 Samuel 27, David fled from King Saul (the king of Israel before David, who suspected David of having designs on the throne) and sought shelter in Gath, a Philistine city. David lived for a considerable time in Philistine territory as a military ally of the Philistine king.

Discerning readers of the Bible may sense that the descriptions of David's cooperation with the Philistines are designed to put the best face on an embarrassing situation. The Philistines had been Israel's dedicated opponents throughout Saul's reign (I Samuel 14:52). Saul and three of his sons, including Jonathan who was allegedly David's closest friend, died during a battle with the Philistines at the very time that David and his followers were serving in the Philistine ranks. In fact, according to I Samuel 28 and 29, David's contingent avoided direct battle with Saul on the Philistine side only because some of the Philistine princes questioned David's loyalty; a charge which David himself protested. After David's ascent to the throne, there are some notices of hostility between the Israelites and the Philistines (II Samuel 5:17–25; 8:1; 21:15–22). On the whole though, peace with the Philistines seems to have prevailed during David's reign. As king, David had Philistine detachments in his army (II Samuel 8:18; 15:18), and his descendants continued to hold the Philistine city of Ziklag, which had been given to David in return for his services to the Philistine king.

As we saw, the closing verse of the Genesis 21 Abraham-Abimelech-well story is, "Abraham resided in the land of the Philistines a long time" (Genesis 21:34). Just as we did with the allegorical connection between David and Abraham in Genesis 14, we can read the Abraham-Abimelech-well story of Genesis 21 as a political allegory, one that serves as an apology for David's pact with the Philistines. If Abraham, the great hero of the past, could cooperate with the Philistines, there was no reason that David could not do likewise.

The covenant with Abraham is initiated by Abimelech, who opens the conversation with "God is with you in all you do." Similarly, we are told in I Samuel 18 that, "David was successful in all his undertakings, for the Eternal was with him." That God is "with" Abraham in "everything" indicates allegorically that God approves of *all* of David's actions, including the continuation of good relations with the Philistines in whose land David had dwelled. At the same time, however, the fact that Abraham resolved his rights to his well indicates to the Israelites that Abraham/David will stand up to the Philistines when it is necessary to defend the precious right to water.

Some final observations on these stories:

- Be'er in Hebrew means "well" and sheba (sometimes written as "sheva") can mean either "seven" or "oath."

- The scene of the pact between Abraham and Abimelech at Beersheba is regularly identified as the southern limit of David's kingdom.[113]

- In the generation after Abraham, his son Isaac goes through the same oath-taking over water rights—also with Abimelech! In Genesis 26, Isaac's servants dig two wells which are then seized by herdsmen living on Abimelech's land. After traveling away from those wells, Isaac is told by God that he has reached a good place to settle, so Isaac's servants dig a new well and he starts to prosper. Abimelech comes to Isaac and says:

> "We now see plainly that the Eternal has been
> with you, and we thought: Let there be a sworn
> treaty between our two parties, between you and
> us. Let us make a pact with you that you will not
> do us harm, just as we have not molested you but
> have always dealt kindly with you and sent you
> away in peace." (Genesis 26:28–29)

44. Jerusalem

The view of Jerusalem is the history of the world; it is the history of earth and of heaven. Benjamin Disraeli (1804–1881), U.K. Prime Minister, 1868, and 1874–1880

The episode in Genesis 14, where Abraham is blessed by the king/priest Melchi-zedek, after which Abraham gives Melchi-zedek a ten-percent tithe, deserves a closer look. Scholars note that the episode feels like an interpolation embedded into the larger story. Without the interpolation, the passage would read as follows:

> When [Abraham] returned from defeating
> Chedorlaomer and the kings with him, the king
> of Sodom came out to meet him in the Valley of
> Shaveh, which is the Valley of the King . . . Then
> the king of Sodom said to [Abraham], "Give me
> the persons, and take the possession for yourself."
> (Genesis 14:18 and 21)

However, in the present form of the text, between those two verses we find the following:

> Melchi-zedek, king of Salem, brought out bread
> and wine. He was a priest of [the god] El-Elyon.
> He blessed him, saying, "Blessed be [Abraham] to
> El-Elyon, Creator of Heaven and Earth. And
> blessed be El-Elyon, who delivered your foes into
> your power." Then [Abraham] gave him a tithe
> of all. (Genesis 14:19–20, translation by the author)

The Melchi-zedek episode is not overly significant to the Abraham story, and the king of Sodom passages would flow more easily if the Melchi-zedek passages were removed. However, scholars have shown that the passages did serve the needs of the Davidic monarchy.[114] Melchi-zedek is identified as *the king of Salem*. Salem is none other than a nickname for Jerusalem.

Keeping in mind that there is no hard evidence about David or his movements, through the biblical reading we can surmise that around 1000 B.C.E. David was the ruler of an area in the southern part of Canaan, perhaps in Judah. His base was in Hebron, and he led a campaign into the northern part of Canaan. David's goal would have been to spread his authority, which would include unifying the people under his sovereignty.

Perhaps in an effort to move closer to the center of his new domain, or perhaps because he believed the location was more defensible, or perhaps for any number of reasons we could speculate about, David chose to move his base, including the main temple of worship for the god of his people, to Jerusalem. Archaeology has shown that a city already existed at the site of Jerusalem by about 3500 B.C.E. Undoubtedly, there were people living at this location and worshipping their own gods at their temple. David's decision to move his base, and to move the center of worship for his people, would have been disconcerting. And causing even more agitation, the Israelite god would now be worshipped at a site where other gods had previously been worshipped.

The scholar Ernst A. Knauf (born: 1953), professor at the University of Bern, is particularly forceful in his assertions about the cultic aspects of Jerusalem:

> Solomon did not build the temple of Jerusalem or any other temple that is presently known, but, he introduced the Israelite and Judaean tribal god Yahweh into the main temple of Canaanite Jerusalem, where he joined El . . . and Asherah as a lesser god.[115]

Even though Knauf overstepped the limits of the available evidence, he is surely on the right track in showing that Genesis 14 fulfills the religious-political objective of justifying the actions of David. For many Israelites, the cultic associations of Jerusalem must have been largely unfavorable. The allegory about Abraham and his dealings with Melchi-zedek claims that the relocation of the cult center of the Israelites to Jerusalem, originally a non-Israelite city, was not an innovation. The site of Jerusalem had always been holy. This fact is echoed in Psalms 76, as follows:

> God has made himself known in Judah,
>   his name is great in Israel;
>   Salem became his abode;
>   Zion*, his dwelling.
> There he broke the fiery arrows of the bow, the
> shield and the sword of war.

David is credited, like the revered ancestor Abraham, with recognizing the holy significance of Jerusalem. Therefore, bringing the worship of God to Jerusalem was right and proper.

The very name of the king/priest Melchi-zedek would have also helped to assuage concerns. People find comfort in the familiar, and Melchi-zedek shares the second element of his name with that of Adoni-Zedek. According to Joshua 10, a tradition with which the Israelites would have been familiar, Adoni-Zedek was a king of Jerusalem contemporary with Joshua. More persuasively, we cannot doubt that the ancient audience would have connected the name Melchi-zedek with the name Zadok, which shares the consonantal root structure ZDK. Keeping in mind that ancient Hebrew and Aramaic were only written with consonants, this similarity would have been even more pronounced. Zadok was a priest at the shrine of Jerusalem during the reign of David, and the sole priest at that same site during the reign of Solomon.[116]

Not only did David change the location of the ruling priesthood, he also appointed his own sons as priests (see II Samuel 8:18) thereby solidifying the power of the Jerusalem priests. There can be little doubt that elements of the native Israelite priesthood(s) would have objected to their loss in authority as they became subordinate to priests located in Jerusalem, who gained a level of seniority because David selected

---

* In this psalm, "Zion" refers to Mount Zion, which in 1000 B.C.E. was topped with a fortress that had been conquered by David and then included within the city walls of Jerusalem. Over time, the meaning of the term "Zion" expanded to indicate the entire city of Jerusalem, or the entire land of Israel or, sometimes, the Jewish afterlife.

their city as his base.

Biblical sources indicate that there was significant opposition to these religious innovations, which would eventually lead to the rejection of Jerusalem's monarchy, calendar and priesthood.

Summary – Part VII

- According to internal biblical dates, if the patriarch Abraham really existed, he would have lived circa 1800 B.C.E.

- The years of 1930–1970 were a fruitful time of archaeological discovery, raising hopes that the biblical stories would be proved to be demonstrably true.

- Careful research demonstrated undeniable anachronisms, such as camels as part of 19th–18th century B.C.E. stories. Archaeology shows that camels were not domesticated in Canaan before the 10th century B.C.E.

- The writers of the Bible attempted to explain phenomena that were well known to their audiences, but whose origins were remote or obscure. One way to do that is by using names that are self-explanatory. For example, Ab means "father" in Semitic languages, and evidence points to a tribe of people called the "Raham." Therefore, Abraham could be the ancestor of the tribe of Raham.

- The Abraham stories sometimes serve as allegories for all the people of Israel. For example, Genesis 12 tells how Abraham went down to Egypt during a famine and, through the intervention of God, emerged wealthy. Abraham's story foreshadows the story of the people of Israel going down into the land of Egypt but emerging with wealth thanks to the support of God.

- Parallels between the stories of Abraham and the stories of King David, the king of Israel circa 1000 B.C.E., are numerous.

- The Abraham stories also served to bolster support for some of the radical changes David introduced into Israelite society. Telling stories about similar actions by Abraham justifies David's actions.

- Because Abraham is a noble warrior and protects his people, and because his actions align so closely with David's, the ancient Israelites could be assured that David would protect them.

- The parallel stories of Abraham and David fulfill the religious-political objective of justifying the actions of David and his successor/son, Solomon. For example, stories about Abraham revering the king/priest of "Salem," the short-form of the name Jerusalem, were written to assuage any angst over David making his capital Jerusalem.

PART VIII
JACOB, JOSEPH & JEROBOAM

Overview: In roughly 922 B.C.E., the northern region of Israel broke away from the southern region of Judah. Writers from the breakaway northern kingdom borrowed heavily from well-known ancient stories and motifs to create legends that justified their separate existence and the innovations of their king, Jeroboam I. But when the northern kingdom was conquered by the Assyrians in 722 B.C.E., the people of the two kingdoms which had been separate for 200 years came together again and a new story was written.

45. A Kingdom Divided

If a house is divided against itself, that house cannot stand.
Mark 3:25

Modern scholarship agrees that before 922 B.C.E. there were tribes of people living in the area of current day Israel who, over time, united. The Bible tells us that Saul was the first king of this united group, followed (briefly) by his son, Ishbosheth, and then by David, whom we studied in the last chapter. David's son Solomon became the king after David. But, according to 1 Kings 11, Solomon:

> . . . had seven hundred royal wives and three
> hundred concubines; and his wives turned his
> heart away [from the Eternal] . . . And the
> Eternal said to Solomon, "Because . . . you have
> not kept my covenant and the laws which I
> enjoined upon you—I will tear the kingdom away
> from you and give it to one of your servants. But,
> for the sake of your father David, I will not do it
> in your lifetime; I will tear it away from your son.
> However, I will not tear away the whole
> kingdom; I will give your son one tribe, for the
> sake of my servant David, and for the sake of
> Jerusalem which I have chosen." (1 Kings 11:3–13)

Sure enough, Solomon's son, Rehoboam, lost the united monarchy of Israel and Judah in 1 Kings 12. The book of Kings tells us that Jeroboam I (a man who had worked for Solomon) and his troops rose up against Rehoboam, dividing the kingdom into the northern kingdom of Israel and the southern kingdom of Judah. We lack supporting evidence that the division of the kingdoms happened exactly the way the Bible claims; however, the existence of the two separate kingdoms—Judah and Israel—is an undeniable fact.

As noted earlier, in 720 B.C.E. the northern kingdom was destroyed by the Assyrians, who deported many of its inhabitants and replaced them with peoples from other conquered territories.

Some of the inhabitants of the defeated northern kingdom migrated to the southern kingdom—bringing their stories and traditions with them. The fact that stories from both the northern kingdom and the southern kingdom have been integrated into the one Bible accounts for some of the inconsistences in the Bible.

The task of recovering the historical background of the northern traditions is simpler than for the southern traditions because the northern kingdom had a briefer existence. Additionally, examination of northern traditions is enhanced by archaeological finds of inscriptions commemorating the battle conquests of Assyrian kings, which sometimes share the same names and sites of battles featured in stories from the biblical books of Kings. It is too much to say that everything in the books of Kings is true, but scholars agree that—absent the miraculous elements—there is a good deal of reliable historical material in Kings.

That said, we must bear in mind that the northern traditions that came south to Judah with the survivors of the Assyrian conquest were often reworked negatively by southern writers, some of whom considered the entire northern kingdom to have been a sinful aberration. As such, the defeat of the northern kingdom of Israel allowed the southerners of Judah to advance their agenda that God was punishing the northerners for their sinfulness, while showing that the southerners merited divine protection. Consequently, any critical modern reading of the Bible must allow for the editorial process that northern documents underwent in Judah, and later in the postexilic Jewish communities.

46. The Twelve Tribes

Each tribe has its characteristics, it is true.
John Hanning Speke (1827–1864), explorer

We have learned that the southern hero David was able to fight off bears and lions, and that he defeated Goliath with just a single shot from his slingshot. As we might expect, the northerners also told stories about their champions, whom they too extolled as legendary heroes of the past. Some of the northern stories were reworked by southern writers to enhance the status of the south. But others were adopted outright, with their regional distinctiveness stripped out.

The biblical hero Joshua, the man who led the Israelites into the Promised Land of Canaan after Moses died, is an excellent example of a hero who lost his regional flavor. By closely examining the geographic data provided by the book of Joshua, scholars have found that the man Joshua was, in all likelihood, originally a local champion from the northern tribe of Ephraim. However, in the final form of the book named for him, written in the 7th century B.C.E. and later, Joshua is portrayed as the great national leader who led a unified Israel forward in the conquest of the Promised Land.[117]

Similarly, the traditions concerning Jacob are an example of where the southern writers made obvious changes to advance their own agenda. Even though Abraham is known as the father of the Israelite people, the name of his grandson, Jacob, is another way to identify the Israelites. For example, in Exodus 19, Isaiah 2, and Psalms 114 the Israelites are referred to as the "House of Jacob." Numbers 23 relates a tale where the prophet Balaam simply uses the name "Jacob" to mean all of Israel, as does the prophet Amos in the book of his own name.

The Bible tells us that Jacob had twelve sons, and there were twelve tribal lands of Israel—however, the sons and the tribal lands are not exactly parallel. Jacob's twelve sons are: Reuben, Simeon, Levi, Judah, Dan, Naphtali, Gad, Asher, Issachar, Zebulun, Joseph and Benjamin (Genesis 35:22). The tribe of Levi has the responsibility of the priesthood. The Levites (offspring of Levi) are not given land. Instead, their members work throughout all the tribal lands administering the priestly duties and maintaining the sanctuaries. The other tribes are expected to support the members of the Levite tribe. That leaves us with eleven tribal lands.

Another brother who does not have a tribal land specifically named for him is Joseph, the favorite son of Jacob. Genesis 48 tells us that Joseph was living in Egypt when Jacob relocated there in his later years. In his final days, Jacob was visited by Joseph and his two sons: Manasseh and Ephraim. During that visit, Jacob designated Manasseh and Ephraim as his own sons, thus assigning to Joseph a double portion of inheritance (Genesis 48:5-7, 22), land which, according to Numbers 34:23–24, was divided between the descendants of Manasseh and Ephraim. Joseph, who had risen to a position of prominence in Egypt, lived out the rest of his days there, and upon his death—like a high-ranking Egyptian—was put in a mummy case (Genesis 50:26).

These are the twelve eponymously named tribal lands of Israel: Reuben, Simeon, Judah, Dan, Naphtali, Gad, Asher, Issachar, Zebulun, Manasseh, Ephraim, and Benjamin.*

---

* Eponyms, which name something after someone in particular, were used by the Assyrians in the 9th century to name the years of the calendar. Greek myth has provided a particularly abundant trove of eponyms: The psychological term "narcissism" is named for the Greek character Narcissus, who loved to stare at his own reflection. Echo was a Greek nymph who could only repeat the last words spoken to her. "Panic" comes from the Greek god Pan, who was known to startle or cause fear. Atlas was forced to carry the world on his shoulders, and today a book of maps is named for him. The inspiration for eponyms is not limited to antiquity. A "watt" is a measurement of electric power and is named for inventor James Watt (1736-1819). The cardigan sweater is named for James Brudenell, 7th Earl of Cardigan (1797-1868). And, the saxophone was invented by Antoine-Joseph "Adolphe" Sax (1814-1894).

47. Jacob

How fair are your tents, O Jacob. Your dwellings, O Israel!
Numbers 24:5

The name Jacob was common in the ancient Near East among the western Semites, meaning speakers of languages closely akin to biblical Hebrew. Inasmuch as forms of Jacob are found from Old Babylonian to early post-Christian times, the name has no implications for dating the biblical sections in which it appears.[118]

Jacob and his twin brother, Esau, are the only children of Isaac and his wife, Rebekah. Jacob struggles with his brother in the womb (Genesis 25:22) and comes out of the womb holding onto the heel of Esau, who is born first (Genesis 25:26). This unruly beginning presages the sibling clashes to come.

As young men, Esau becomes a hunter and Jacob is described as a "mild man who stayed in camp" and, apparently, can cook. One day, Esau comes home famished and requests some of the lentil stew that Jacob has made. Jacob offers Esau stew in exchange for the birthright that rightfully belongs to Esau, a deal to which Esau impulsively agrees (Genesis 25:28–35). The "birthright" is the right of the firstborn son to be first in line to receive inheritance from the father, including a double portion of the father's possessions (Deuteronomy 21:17).

Years later, when the now blind Isaac is on his deathbed and wants to bestow his blessing on his firstborn, Jacob tricks his father into thinking that he is actually Esau. (Even though they were twins, Jacob and Esau looked quite different, so this deception took the combined efforts of Jacob and his mother, Rebekah, who favors Jacob (Genesis 25:28).) Realizing that Jacob has gotten both the birthright and the blessing, Esau:

> . . . harbored a grudge against Jacob because of the
> blessing which his father had given him, and Esau
> said to himself, "Let but the mourning period of
> my father come, and I will kill my brother Jacob."
> (Genesis 27:41)

Rebekah, learning of Esau's threat against Jacob, encourages Jacob to flee for his life. Jacob leaves his home and begins a series of complex and compelling adventures, which are very revealing once we realize that they were written as political allegory. We illustrate this by turning to the best-known episode in the Jacob tales—his wrestling match. According to Genesis 32, Jacob, fearing for his safety, took his wives and children across the Jabbok River ford. When he was alone, a mysterious stranger arrived and:

> wrestled with him until the rising of the morning
> star ... [That man] wrenched his hip at the
> socket, so that the socket of Jacob's hip was
> strained ... Then he said, "Release me, for the
> morning star has risen." But he answered, "I will
> not release you unless you bless me." So he said to
> him, "What is your name?" [He answered,]
> "Jacob." He replied, "Your name shall no longer
> be spoken "Jacob," but "Israel" (Hebrew: *Yisrael* =
> God's striver), for you have striven with
> divinities and with humans and have prevailed."
> Jacob asked, "Pray speak your name." But he said,
> "Why do you ask my name?" But he blessed him
> there. So Jacob named the place Peniel (God's
> face), "for [said he], I have seen a divinity face to
> face, yet my life has been saved." The sun rose
> upon him as he passed Penuel*, limping on his
> hip. That is why the children of Israel to this day
> will not eat the thigh muscle that is on the socket
> of the hip, since he wounded Jacob's hip socket at
> the thigh muscle. (Genesis 32:23–33, translation by
> the author)

---

* The location of Jacob's wrestling with a divine being in Genesis 32:31 is written as "Peniel" (פניאל), but in Genesis 32:32 as "Penuel" (פנואל). The Hebrew letters YOD= י and VAV= ו are similar and the difference may be due to variant scribal practices.

Folklorists, comparative religionists, and academics in the field of "Bible as literature" have deservedly emphasized the literary elements of Jacob's struggles with God. Taking a different approach, scholar Stanley Gevirtz (1929–1988), who taught at University of Chicago and Hebrew Union College, Los Angeles, noted that "The entire incident was fraught with geo-political significance."[119] Gevirtz pointed out that the incident is set in the Gilead region, an area just east of the Jordan River, located in modern-day Jordan. At the start of the story, Jacob travels through a place that he names Mahanaim, meaning "two camps" (Genesis 32:3). After the struggle with the angel, Jacob names the site Penuel meaning 'God's face,' for:

> I have seen a divine being face to face, yet my life
> has been preserved. (Genesis 32:31).

When Jacob reached his destination, he:

> . . . built a house for himself and made stalls for
> his cattle; that is why the place was called
> Succoth. (Genesis 33:17)

The word *succoth* translates to "booths," e.g. structures for dwelling. In just these few passages, the writers indicate that it was Jacob who named the areas Mahanaim, Penuel, and Succoth. Since Jacob named them, he must have been there first and his descendants can claim a kind of ownership.

Another story, known informally as Jacob's Ladder, is arguably the second most popular Jacob story. As he travels, Jacob is unaware that he has come to a holy place, but he does know he is tired. Jacob decides to rest, and there he has a dream:

> There was a stairway resting on the ground, with
> its top reaching to heaven and angels of God
> ascending and descending it. There was God
> standing atop it. He said, "I, the Eternal—the god
> of Abraham, your father, and the god of Isaac—
> will give you and your descendants this land on
> which you sleep. Your offspring will be as

numerous as the dust of the earth, so that you will
break out west and east and north and south. And
all the families of the earth will bless themselves
through you and your offspring. Remember it is I
who am with you, who will protect you wherever
you go and bring you back to this land. For I shall
not leave you until I have done what I promised
you." (Genesis 28:12-15, translation by the author)

When Jacob awakes, he realizes that he has slept in a holy place,
God's very house—the gateway to heaven. He marks the place as holy
by the ritual of standing up the stone he had slept on and pouring oil
over it. Then he changes the name of the place, Luz, to Bethel,
meaning "House of God." Lastly, Jacob vows that if God will provide
him with safe passage, food, and clothes on his journey, he will make
the stone he had slept on the foundation of a temple where he will
tithe to the Eternal.

Once again, geography is crucial. The story illustrates that Bethel is
a holy location and tells us that Jacob was the first to recognize its
holiness and then, prophetically, name it.

These biblical stories are awe-inspiring and have ignited the
imagination of painters, musicians, authors and, in the case of Jacob's
Ladder, even toy makers! But Jacob was surely not a historical figure.
Entire peoples do not spring from the loins of individuals. Historical
figures do not wrestle with divinities, nor do they live to be 147 years of
age (Genesis 47:28). It is necessary, therefore, to find a historical figure
associated with the geopolitical significance of these particular locales.

48. Jacob as Allegory of Jeroboam I

No state, upon its own mere motion, can lawfully get out of the Union.
Plainly, the central idea of secession is the essence of anarchy.
Abraham Lincoln (1809–1865), U.S. President, 1861–1865

When the kingdoms of Israel and Judah divided circa 922 B.C.E., Jeroboam I was the northern hero of the division. While currently there is no direct evidence that Jeroboam I existed, the chronology of his reign, and that of his successors, fits nicely with substantiated historical information. Although the stories in the books of Kings are romanticized, we are still able to glean useful information from them.

According to 1 Kings 12, when Solomon died and Rehoboam ascended the throne of the united Israelite kingdom, Rehoboam proved to be a merciless king. The text tells us that, in the early days of his reign, Rehoboam visited the people in the northern city of Shechem and made his intentions clear:

> My father made your yoke heavy, but I will add
> to your yoke; my father flogged you with whips,
> but I will flog you with scorpions.[*] (1 Kings 12:14)

"Yoke," in this context, refers to forced labor or corvée. In 1 Kings 11 we are told about an able man who was appointed by the king to be one of the enforcers of this yoke:

> Jeroboam son of Nebat, an Ephraimite from
> Zeredah whose mother Zeruah was a widow, was
> a servant of Solomon . . . When Solomon built
> the Millo and closed up the breach [of the wall] of
> the City of David his father, he saw how highly
> capable the young man was, for Jeroboam was a
> man of great ability. The king appointed him as
> overseer of the corvée labor of the House of

---

[*] Possibly, a sharp object attached to the end of a whip or cat-o'-nine-tails.

Joseph. (1 Kings 11:26-28, translation by the author)

The allegorical identification of Jacob with Jeroboam I is evident when we compare their stories which, according to inner biblical chronology, are set hundreds of years apart. Genesis 32 tells us that the allegorical Jacob, circa 17th century B.C.E., wrestles through the night with a divine being who, at the conclusion of the wrestling, says:

> Your name shall no longer be Jacob, but *Israel*, for you have striven with divine beings and have prevailed. (Genesis 32:29)

Jeroboam, the capable and able young man of the 10th century B.C.E., dons a new cloak and travels outside Jerusalem alone, where he is accosted by a prophetic man of God, Ahijah of Shiloh. Ahijah tears Jeroboam's cloak into twelve pieces and gives Jeroboam a new title: King of Israel.

> . . . Ahijah pulled the new cloak off Jeroboam and ripped it into twelve pieces. He said to Jeroboam, "Take ten fragments for yourself, for thus says the Eternal, the god of Israel; I am ripping the kingdom from Solomon and giving you the ten tribes . . . for I have taken you to rule over all your heart desires, for you shall be king over Israel." (1 Kings 11:29-32, translation by the author)

Affirming the 10th century B.C.E. division between Jeroboam's northern kingdom of Israel and Rehoboam's southern kingdom of Judah, and squelching any idea to reunite the kingdoms, Rehoboam is told by a man of God that "this thing is from me" (1 Kings 12:24). The allegorical story of the 17th century B.C.E. change of name from Jacob to Israel declared by the divinity reflects the new political reality of the kingdom established by Jeroboam I. A twice-told tale!

Another allegorical connection between Jacob and Jeroboam I is the importance attached to the place named "Penuel." After wrestling with the divine being, our hero Jacob names the spot Penuel, "for [said

he], I have seen a divinity face to face, yet my life has been saved"
(Genesis 32:31). Although it does not have the poetry of divinity
attached to it, a clear connection of Jeroboam I to Penuel is provided
when we are told that, after rebelling against Rehoboam and founding
the northern kingdom:

> Jeroboam built Shechem in the hill country of
> Ephraim and took up residence there; from there
> he went out and built Penuel. (1 Kings 12:25)

We do not know why Jeroboam I abandoned Shechem, located
in the heart of the Ephraimite hill country, and chose Penuel—a city
across the Jordan River—as his capital. It has been speculated that
he needed an area more secure from his southern rival, Rehoboam,
or from Pharaoh Shoshenq I (reign: circa 943–922 B.C.E.), initially a
supporter of Jeroboam I but later an enemy of the northern
kingdom.[120] Another biblical tale indicates that Penuel might have
once been an established stronghold that could be efficiently rebuilt
into a new and protected home base. According to the story in
Judges 6–8, the northern hero Gideon overcame great odds to
deliver a military victory, during which he smashed the tower at
Penuel and slaughtered all the inhabitants. Penuel was a known
locale.[*]

Important to us in trying to discern the underlying meaning in the
Bible is the fact that the claim to Penuel is another biblically twice-told
tale: once realistically and once allegorically.

Now ruling over his own domain, Jeroboam would have wanted
to complete the separation from Rehoboam's southern kingdom. 1
Kings tells us that Jeroboam I was concerned that the northerners
would continue to revere the temple in Jerusalem, built by Solomon
(Rehoboam's father) and travel to Rehoboam's land to celebrate

---

[*] Fun Fact: In 1899 the evangelical Christian organization, The Gideons
International, was founded by traveling businessmen who were inspired by
Gideon's faith, and who wanted to share their Christian faith with others.
You may be familiar with the Gideon's Bibles that can be found in many
hotel rooms. The organization placed its first Bible in a hotel room in 1908
and, as of 2016, had distributed more than 2 billion Bibles.

important festivals. This, Jeroboam believed, would diminish the status of the new kingdom he was establishing. So, on the advice of his counselors, Jeroboam made two golden calves, one of which he places at Bethel, at this southern border, and the other at Dan, at his northern border. And he tells his people:

> "It is too far for you to go up to Jerusalem. O
> Israel, the gods (Hebrew: *elohim*) who brought
> you up out of Egypt are right here." (1 Kings 12:28,
> translation by the author)

Then, according to this same southern author, Jeroboam invents:

> . . . a festival in the eighth month on the fifteenth
> day of the month, like the festival that is in
> Judah, and ascended the altar . . . He ascended
> the altar he had made in Bethel on the fifteenth
> day of the eighth month, in that month in which
> he himself had invented a festival for Israel. (1
> Kings 12:32–33, translation by the author)

Numerous scholars have noted that Jeroboam's activities were performed in God's name and sanctioned by prophets of God. Jeroboam's decision to hold the harvest festival in the eighth month corresponds closely to the climate conditions of the northern kingdom. In general, Jeroboam's activities, should be viewed as well within the norms of religious worship of the time.[121]

This includes the use of graven images of worship. Many people are aware that one of the Ten Commandments is, thou shalt not make idols; an "idol" is any representation, either image or statue, of a god that can be used as an object of worship. This includes idols of the Israelite god. Scholars note that, elsewhere in the Bible, images are not only permitted but they are actually demanded by God. For example, in Exodus 25, God specifies to Moses the creation of cherubim which will be affixed to the ark (Exodus 28:18-20), and lampstands in the shape of blossoming trees (Exodus 25:33–35). Also, at God's direction "Moses made a copper serpent and mounted it on a standard" (Numbers 21:9) to work as a healing talisman.

Archaeology has shown that images of calves and bulls were used in communities throughout the region to symbolize the strength of their gods. One example is an Iron Age I (roughly 1200–1000 B.C.E.) find of a bronze bull figurine in the northern Samaritan hills. As archaeologist Amihai Mazar noted:

> A unique find from this site is a bronze bull figurine, evidently the work of a highly skilled craftsman. It must have been the central cult at the site and is reminiscent of the golden calves described in the exodus and the shrines erected by Jeroboam at Bethel and Dan.[122]

The sacredness of Bethel is evidenced by the enthusiastic praise in the book of Genesis of religious practices observed there. Recall from the "Jacob's Ladder" story that Jacob named the area Bethel, and left a holy marker there, after he dreamed of angels ascending and descending a nearby stairway while God promised him an abundance of land and offspring (Genesis 28:11–15). Additionally, Jacob returned to the same location in Genesis 35 to build a shrine at Bethel where tithes were offered to God. The religious practices instituted by Jeroboam I echoed those of Jacob, the hero from generations before. The tales of Jacob's activity at Bethel legitimate—indeed commend—the cultic activity at Bethel by Jeroboam I when he erected an altar there.

The northern traditions preserved in the Bible celebrate Jeroboam's actions. But the southern traditions disparage Jeroboam's activities. One passage reflecting that viewpoint is preserved in 1 Kings 12, with a snide comment about Jeroboam's innovations:

> This matter led to sin. (1 Kings 12:30, translation by the author)

49. Haters, Hosea and Hyperbole

I think writers are prone to hyperbole.
John Legend (born: 1978), entertainer

Hosea was an 8th century B.C.E. prophet who lived in the northern kingdom. His prophecies, which were canonized in the Bible in the book bearing his name, raise the alarm that the people were not following God's ways. The prophet Hosea likened the behavior of the people to cheating lovers who "have strayed away from your God" (Hosea 9:1):

> And now they go on sinning;
> They have made them molten images,
> Idols, by their skill, from their silver,
> Wholly the work of artisans.
> They say, "To them Sacrifice;"
> Humans are wont to kiss calves!
> (Hosea 13:2, translation by the author)

A critical reading of 1 Kings shows that Jeroboam I created images of calves to honor God. But the prophet Hosea, two centuries later, makes known his disdain for the figures and for the inhabitants of the northern kingdom, whom he considers cheats and fools.

Bible scholar H. L. Ginsberg (1903–1990), who taught at the Jewish Theological Seminary, noted that Hosea's disgust was channeled all the way back to the ancestor Jacob! In Hebrew, the name Jacob is spelled Ya'qob, which is similar to the Hebrew word *āqab*, meaning "cheated." Remember that biblical names are often assigned meaning, like Tubal-Cain for "metalworker-smith," or Abraham for "father of the Raham tribe." In Genesis 27:36 Esau says, "Was he, then, named Jacob that he might supplant me these two times? First he took away my birthright and now he has taken away my blessing!" Esau makes a pun that the name Jacob is so close to the word meaning "cheater," and now we know he was well-named!

Hosea attacks the existence of a temple at Bethel as yet another corruption by Jacob:

> In the womb, he [Jacob] cheated his brother.
> Grown to manhood, he fought with a divinity; he
> fought with an angel and triumphed; the other did
> weep and implore him. It was at Bethel that he
> met him, so there he invokes him by that name!
> But the Eternal, the God of the Hosts, cannot be
> invoked but as the Eternal! (Hosea 12:4–6,
> translation by the author)

Hosea's accusations that Jacob "cheated" his brother in the womb is more extreme than that of Esau's, whose complaint in Genesis is limited to Jacob's actions in adulthood. Hosea says that Jacob was a cheat even before he was born, and Hosea adds two additional details to the story that are not found in the Torah: Hosea claims that Jacob did not struggle with an angel of God, but with some lesser divinity named Bethel, after whom the shrine is actually named. And Hosea says that the divinity was brought to tears. Even though Jacob was the victor and his opponent cried, Jacob, in his stupidity worships that same divinity, invoking Bethel by name rather than calling on God. Therefore, according to Hosea, the shrine should not be called Bethel, "House of God," but Beth-Aven, or as Ginsberg put it, "Delusionville." [123]

The Assyrian attacks on Israel began during Hosea's lifetime, making him a witness to their terror and destruction. Would Hosea have told his followers that the Assyrian god must be more powerful than the Israelite God? No! Hosea would have said that the fault lay with the people who were not worshipping God properly. According to Hosea, the earlier leaders, Jacob and Jeroboam I, had led people down the wrong path. Thankfully, Hosea shows the people that the correct path is open and, like an adulterous partner ready to come home, they may "Return, O Israel, to the Eternal your God, for you have fallen because of your sin. Take words with you and return to the Eternal" (Hosea 14:2–3).

The prophecy of Hosea tells us that the Assyrian destruction of the northern kingdom of Israel was a form of punishment from God. Meanwhile, historians tell us that the Assyrian conquest was part of the

Assyrian westward expansion. In any event, the end result is the same and the northern kingdom fell in 722 B.C.E., after almost twenty years of attacks. Following the typical Assyrian pattern, the Assyrians would have forced the local inhabitants out of the northern kingdom of Israel, and many would have undoubtedly migrated south to Judah, bringing their stories with them. But then calamity struck in 587 B.C.E. and the people were invaded again, this time by the Babylonians who also forced many of the natives out of Israel by 586 B.C.E. Then in 539 B.C.E., the Persians defeated the Babylonians and invited the Israelites to return. Scholars agree that during the 6th century B.C.E. there was a concerted effort by the community to save as much of their culture as possible. The people gathered histories, parables, and poems of all the tribes. The different tribes had different customs, which can account for discrepancies between the stories.

At some point, the 1 Kings stories of the northern hero Jeroboam I were reworked by a southern writer (or writers) from Judah who was disdainful of the northern tribes. The writer of 1 Kings 12 knows Jeroboam's innermost fears: Jeroboam's "Israelites" would be swayed by their cultic loyalties to the Jerusalem temple and would return to the service of Rehoboam, king of Judah. The story says that, outwardly, Jeroboam I presented his actions as motivated by concern for the hardship that his people endured when they had to make long pilgrimages to worship in Jerusalem. But, to expose Jeroboam's insincerity, the writer has him inwardly recoil in fear that:

> ... this people will return to their lord, to Rehoboam. (1 Kings 12:27, translation by the author)

In 1 Kings 12:28, Jeroboam tells the people that "the gods (Hebrew: *elohim*) who brought you up out of Egypt are right here. The use of *elohim* is deliberate. Although the term is frequently used as a synonym of God, or an alternative to it depending on the context, *elohim* can also refer to a "false" god, an angel, or even a ghost. Complicating matters, but extremely useful to our southern author, is the fact that *elohim* is grammatically plural.[124] In this context, the audience is encouraged to interpret *elohim* as a reference to the calves and, accordingly, to identify Jeroboam I as a maker of calf-gods.

Another device the author employs to vilify Jeroboam I is his repeated use of the verb *make* (Hebrew: *'āśah*), which often has the connotation of "make something up." Jeroboam I not only "makes" the golden calves (where the verb is appropriate), he also "makes [up]" priests and "makes [up]" a festival to rival the one in Judah. Lest this technique prove too subtle, the writer concludes the section by informing the audience that the festival was "invented" by Jeroboam I.

50. Old Stories/New Stories

The power of storytelling is exactly this: to bridge the gaps where everything else has crumbled.   Paulo Coelho (born: 1947), author

Sometimes old stories are the best. When people hear a familiar story, they often find wisdom or comfort in it. They tend to believe that the story must be true because they already *know* it. The people who preserved the memory of Jeroboam I borrowed snippets from even older stories, which helped the hero-story of Jeroboam I stay relevant.

In Part VI of this book, we provided a plausible rough outline of the history of the Israelite people. It would be helpful now to provide a plausible rough outline of the literary history of the Israelite people. Readers must bear in mind that the present order of biblical books, and chapters within biblical books, tells us nothing about their date of composition. In a like manner, the time in which a story is set does not tell us when it was written. For example, a story about Adam and Eve might have been written later than a story about David and Bathsheba.

Possibly the oldest composition in the Bible is the Song of Deborah (Judges 5). The passage is a celebratory hymn recounting the victory of a group of northern Israelite tribes over a Canaanite oppressor. It may have originated as early as the 12th century B.C.E., which makes it roughly contemporary with some Egyptian and Mesopotamian hymns.

Another early Israelite composition was Miriam's Song at the Sea (Exodus 15:20-21). The poem celebrates the Exodus from Egypt and is part of what we have called the Foreignness Tradition: asserting that, after 400 years of enslavement in Egypt, Israel conquered Canaan. The Song of Moses (Exodus 15:1-18) is also an ancient celebration of the Exodus from Egypt, but the inclusion of a reference to the temple in Jerusalem alerts us to the fact that it is a later expansion of Miriam's poem. The traditions of the Exodus narrative originated among the northern tribes.

The rise of a united Israelite kingdom under David laid the foundation for a national literature. Developed over centuries, this literature uses prose and poetry to attempt to explain Israel's origins and its relationship to its god. Additionally, the creation of prayer literature—and its expansion—resulted from the increased significance of the temple in Jerusalem in the lives of the people from the time that David planned for its establishment, through the time of his son and successor, Solomon, and beyond. The prayer literature is preserved most notably in the book of Psalms, whose earliest compositions may go back to the time of David but whose latest poems are products of the Hellenistic period.

Classical prophecy is often considered the greatest contribution of ancient Israel, both for its literary quality and its religious teachings. The westward expansion of the Assyrian empire in the 8th century B.C.E. led to the rise of prophets such as Amos, Hosea, (1st) Isaiah, and Micah. These prophets explained Assyria's movements as part of God's plan to punish Israel for its faithlessness and moral corruption. The original writings of these prophets and their successors were greatly expanded and adjusted by later writers in order to meet new circumstances. Similarly, the westward expansion of Babylonia in the 7th and 6th centuries B.C.E. inspired prophecy—most famously those of Jeremiah and Ezekiel—that, likewise, was greatly expanded.

The production of what became biblical literature survived the downfall of the northern and southern kingdoms. Such great biblical books as Job, Ecclesiastes, Ruth, Jonah, the Song of Songs, Lamentations, Esther and Daniel, not to mention less popular works like Ezra, Nehemiah and Chronicles, happened post-downfall.

A few brief remarks are in order about canonization, or the acceptance of the ancient Hebrew writings as authoritative. The Torah was probably canonized during the 3rd century B.C.E., and the entire Hebrew Bible by the 2nd or 3rd century C.E. (these dates are highly speculative). There are at least 800 years of collected material in the Bible. This material has been lovingly preserved but also edited over the centuries, leading to the creation of the Hebrew Bible we have today. (It is worth noting that some compositions with significant religious value, such as the books of Maccabees and Ecclesiasticus (also called *Ben Sira*), did not become part of the Jewish biblical canon but, fortunately, were preserved in some Christian biblical collections.)

Canonization of the Bible was accompanied by the gradual

extinction of prophecy.

51. Joseph, and Other Stories of Sibling Rivalry

[Regarding brothers:] *We must love one another, yes, yes, that's all true enough, but nothing says we have to like each other.*
Peter De Vries (1910–1993), author

At thirteen chapters, the gripping story of Joseph is the longest coherent narrative in the Torah. The tale of the biblical Joseph has long been compared with the "Tale of Two Brothers," an Egyptian story from the 12th century B.C.E. The Egyptian and biblical stories share important elements: sibling rivalry leading to violence; false accusation of sexual misconduct; and the hero's unlikely rise to prominence in the Egyptian royal court. But whereas "Two Brothers" is a folktale, the story of Joseph is a significant political allegory which serves the literary function of getting the ancestors of Israel to Egypt.

Joseph is the first-born of Jacob's favorite wife, Rachel, and unsurprisingly Jacob favors Joseph over his brothers. In addition to having the status of "pet" child, Joseph has the ability to interpret dreams. Joseph's brothers become jealous of Joseph's elevated status with their father, and plot to kill him. Before they can inflict any physical harm, the brothers spot a caravan traveling toward Egypt and decide that instead of killing Joseph it would be more profitable to sell him into slavery. After a series of adventures, Joseph finds himself in the court of Pharaoh where Joseph uses his ability to interpret dreams to warn Pharaoh about an upcoming famine. Joseph's foresight enables him to rise to a position of prominence, second only to Pharaoh.

A generation ago, scholars believed it was possible that Joseph was a historical figure who served as a ruler over Egyptian lands during the "Hyksos" period. "Hyksos" is based on an Egyptian phrase meaning "rulers of foreign lands"—that is rulers who were not Egyptian but instead, like the Hebrews, are related to Canaanites. The Hyksos reigned over portions of lower Egypt beginning about 1630 B.C.E. Under Hyksos reign, it was argued, Joseph, one of the Hyksos, could have risen to power. That theory has not held up for a number of reasons, not the least of which is that a Hyksos background completely negates the fundamental premise of the story; that Joseph and his brother are foreigners whose "Hebrew" origin is manifest in their language and dietary customs.[125] Additionally, while the Joseph story is set (by our reckoning) in the 15th century B.C.E., the story contains mentions of realia, or objects that would not have been commonplace until centuries later, leading many scholars to date its composition to the 8th century B.C.E.

Given that the Joseph story is not historical, it should be taken as political allegory. I noted earlier that Jacob allegorically stood in for Jeroboam I, but Jacob was not Jeroboam's only allegorical representative.

Let's compare the central elements of the Joseph story with the narrative about Jeroboam I: While Joseph is still living among his brothers, he dreams that he and his brothers are represented by sheaves of wheat. In the dream, Joseph's sheaf stands up straight while the other sheaves bow down to his sheaf. When Joseph relates this transparent dream to his brothers they accuse him of grandiosity, saying:

> Will you rule over us as king? Will you have
> complete dominion over us? (Genesis 37:8
> translation by the author)

As a result of this dream, and an even more transparent one that Joseph relates to his brothers and their father, Joseph's brothers plot to kill him. He finds sanctuary in Egypt, where he is protected and elevated by Pharaoh.

Similarly, according to 1 Kings 11, Jeroboam (the son of Nebat) was told by the prophet Ahijah that he would be king of the breakaway Northern Israel. Hearing about this prophecy:

> . . . Solomon sought to kill Jeroboam, so he arose
> and fled to Egypt, to Shishak, king of Egypt. (1
> Kings 11:40, translation by the author)

Scholars are unanimous in identifying Shishak, the earliest-named pharaoh in the Bible, with Shoshenq I, the Libyan who founded the twenty-second Egyptian dynasty. 1 Kings makes clear that Shoshenq I had developed a policy of undermining strong rulers who were potential enemies of Egypt by encouraging their rivals. According to I Kings 11:14-22, Shoshenq provided a haven to the Edomite Hadad in order that he might cause trouble for Solomon, In keeping with this strategy, Shosheq also provided a haven for Jeroboam, which allowed Ahijah's prophecy to be fulfilled and allowed Jeroboam to establish the independent northern kingdom and rule it as Jeroboam I. It is also possible that Shoshenq I provided military support to Jeroboam I, not just a haven. If Shoshenq I agreed to back Jeroboam's rebellion against Rehoboam in Judah, Judah would have been able to assess the futility of fighting back against Jeroboam I.[126] According to 1 Kings, Rehoboam accepts the split as having come from God:

> But the word of God came to Shemaiah, the man of
> God: Say to King Rehoboam of Judah, son of
> Solomon, and to all the house of Judah and
> Benjamin and to the rest of the people, "Thus,
> says the Eternal, you shall not go up or fight
> against your kindred the people of Israel. Let
> everyone go home, for this thing is from me." So
> they heeded the word of God and went home
> again, according to the word of God. (1 Kings
> 12:22–24, translation by the author)

In these verses, the man of God, Shemaiah, warns Rehoboam not to wage war against Jeroboam. He refers to Rehoboam's domain as the "house of Judah" but affirms Jeroboam's claim to "Israel," the official name of the northern kingdom.[1*]

In Part IV of this book, we saw that there is no archaeological evidence that the Israelites were ever slaves *in* Egypt. Israelites were clearly slaves *to* Egypt, but within their own homeland. We know that by the 10th century B.C.E. the allegory of Israel in Egypt already existed

---

* Point of Interest: Finding refuge in Egypt also served the writer of Matthew 2:13–15 in the New Testament, who described the flight to Egypt by Joseph, husband of Mary. In her book, *The Origin of Satan*, Elaine Pagels points out the irony of the holy family fleeing to Egypt to seek refuge from a Jewish king.

in the Foreignness Traditions of the northern kingdom. By placing one of Jacob's sons in Egypt and having him rise to power, the story very nicely comes full circle.

Another motif the writers utilized is that of the rejected brother who rises to power outside his homeland and then returns in triumph. Outside the Bible, there is the story of King Idrimi of Alalakh in Syria who ruled in the 15th century B.C.E. The story— inscribed on the base of a statue of the king—was written no later than the 13th century B.C.E. and purports to be his autobiography.[127] Idrimi begins by explaining that, of his brothers, "none had the plans I had." Idrimi goes off on his own, rises to great power, and is reconciled with his brothers, to whom he gives positions of authority.

Within the Bible, we see the motif repeated in the story of the warrior Jephthah in Judges 11. Jephthah was driven from his childhood home by his half-brothers who were unwilling to give Jephthah a share of their father's property. Jephthah joins a gang of raiders and becomes known for his fighting ability. When war is declared on his hometown, the townspeople ask Jephthah to return and lead them. Jephthah becomes the commander of the army and routs the enemy.

The propagandists of Jeroboam I were able to rely on existing material and did not have to create new motifs when they introduced the figure of Joseph—an ancestor of the group from which Jeroboam I claimed ancestry—into the Exodus traditions. As with "Joseph" before him, Jeroboam I had been protected by Pharaoh and risen to great power under the ultimate protection of God.

In the section titled "Twelve Tribes" we clarified why Joseph does not have a land in the northern kingdom specifically named for him. In Genesis 48, Jacob adopts Joseph's sons, Manasseh and Ephraim, as his own. Jacob also assigns to Joseph a double portion of inheritance— land which, according to Numbers 34:23–24, has been divided between the descendants of Manasseh and Ephraim. Of course, this story has the added benefit of providing an explanation for why Joseph, the favorite son of his father Jacob, does not have a tribal land named after him.

In some biblical texts, the traditions refer to the northern kingdom of Israel as the "House of Joseph." The prophet Amos lived in the 8th

century B.C.E. and was contemporary with the prophets Hosea and
Isaiah. Amos warns the Israelites:

> Seek the Eternal, and you will live,
> Else he will rush like fire upon the House of
> Joseph
> And consume Bethel with none to quench it.
> (Amos 5:6)

This fits in nicely with an 8th century introduction of the Joseph
legends. The title "House of Joseph" might have been retroactively
applied in an effort to support the Foreignness Traditions and the
Exodus out of Egypt—which archaeology proves did not happen. It
is interesting to note, however, that the Foreignness Tradition is the
tradition that won out. The story of the Jewish people is that their
ancestors wandered for 40 years until they reached the Promised Land
of Canaan—a journey celebrated every year during Passover.

The kingdom of Israel, with the title "House of Joseph," was the
kingdom that was destroyed by the Assyrians. The kingdom of Judah
survived for more than a century thereafter. Had the House of Joseph
survived, the people who claim descent from these people might have
called themselves "Joes," not "Jews."

52. Reconciliation

This world is full of conflicts and full of things that cannot be reconciled. But there are moments when we can . . . reconcile and embrace the whole mess, and that's what I mean by "Hallelujah."
Leonard Cohen (1934–2016), poet and singer-songwriter

The prophet Ezekiel lived circa 622–570 B.C.E. According to the book of his name, he was the son of a Temple priest, which by default meant he was part of the upper echelon of Judahite society. Ezekiel knew about the gut-wrenching defeat of the northern kingdom by the Assyrians, and he experienced first-hand the Babylonian devastation of Jerusalem. When people cried out to their leaders for comfort, Ezekiel prophesied a time when the northern kingdom ("House of Joseph") and southern kingdom would be reunited as one people:

> The word of the Eternal came to me: "Mortal,
> take a stick and write on it: 'For Judah and the
> children of Israel associated with him.' Then take
> another stick and write on it: 'For Joseph and all
> the house of Israel associated with him' and join
> them together into one stick, so that they may
> become one in your hand. And when your people
> say to you, 'Will you not tell us what you mean by
> these?' say to them, 'Thus says my lord, the
> Eternal: Behold I am about to take the stick of
> Joseph and the tribes of Israel associated with him
> and I will join it with the stick of Judah.'"
> When the sticks on which you write are in your
> hand before their eyes, then say to them, "Thus
> says my lord, the Eternal: 'Behold, I will take the
> children of Israel from the nations among which
> they have gone . . . and make them one nation in
> the land on the mountains of Israel, and one king
> shall be king over them all, and they shall be no
> longer two nations, And no longer be divided in

> two kingdoms . . . My servant David shall be king
> over them'" (Ezekiel 37:15–24, translation by the
> author)

Ezekiel paints a picture of reunited harmony, with just one king. His prophecy must have been comforting to those who were familiar with the southern traditions, promising that a descendant of David, the revered king of Israel, would always be on the throne. But it would have been much less comforting to those who supported the northern, or Joseph/Jeroboam I, traditions. And Ezekiel's prophecy goes directly against what the northerners knew from the Joseph story as found in Genesis 44, when Judah, the older brother, humbled himself before Joseph:

> Please my lord, let your slave appeal to my lord,
> and do not be impatient with your slave, you who
> are the equal of Pharaoh . . . Let your slave remain
> as a slave to my lord. (Genesis 44:18 & 33,
> translation by the author)

In Ezekiel's version, it is not Judah who humbles himself to Joseph—it is the exact opposite. At the time that Ezekiel prophesied, the northern Israelite monarchy and the state itself had been gone for more than a century. Judah had only recently fallen to the Babylonians, and members of the Davidic dynasty were alive and treated with some respect by the conquerors.[128] Accordingly, it was at least a visionary possibility that Judah's fortunes might soon rise and that an Israelite state under Judahite leadership might reemerge. Ezekiel reversed the terms of the reconciliation to suit his own purposes, or the purposes of his fellow Judahites!

Although Ezekiel's prophecy contrasts sharply with the culmination of the Joseph story, it is interesting that the grand design neatly fits the political situation in the reign of Jeroboam II. Jeroboam II lived eight generations after Jeroboam I and, according to 2 Kings 14:23, ruled the northern kingdom for forty-one years (reign: circa 789–748 B.C.E.). Immediately after introducing Jeroboam II, the writer throws him under the bus by stating that Jeroboam II "did evil in the sight of the Eternal" (2 Kings 14:24, translation by the author).

However, the same writer admits that Jeroboam II's victories reestablished the territorial limits of Solomon's reign:

> It was he who restored the boundaries of Israel
> from Lebo-Hamath to the sea of the Arabah, in
> accordance with the word of the Eternal, the god
> of Israel. (2 Kings 14:25, translation by author)

The description of the "boundaries of Israel," which leaves no room for Judah, is completely consistent with the biblical description of events immediately before the ascent of Jeroboam II to the throne of his father Jehoash. According to 2 Kings 14:8-14, Amaziah, king of Judah, foolishly started a war with Jehoash, son of Jehu, king of Israel, which turned out very badly for Amaziah:

> Judah was defeated by Israel, and everyone fled to
> his tent. But Jehoash, king of Israel, captured
> Amaziah, king of Judah, at Beth-Shemesh. Then
> he marched to Jerusalem and breached the walls
> of Jerusalem . . . He carried off all the gold and
> the silver and all the vessels to be found in the
> temple of the Eternal and the royal treasuries, and
> hostages as well. He then returned to Samaria. (2
> Kings 14:12–14, translation by author)

The capture of the king, the breaching of the walls of the capital city, and the taking of hostages—probably from the royal family and the nobility—indicate that Judah became subordinate to Israel during the reign of Jeroboam II's father, Jehoash. The territorial descriptions of Jeroboam II's reign indicate that Judah's subordinate status did not improve for a generation. Against this historical background, it appears that the Joseph story originated as an allegory regarding Jeroboam I.[129] Expelled by his brothers, Joseph was exalted by the king of Egypt and rose to great power. Likewise, Jeroboam I was expelled from his group and found political backing from Egypt. But the great heights predicted by the "Joseph" dream had to wait until the reign of the second "Joseph," Jeroboam II, in whose court the story was further elaborated.

Summary – Part VIII

- The unified kingdom that King David ruled over became divided in 922 B.C.E. Jeroboam I rebelled against Rehoboam (the grandson of David), resulting in two kingdoms—Israel and Judah.

- Jeroboam I was an upstart. Over the years (centuries), traditions were created to justify his rebellion and to support the separation of the unified kingdom.

- The allegory of the hero Jacob, who defeated angels in hand-to-hand combat and founded temples to God, bolstered the Jeroboam I story, as did the allegory of the story of Joseph who broke away from his brothers and rose to prominence with the support of an Egyptian ruler.

- When creating a new origin story, one will always find detractors. The prophet Hosea predicted doom and gloom for the northern kingdom.

- Doom and gloom crashed down on the northern kingdom of Israel when it was defeated by the Assyrians in 722 B.C.E. Some northerners fled to the southern kingdom of Judah and brought their 200 years of separate traditions with them.

- In the 6th century B.C.E. the Babylonians invaded Judah. By 586 B.C.E., people were dispersed again due to the Babylonian-enforced exile of many local inhabitants.

- An effort to preserve Israelite culture got underway. Stories, poems, and songs were collected. In order to keep the people unified, a single story had to be created from the wide variety of collected material. The variety helps to explain some of the inconsistencies in the Bible.

- Editorial input over the centuries attests to the desire of the transmitters of both traditions, northern (Israelite) and southern (Judahite), to dominate the final story. But the fact that the leaders of Judah were still in control gave them an obvious advantage.

PART IX
AARON & JEROBOAM

Overview: Aaron, the forerunner of the Israelite priesthood, is identified in biblical writings positively as God's chosen priest, and negatively as a spineless collaborator with the sinful Israelites. Which is it? Analysis shows that the status of Aaron shifted with the political winds. Aaron, like the biblical Jacob and Joseph, was a fictional character used to allegorize the religious innovations of King Jeroboam I.

53. Aaron

You can be my wingman anytime.
the character "Iceman" in the 1986 movie Top Gun

We first meet Aaron in the Bible in Exodus 4. Moses has been ordered by God to go to Egypt and free the Israelite people from Pharaoh's oppression. But Moses hesitates, claiming "I am slow of speech and slow of tongue . . . Please, oh Eternal, make someone else your agent" (Exodus 4:10–13). So Moses gets a wingman—Aaron.

In some biblical traditions, Aaron is depicted as the older brother of Moses. However, there are several passages in the Bible that cast doubt on that depiction, as well as that of the relationship with their "sister," Miriam. In Exodus 2, the older sister who watches the baby Moses float down the Nile in the wicker basket is unnamed, and there is no mention of an older brother.

The Song of Moses and Miriam's Song of the Sea, both in Exodus 15 and celebrating the Exodus from Egypt, would have been an obvious place to make a sibling connection between Moses and Miriam. Miriam's position as a prophet and sister to Aaron is specified in the Song of the Sea, but there is no mention of Moses. Miriam is not mentioned together with Moses and Aaron as a sister until a genealogy of Levites in Numbers 26:59.

Joshua 24, a chapter of the Bible we reviewed in some depth in Part VI of this book, is widely believed to have been written in the 8th century B.C.E. and gives us what most scholars agree is the chronologically earliest mention of Aaron and Moses together. In Joshua 24:5 Aaron is named along with Moses as one of two men whom God "sent" (Hebrew: *šālaḥ*) to "smite" the Egyptians, but there is no indication that Aaron is related to Moses. Similarly, Micah 6:4 is another 8th century B.C.E. writing that mentions Moses, Aaron, and Miriam as the three people "sent" (Hebrew: *šālaḥ)* before Israel to bring them up out of Egypt, but a biological connection between the three is not proffered.

In Exodus 3–4 Moses receives instruction from God along with a toolbox of wonders, including the ability to turn a staff into a crocodile and water into blood. (The wonders are meant to demonstrate to Pharaoh that it is God who stands behind Moses's demand to free the Israelites.) It is at this point that Moses expresses his reluctance to be God's spokesperson, which angers God. A compromised is reached when God tells Moses to enlist the services of his brother, Aaron. To seal the deal, God tells Moses that he, God, will "be with you (Moses) and with him (Aaron) as you speak, and tell both of you what to do—and he shall speak for you to the people. Thus, he shall serve as your spokesperson" (literal translation, "your mouth"; Exodus 4:15–16). Moses informs Aaron that God has handpicked Aaron to be his assistant, and then informs Aaron of all that God instructed. Next the two men assemble the elders of Israel and advise them of the plan. Following the instructions of God, it is Aaron who relates the divine word given by God to Moses, and it is he who demonstrates the wonders.

In these passages Aaron has quickly become a major character in the narrative and is bestowed with divine abilities close to those of Moses. When Moses and Aaron arrive in Egypt, Moses again expresses his reluctance to speak directly with Pharaoh and is once again told that Aaron will fill the role of spokesperson. Just as God speaks to the people through his prophets, Moses will speak to Pharaoh through Aaron:

> God said to Moses: "Observe, I have designated
> you as God (elohim) to Pharaoh, and Aaron, your
> brother, shall be your prophet (nabi). You shall
> speak [to Aaron] whatever I command you. Then
> Aaron, your brother, will speak to Pharaoh that he
> send the children of Israel from his land." (Exodus
> 7:1-2, translation by the author)

Although Moses is reluctant and Aaron is given the position of spokesperson, during their first audience with Pharaoh both Moses and Aaron speak, and Pharaoh speaks to the two of them (Exodus 5:1, 3, 4). But when it comes to working the wonders in Exodus 7, Moses gives the instruction to Aaron, and Aaron performs the deeds. It is Aaron's rod that turns into a crocodile (Hebrew: *tannin;* 7:10), swallows the crocodiles of Pharaoh's lector priests (7:12), turns the Nile into blood (7:20), causes the plague of frogs (8:2), and brings vermin/lice upon man and beast (8:13).

The elevated status of Aaron is clear. What is not mentioned in any of these passages is Aaron's association with the priesthood or with priestly functions.

54. Aaron and the Golden Calf

For every high priest chosen among men is appointed to act on behalf of men in relation to God, to offer gifts and sacrifices for sins . . . And one does not take the honor upon himself but is called by God, just as Aaron was. Hebrews 5:1–4

While there are lingering questions about Aaron's biological relationship to Moses, it is certain that Aaron enjoyed an elevated status and was authorized to perform sacred rituals. Aaron is called *kohen. Kohen* is the Hebrew word for "priest," and there are Jewish men today who claim direct lineage from Aaron, making them "sons of Aaron" and members of the priestly class. One way the elevated status of members of the priestly class continues to be recognized today in Orthodox, and in some Conservative, Jewish congregations is during the Torah reading portion of religious services, when people are called upon to ascend the altar and recite blessings (*aliyot*) over the Torah: the privilege of reciting the first blessing (*aliyah*) is reserved for a *kohen*. (The Reform movement, and some liberal Conservative Jewish congregations, have discontinued this practice.)

According to the Torah, Aaron and his descendants were first chosen for the priesthood in the wilderness when Moses was given the following instruction:

> You yourself are to go, and from the midst of the
> Israelites bring near to you Aaron your brother,
> along with his sons, to officiate for me as priests.
> (Exodus 28:1, translation by the author)

Recall from Part II of this book (chapter "J, E, P, and D"), the outline of Julius Wellhausen's theory that there were four different contributors, plus a Redactor, R, to the final version of the Hebrew Bible: the J source, the E source, the P source, and the D source. Although the details are debated, virtually all scholars agree about the existence of the P, or "Priestly," source, which contains the rules about ritual sacrifice and the functions of the priests at the Temple, as well as genealogies. According to biblical tradition, Aaron was the founding father of the only legitimate priestly line, and therefore a major figure in P source passages.

In classical rabbinic sources as well as modern scholarship, Aaron has often been described as a paradigm of the Israelite priesthood, so that regulations pertaining to Aaron apply to all priests. But "paradigm" does not adequately describe the varied images of Aaron presented in the Torah. Scholars have observed two conflicting traditions at work. Sometimes Aaron is portrayed in a strong, positive image as God's chosen priest, as in when he protects the Israelites against the spread of plague by placing himself between the dead and the living (Numbers 17). At other times Aaron is vilified or tainted, as in the story of the golden calf (Exodus 32) in which he appears at worst as the somewhat willing sculptor of the calf, and at best as a spineless collaborator with the sinful Israelites.[130]

To trace the evolution of the figure of Aaron the Priest in Israelite tradition we begin with the episode of the golden calf, which has been the subject of study for over two millennia.[131] According to the story, Moses ascends Mount Sinai to receive "the stone tablets with the teachings and commandments . . . and Moses remains on the mountain forty days and forty nights" (Exodus 24:12–18). Forty days and nights was a long time for the people to wait for Moses. The people become agitated, and they press Aaron into service to help fill the void caused by the absence of Moses:

> When the people observed that Moses was so late in coming down from the mountain, they mobbed Aaron and said to him, "Come, make us gods [elohim; plural] who shall go at our head, for this Moses—the man who took us up out of Egypt—we don't know what has become of him." Aaron said to them, "Break off the gold rings that are in the ears of your wives, your sons, and your daughters, and bring them to me." Then all the people broke off the gold rings that were in their ears and brought them to Aaron. What he took from them he tied in a bag, and then made into a molten calf. They declared, "These are

> your gods, O Israel, who brought you up out of
> the land of Egypt." When Aaron saw this, he
> built an altar before it. He then proclaimed as
> follows: "Tomorrow is a festival to the Eternal."
> (Exodus 32:1–5, translation by the author)

In response, the people offer sacrifices and then get up "to make merry" (Exodus 32:6).

Aaron's construction of the calf fits well with the use of bovine symbolism and zoomorphic imagery all over the ancient Near East. The bull, a symbol of strength and potency, was a natural choice to represent significant aspects of divinity. In Ugarit (now Ras Shamra in modern-day Syria), the god El was referred to as "Bull-El," and there are clear indications that Baal—the ancient god of rain, storms, and fertility who was worshiped all over Syria-Palestine—had bovine aspects.

The people's request for "gods to go before us" is entirely in keeping with the function of Near Eastern gods as guides and forerunners, and it fits chronologically with the setting of the tale.[132] One motif that runs through ancient Near Eastern literature is divine guidance in military campaigns. An Assyrian inscription from the royal court of Adad Nerari II, king of Assyria in the 10th century B.C.E., refers to the goddess Ishtar as *ālikat panât ummanātiya rapšāti,* "the one who goes at the head of my extensive army." Because the Torah regularly depicts the Israelites as an army on the march, we should not be surprised to find in the Exodus tale a very close parallel to a king's religious-military imagery. The Akkadian phrase *ālikat panât* regarding the goddess Ishtar is etymologically and semantically equivalent to the Hebrew phrase *yelĕku lĕpanenu,* which is the Israelite request for divine leadership in the Torah passage. (Literally translated as "go at the face," but is semantically a call for a divine presence to lead an action.)

The tale continues when Moses descends from Mount Sinai and accuses Aaron of leading the people to "great sin" (Exodus 32:21) by providing a calf for them to worship. Aaron responds to Moses:

> I said to them, "Whoever has gold, break it off
> of you." They gave it to me, I threw it in the fire,

and out came this calf. (Exodus 32:24, translation
by the author)

Most modern scholarship has ridiculed Aaron's statement as a
weak attempt at an alibi: Aaron was not really responsible for the
construction of the calf, which emerged from the fire fully formed.
But the "alibi" interpretation is based on an inaccurate translation of
Exodus 32:4, which I have translated as "What he took from them
he tied in a bag, and then made into a molten calf." The Hebrew for
"tied in a bag" is *vayatzar ba-ḥeret,* which has often been translated as
"cast in a mold." As the American biblical scholar Stanley Gevirtz
pointed out, the Hebrew word *ḥeret* does not refer to a mold or to
any tool that Aaron used in making a calf.[133] The *ḥeret* denotes the bag
in which the precious metal was collected and then thrown into the
fire, and the calf came out fully formed.

Israeli scholar Samuel E. Loewenstamm (1907–1987), who
taught at Hebrew University in Jerusalem, noted in his book,
Comparative Studies in Biblical and Ancient Oriental Literatures that
"Neither the author nor Moses stigmatizes Aaron's statement as a
lie. On the contrary, the context proves that the author believed in
Aaron's words."[134] Moses's lack of reaction to what some have
interpreted as a bald-faced lie shows that the original meaning has been
misinterpreted. Instead, this passage reflects a widespread motif
portraying the wondrous production of cultic objects without the
benefit of workmanship.

A 13th century B.C.E. Ugaritic text relates the creation of a new
house (temple) for the god Baal. The story goes that Baal, the god of
storms and fertility, brings silver and gold for the construction of his
house. A fire consumes the gold and silver for six days, after which
the house is described as having spontaneously been completed.
Interestingly, Medieval rabbis (10th–12th century) were not aware of
the miraculous origin of Baal's temple, but independently came up
with the notion that God's temple was constructed in the same way:

The holy spirit alighted on him (Moses), and he
erected the tabernacle. You must not say that it
was Moses who erected it. But miracles were
performed through him, and it rose on its own

accord. (Midrash Exodus Rabbah 5:2, in
reference to Exodus 40:18)

In keeping with this ancient mythical motif, Aaron was not
actively involved in constructing the calf. After collecting the precious
metals, Aaron bound them in a bag and waited for the fire to
become sufficiently hot and then he cast the metal into the flame. The
golden calf spontaneously emerged from the flames—a clear
indication that the image represented the divine presence. Aaron
was inspired to build an "altar before it" because the calf was a
legitimate representative of God's presence, which could be
credited with leading the people out of Egypt. Its inauguration would
more than justify a "festival to the Eternal."

Why, then, did Moses descend from Mount Sinai and accuse Aaron
of leading the people to "great sin" by providing a calf for them to
worship? And how "great" a sin was the golden calf episode? At first
the question appears naïve. Stephen (5–34 C.E.), an early avid
devotee of Jesus who later attained sainthood as the first martyr in
Christianity, is purported to have given a speech just before being
stoned to death (Acts 7:41) where he specifically refers to the calf
as an "idol" (Greek: *eidōlon)*, and generations of readers have concurred
with Stephen's assessment.

Although the consensus belief of calf-as-idol has been adopted, it
fails to explain the fact that there are other biblical passages where the
image of a bull representing the divine is perfectly acceptable. The 8th
century B.C.E. prophet Isaiah speaks of God as "the bull of Israel:"

> Therefore, word of the Eternal
> The Eternal of Hosts (i.e. heavenly bodies),
> Bull of Israel.
> Ah, I will get satisfaction at the expense of my
> foes
> and take vengeance on my enemies.
> (Isaiah 1:24, translation by the author)

Isaiah's 6th century B.C.E. successor, Deutero-Isaiah, the
Bible's most militant monotheist, speaks of God as the "bull of
Jacob" (Isaiah 49:26). It would be easy to dismiss these statements as

verbal imagery. However, 1 Kings 7:23–31 describes in great detail the laver, or priestly washing basin commissioned by Solomon for the House of the Eternal, which sat upon twelves statues of bulls. Solomon felt no compunction about using the image of bulls to symbolize the strength of God.

At some point, the image of bull as representation of the strength of God became tainted. It is important to bear in mind that cultic objects and religious rituals are usually not evaluated on their own. Much depends on the people or institutions with whom the rituals are associated. From the perspective of the Judahite narrator, if Jeroboam did it, it was bad. The northern hero Jeroboam I was known to have used calves in his northern temple. Southern writers who wanted to bolster their own superiority pointed to this action as something to be denigrated, casting aspersions on both Jeroboam I and the allegorical Aaron who performed the same action. Before we look at the parallels between the stories of Jeroboam I and Aaron, we will take a slight detour to look at other "idols" in Bible stories.

55. Other Graven Images

Every one of us is, even from his mother's womb, a master craftsman of idols. John Calvin (1509–1564), theologian, reformer and father of Calvinism

The prohibition against creating idols is stated seven times in the Torah:

- You shall have no other gods besides me. You shall not make for yourself a sculptured image, or any likeness of what is in the heavens above, or on the earth below, or in the water under the earth. You shall not bow down to them or serve them. (Exodus 20:3–5)
- You shall not make any gods of silver, nor shall you make for yourselves any gods of gold. (Exodus 20:20)
- You shall not make molten gods for yourselves. (Exodus 34:17)
- Do not turn to idols or make molten gods for yourselves: I the Eternal am your god. (Leviticus 19:4)
- You shall not make idols for yourselves, or set up for yourselves carved images or pillars, or place figured stones in your land to worship upon, for I the Eternal am your god. (Leviticus 26:1)
- For your own sake, therefore, be most careful . . . not to act wickedly and make for yourselves a sculptured image in any likeness whatever: the form of a man or a woman, the form of any beast on earth, the form of any winged bird that flies in the sky, the form of anything the creeps on the ground, the form of any fish that is in the waters below the earth. (Deuteronomy 4:15–18)
- Cursed be anyone who makes a sculptured or molten image, abhorred by the Eternal, a craftsman's handiwork, and sets it up in secret. (Deuteronomy 27:15)

The message is crystal clear: Do not make idols. Do not keep idols. Do not bow down and worship idols. Scholars know that when a prohibition is repeated often it is because people were performing the offensive action.

In reality, it is hardly surprising that ancient Israelites made images of items found in nature because there are other biblical passages that call for it. Exodus 25 specifies that the ark that holds the "tablets of the Pact" (a.k.a. Ark of the Covenant) should be adorned with "two cherubim of gold . . . with their faces turned toward the cover" (Exodus 25:18–20). And the passage goes on to require a lamp with branches and "cups like almond-blossoms" (Exodus 25:31–34). The laver, or priestly washing basin, was quite large, measuring 10 cubits* across with a circumference of 30 cubits; its depth was 5 cubits. The twelve bull statues that held this massive basin aloft in Solomon's temple must have also been massive (1 Kings 7:23–26). Additionally, there were ten, smaller lavers in the temple which were adorned with lions, bulls, palms and cherubim (1 Kings 7:29–36).[135]

Another story about a biblical idol comes from Numbers 21. The story goes that the people began to complain about their living situation while wandering in the desert after the Exodus. God, annoyed by their lack of belief and/or gratitude, sends snakes to attack the people. Many Israelites were bitten and died, prompting the survivors to regret their insolent behavior and to ask Moses to intercede on their behalf, which he does:

> Then the Eternal said to Moses, "Make a seraph
> (venomous snake)-figure and mount it on a pole,
> and if anyone who is bitten looks at it, he shall
> recover." Moses made a copper snake and
> mounted it on a pole; and when anyone was
> bitten by a snake, he would look at the copper
> seraph-figure and recover. (Numbers 21:8–9,
> translation by the author)**

---

* 1 Cubit = 1.5 feet, or 0.46 meters

** Snakes have long been worshipped. Snakes shed their skin, which gives the impression of rebirth, and their venom is both feared as lethal and respected for medicinal purposes. The ancient Greeks worshipped Asclepius, the god of medicine, healing, rejuvenation and physicians. Asclepius is depicted as a god with a serpent (snake) entwined staff, known as the Rod of Asclepius; a symbol that has been adopted by many medical associations. According to Greek mythology, Asclepius fathered many children, including Hygieia (hygiene), Panacea (remedy), and Meditrina (health, longevity, and wine).

This story may leave some people perplexed. Why was Moses directed to create an idol, but when Aaron created an idol it was a "great sin?" The ancient rabbis pointed to the fact that God specifically directed the action by Moses, so that must have made it all right. But, at some point, this inconsistency was addressed. 2 Kings tells us that King Hezekiah, "broke into pieces the bronze seraph-figure that Moses had made, for until that time the Israelites had been offering sacrifices to it" (2 Kings 18:4).

It is a human impulse to make images, and ritual often requires something for people to look at. Even today the Torah scrolls used in a sanctuary have become revered objects. The Torah scrolls are typically kept in a wall enclosure of a synagogue, known as an ark (Hebrew: *aron*). Before speaker systems became commonplace, a scroll was taken out of the ark and marched to a podium in the center of the synagogue from where it would be read, ensuring the entire congregation could hear the reading. Today there are wonderful sound systems, and frankly it would be easier to read the Torah portion on any number of electronic, handheld devices. But people need symbols and something to focus on, so congregants continue to march the Torah around the room. Also, while the Torah is being paraded about, people will often reach out their hand, or a prayer book, or a prayer shawl to touch or kiss the Torah. There is no textual basis for this custom, but people like the symbolism. Our environment has changed over the millennia, but our minds still seek out a visual object toward which to direct our attention.

56. Etched in Stone

*Historical fiction is not history. You're blending real events and actual
historical personages with characters of your own creation.*
George R. R. Martin (born: 1948), author

1 Kings 12 tells us that Jeroboam I set up two calves, one at Dan
and one at Bethel, for his entire population to be able to worship closer
to their homes. In our chronology, this would have been the 10th
century B.C.E. And Exodus 32 tells us, again in our chronology, that
in the 14th/13th century B.C.E., at the request of the people, Aaron
coordinated the collection of valuables to enable the creation of a
golden calf for the people to follow. However, analysis of the Exodus-
32-golden-calf text provides linguistic and historical clues pointing to
a much later date of composition. A starting point is Exodus 31:18:

> When he [God] had finished speaking with him
> at Mount Sinai, he gave Moses two tablets of the
> pact, stone tablets written with the finger of God
> [elohim; singular]. (Exodus 31:18, translation by the
> author)

The Hebrew words used to describe the "two tablets of the pact"
given to Moses are, *šenē luḥot hā'edut*, To truly understand the linguistic
clues, we need to compare the word usage:

Akkadian	Hebrew	Aramaic	English
adê	*'edut*	*'iddaya*	pact/treaty/covenant
ṭuppī adê	*luḥot hā'edut*	(no attested word in this context)	tablets of the pact

Although scholars continue to debate the precise etymological
connections among the Hebrew, Aramaic, and Akkadian terms,
there is no question that in roughly the middle of the 8th century
B.C.E. the word *adê* entered the lexicon and became common in
Akkadian sources for pacts, treaties, covenants, and loyalty oaths.[136]
Also in the 8th century B.C.E., the Hebrew language developed its

own word, *'edut*, with the same range of meanings.

Historically significant is the detail that the text of the "covenant" or "pact" was etched in stone. Although treaty texts are known as far back as the early 2nd millennium B.C.E., none of these has thus far been discovered in stone. But from the middle of the 8th century B.C.E., we have three texts of treaties found at Sefire, a small town in the vicinity of present-day Aleppo, Syria. These texts—which describe their contents as *'iddaya*, "pacts," between a local Syrian ruler, Matiel of Arpad, and a powerful Mesopotamian overlord, Shamshi-ilu—were written on stone.

From a slightly earlier period we have the only surviving treaty between Assyria and Babylonia. Concluded between Marduk-Zakir-Shumi I of Babylonia and Shamshi-Adad V of Assyria, and written in or shortly after 821 B.C.E., the document is the only known Mesopotamian treaty written on stone. Admittedly, we are arguing from a small amount of evidence. Nonetheless, given the present state of that evidence, if we wish to fix a plausible date for the biblical image of a pact said to be written in stone, the 9th or 8th century B.C.E. is justified.

57. Aaron as Allegory of Jeroboam I

To me, the drive for monumentality is as inbred as the desire for food and sex, regardless of how we denigrate it. Monuments differ in different periods. Each age has its own.
Philip Johnson (1906–2005), architect

In 1967, scholars Moses Aberbach (1924–2007) and Leivy Smolar (1938–2007), both of Baltimore Hebrew University, published an article comparing the Aaron story and the Jeroboam I story. The more significant parallels are listed below:[137]

Aaron	**Jeroboam**
Aaron makes a molten calf Exodus 32:4	Jeroboam makes two golden calves 1 Kings 12:28
Aaron declares, "These are your gods, O Israel, who brought you up out of Egypt" Exodus 32:4	Jeroboam declares, "O Israel, the gods who brought you up out of Egypt are right here." 1 Kings 12:28
Aaron builds an altar for the calf. Exodus 32:5	Jeroboam builds altars (platforms) for the calves. 1 Kings 12:31
Aaron proclaims, "Tomorrow is a festival" Exodus 32:5	Jeroboam establishes a festival 1 Kings 12:32
Aaron oversaw as people, "offered holocausts [animals] and brought sacrifices Exodus 32:6	Jeroboam, "ascended the altar . . . to sacrifice to the calves he had made" 1 Kings 12:32

Moses tells Aaron that he brought "great sin upon" the people. Exodus 32:21	Jeroboam's actions "led to sin" 1 Kings 12:30
Aaron's sons are Nadab and Abihu Exodus 6:23	Jeroboam's sons are Nadab and Abijah 1 Kings 14:1 and 1 Kings 14:20
Aaron is the object of God's extreme displeasure, yet he serves until his death at the age of 123. Numbers 33:39	Jeroboam is the object of God's extreme displeasure, yet he serves out his reign in peace. 1 Kings 14:20

As with the allegorical stories of Jacob and Joseph, Aaron belongs to the realm of fictional characters. The hero stories of Jeroboam I reflected a historical account that honored the cultic changes Jeroboam I instituted in the northern kingdom of Israel. The Aaron stories are allegories, created to lend credibility to Jeroboam's changes.

When Jeroboam I became ruler of the northern kingdom of Israel, which was made up of ten of the original twelve tribal lands, his subjects were spread out over a large geographic area. It would not have made any sense for the Israelites to worship in Jerusalem, which was located in Judah and under the sovereignty of Rehoboam. Furthermore, Rehoboam had not done anything to endear himself to the northerners. Rehoboam celebrated the great harvest festival in the seventh month, in keeping with the Judahite agricultural calendar, a full month before the northern crops would be ready for harvest. Additionally, he insisted that people worship at the royal sanctuary in Jerusalem, which was convenient for Judahite pilgrims but not for the northerners.

Jeroboam's actions in establishing new centers of worship were not unprecedented. Two generations earlier, David had established his capital at Jerusalem because it was a much better location for a unified Israelite kingdom than Hebron, some 18 miles further south. David's choice was justified in the allegory of Abraham's recognition of the sacred character of Jerusalem. Similarly, Jeroboam's actions were justified in the allegory of Aaron's creation of idols and altars, and his presiding over worship.

As a champion of his people, Jeroboam I installed the ancient symbolism of God—that of the bull calf—in the sanctuaries at Dan in the northernmost part of his kingdom, and at Bethel in the southernmost part of his kingdom, thereby meeting the religious needs of his people at both extreme ends. At these locations, he celebrated the harvest festival in the eighth month, in keeping with the cooler climate of the north where the autumn crops ripen later.[138]

To be sure, some northerners—the prophet Hosea, for example—opposed the bovine imagery related to God. But that was in the 8th century and there is no reason to believe that Hosea's viewpoint was widespread in the north in his own time, and certainly not in the time of Jeroboam I.

58. Aaron vs. Korah

Lo and behold.   Numbers 17:23

Let's return to the biblical 14th/13th century B.C.E. setting of Moses and Aaron in the wilderness.

Moses is the leader of the Israelites and Aaron is anointed the High Priest (Leviticus 8:12). According to the "P," or "Priestly," narrative, Moses and Aaron are descendants of Levi, who was one of the twelve sons of Jacob. The tribe of Levi is not assigned tribal land because its members are expected to work throughout all the tribal lands, administering the priestly duties and maintaining the sanctuaries. The other tribes are expected to support the members of the Levite tribe (see Numbers 18:21).

Although all Israelite priests are Levites, not all Levites are priests. The actual "priestly duties" are delegated to Aaron and his offspring. The non-priestly Levites are, "attached to the priests (Hebrew: *kohanim*) and discharge the duties of the Tent of Meeting." But, unlike the priests, the Levites are not permitted any physical contact with the furnishings of the Shrine or with the altar—on pain of death! (Numbers 18:3–4).

Korah is another descendant of Levi, and a first cousin to Moses and Aaron. Understandably, Korah, as the leader of the non-priestly Levites, does not appreciate being relegated to the position of "assistant" and he vehemently challenges the appointment of Aaron as God's chosen priest. Unlike the story in Exodus where the character of Aaron is tainted by his involvement in the creation of the golden calf, the interactions with his cousin Korah leave Aaron solidly in the position of God's chosen High Priest.

Bible scholar Baruch Levine (1930-2021), who taught at New York University, theorized that the Numbers 16–17 story is a result of "braiding" together tales of tribal opposition to the concentrated political power of Moses.[139] Using excerpts from Numbers 16 & 17 (translated by the author), we will attempt to untangle the braids in order to allow us to concentrate on the internal struggle within the clergy.

Korah and his followers gang up on Moses and Aaron, saying:

> You have too much! For the entire community is
> holy [plural, Hebrew: qedošim], the Eternal being
> in their midst. Why then do you exalt yourselves
> over the Eternal's congregation? (Numbers 16:3)

Moses responds to Korah with a challenge of his own:

> On the morrow, let the Eternal make known who
> is his holy one [singular with definite article, ha-
> qādoš] by bringing that one close to him. The one
> he chooses he will bring close to him. (Numbers
> 16:5)

And, as an extra warning against the bravado of Korah, Moses adds:

> It is you who have too much, sons of Levi!
> (Numbers 16:7)

Korah's challenge seems to make sense: If every Israelite is "holy," qādoš, how can the holy priesthood be restricted to a specific line? The answer given by Moses is that there is a hierarchy of holiness. There may be many who are imbued with holiness, qedošim, but there is only one that God calls "the holy one"—ha-qādoš, with the definite article.

The Korahites should be satisfied that they have been designated to assist the priests. Aaron, as High Priest, owes his position at the top of the hierarchy of holiness to divine decree. As Moses puts it:

> Truly, it is against the Eternal that you and your
> community are making common cause. As for
> Aaron, who is he that you lodge complaint
> against him? (Numbers 16:11)

To demonstrate that Korah's claim to the priesthood is in opposition to the will of God, Moses instructs Korah:

You and your entire community be present
before the Eternal, you and they and Aaron on the
morrow. Let each one take his fire pan and place
incense in it and offer it, each one of you with his
fire pan in the presence of the Eternal, 250 fire pans,
and you and Aaron, each one his fire pan.
(Numbers 16:16–17)

As instructed, Korah and his people place hot coals and incense in
their fire pans and:

> . . . stood at the entrance to the tent of meeting, as
> did Moses and Aaron. Korah then rallied his
> whole community against them by the entrance to
> the tent of meeting. Then the physical presence
> (Hebrew: *kābod*) of the Eternal appeared to the
> entire community . . . Then Moses said, "By this
> you shall know that it is the Lord who has sent
> me to carry out these actions, that they are not of
> my own devising. If these people die the death of
> every mortal, if the fate of mortals is theirs, then
> it is not the Eternal who sent me. But if the
> Eternal fashions something entirely new, so that
> the earth opens its mouth and swallows them up,
> along with everything they possess, so that they
> descend alive into the underworld [Sheol], then
> you will know for yourselves that these persons
> have rejected the Eternal." (Numbers 16:18–31)

The condition set forth by Moses is fulfilled:

> Just as he finished speaking all these words, the
> earth split open beneath them. The earth opened
> its mouth and swallowed them up, along with
> their families, all the people belonging to Korah,
> and all the property. They and everything
> belonging to them descended live into the

underworld. The earth covered them over so that
they vanished from the congregation. All the
Israelites in their proximity fled at the sound of
their cries, for they said, "The earth may swallow
us, too." A fire issued forth from the Eternal and
consumed the 250 men, the offerers of the incense.
(Numbers 16:31–35)

That "the earth covered them over so that they vanished" is a
particularly nice touch. Korah leaves no descendants or any
physical reminder of his presence on earth. He dies without leaving
a trace (this, despite the fact that Numbers 26:11 explicitly states that,
"the sons of Korah did not die"). At God's behest, Moses
commands Eleazar, Aaron's son, to collect the fire pans and
hammer them into plating for the altar:

This was a reminder to the Israelites to ensure
that no outsider, that is, one not of the legitimate
seed of Aaron, would ever come close to the
Eternal's presence to offer incense and become
like Korah and his community. (Numbers 17:5)

The death of Korah and his supporters leaves the priesthood
in Aaron's hands. But rather than content themselves with an
Aaronic victory by default, the writers add two wonder tales to
show that Aaron truly merited his office. First, an angry God afflicts
Israel with a plague. But a plague sent by God in punishment of evil
doers can harm innocent bystanders. So God warns Moses:

Withdraw from the midst of the community, and
I will instantly annihilate them. (Numbers 17:10)

Then Moses commands Aaron to quickly:

Take your fire pan and put hot coals from the
altar in it and add incense. Quickly carry it over
to the community and perform a ritual of

expiation over them, for the foaming rage has issued from the face of the Eternal, the plague has begun! (Numbers 17:11)

Aaron hurries to the midst of the congregation, and he finds:

> . . . indeed, the plague had begun. He put on the incense and performed the expiation ritual over the people. He stood between the dead and the living, and the plague was contained. (Numbers 17:12–13)

Whereas the fire pans filled with incense had brought about the death of those unqualified for the priesthood, Aaron's fire pan saves most of the congregation from annihilation.

God then instructs Moses to provide another demonstration of Aaron's unique qualifications for the priesthood to the exclusion of all pretenders. Moses is to take a staff from every tribal leader and write each leader's name on it. On the staff of Levi, Moses is to write Aaron's name. God then commands that Moses place the staffs:

> . . . inside the tent of meeting, in front of the ark of the covenant, where I meet you. The man whom I select—his staff will sprout, and then I will be relieved of the complaints of the Israelites that they incite against you. (Numbers 17:19–20)

Moses follows God's instructions, waits until the next day to enter the tent again, and there:

> . . . lo and behold, the staff of Aaron of the house of Levi had sprouted. It gave forth a sprout, produced blossoms, and bore almonds . . . God then said to Moses: "Replace Aaron's staff in front of [the ark of] the covenant for safekeeping, as a warning to rebellious persons, so that their

complaints against me cease and they do not die."
Moses did as God commanded him, so he did.
(Numbers 17:23–26)

In 1962 the Israeli archaeologists Ruth Amiran (1914–2005) and Yohanan Aharoni (1919–1976), on behalf of the Institute of Archaeology at the Hebrew University of Jerusalem, began excavations at Arad, a town in the southern Negeb of Judah. The Arad expedition discovered more than one hundred Hebrew inscriptions in archaeological levels of the Iron Age.[140] Inscriptions from an 8th century B.C.E. temple compound provided evidence of cultic life that must have been known to the writers of the Torah stories. For example, one inscription indicates the "sons of Bezal"—likely a shortened form of "Bezalel," a name that means "in God's protection." According to Exodus 35:30, Bezalel was one of the two leading artisans named by God to carry out the design and construction of the desert tabernacle.

Pertinent to the analysis of the Aaron and Korah account is an inscription from Arad referring to the *bny qrḥ,* the "sons of Korah," or "Korahites," as cultic personnel. In other words, the "Korahites," if not Korah himself, were real, historical cultic personnel of the pre-exilic period. The compliers of the book of Psalms, a book that contains prayers and songs from every biblical period of Israel's history, were certainly aware of the Korahites. They included many passages ascribed to them (see Psalms 42, 44–49, 84, 85, 87, 88).

The Korahites might have been prescient when they chanted:

I say to God, my mountain,
Why have You forgotten me,
Why must I walk in gloom,
Oppressed by my enemy?
        Psalms 42:10

59. Revisionist History

What we remember is not what actually happened, not history, but merely that hackneyed dotted line they have chosen to drive into our memories by incessant hammering. Aleksandr Solzhenitsyn (1918– 2008), from *The Gulag Archipelago*

In the chapter titled "Etched in Stone," I described how scholars analyze linguistic, historical, and archaeological clues to deduce when a biblical story was written. From that kind of analysis, it is clear that the golden calf story, a story set in the 14th/13th century B.C.E., could not have been written any earlier than the 9th century B.C.E. Similar analysis reveals that the traditions about Korah's challenge to the Aaronide priesthood, also set in the 14th/13th century B.C.E., could not have been written any earlier than the 6th century B.C.E.

As scholars have long observed, Aaron is never identified as a priest in the prophetic literature of the pre-exilic period (pre-586 B.C.E.). Therefore, the following passage, where Moses is directed by God to identify Aaron and his descendants, a passage set in the wilderness in the 14th/13th century B.C.E., is chronologically suspect:

> Go personally and bring near to you Aaron, your
> brother, and his sons with him from the midst of
> the Israelites to officiate for me as priests.
> (Exodus 28:1, translation by the author)

If the priesthood had been established as the passage suggests, then in the 7th century B.C.E. the prophet Jeremiah would surely have been aware of the Aaronide priesthood. Jeremiah lived between the years of roughly 644–570 B.C.E. According to the words of his own eponymously named book, Jeremiah "was one of the priests (*kohanim*) at Anathoth" (Jeremiah 1:1). Today, Jeremiah is recognized as one of the major prophets of the Bible. The words of Jeremiah span the reigns of five Israelite kings, but the long-lived Jeremiah rarely liked what he saw. Prophets were political commentators in many ways, and Jeremiah frequently prophesied that the king was leading his people down the wrong path, resulting in their sinning before God. As a priest, surely

Jeremiah would have made mention of the Aaronide priesthood and its responsibility to help the people worship God properly. But Jeremiah makes no mention of Aaron the priest.[*]

More significant than the silence of Jeremiah, however, is the eloquence of Ezekiel (circa 622–570 B.C.E.). Ezekiel is another major prophet of the Bible and, like his contemporary Jeremiah, he was priest (*kohen*). The book of Ezekiel devotes a good deal of space to questions of priestly conduct and ritual, and the role of the High Priest—identified as Zadok. According to the Bible (2 Samuel 8:17; 1 Kings 1:8, 4:4), Zadok was a priest during the reigns of David and Solomon.[**] Regarding the priests descended from the line of Zadok, Ezekiel relays God's message that:

> They alone may enter my sanctuary and they
> alone shall approach my table to minister to me,
> and they shall keep my charge. (Ezekiel 44:16)

Ezekiel makes no mention of the "sons of Aaron."

During the first half of the 1st millennium B.C.E., there was a good deal of diversity in the priesthood. The existence of the Korahite priests has been substantiated by archaeological finds that complement the Torah narrative. Ancient Israel's division into the northern kingdom and the southern kingdom—two distinct states with numerous shrines—had not allowed any single priesthood to control all the cultic offices.

There is no archaeological evidence of the priest Aaron. The earliest biblical traditions regarding Aaron portrayed him as a hero of the Exodus with no connection to the priesthood. This narrative changed with the 10th century B.C.E. accession of Jeroboam I; a leader who was also a priest of a cult in which calves played a prominent role.

---

[*] Fun Fact: Because of his doom and gloom predictions, Jeremiah is known as the Weeping Prophet. The term "jeremiad" is used for a long literary work in which the author bitterly laments the state of society.

[**] Another Fun Fact: 1 Kings 1:38-40 is a passage that describes Zadok the Priest anointing Solomon to become king after David, even though Solomon was not next in line to the throne. That passage has been used since 973 in coronations of the British monarch. In 1727, George Frideric Handel set the words to music for a coronation anthem "Zadok the Priest."

Positive stories of Aaron were meant to allegorically elicit positive associations with the king-priest Jeroboam I. The character Aaron served the purpose of legitimizing the northern kingdom cult of God.

When studying ancient cultures, archaeologists work closely with art historians in analyzing artistic depictions on artifacts to glean vital information about the way cultural identity was expressed and how everyday lives were led. Art historians show us that Exodus 28, the claim of priesthood for Aaron and his descendants set in the 14th/13th century B.C.E., could not have been written earlier than the 6th century B.C.E. Exodus 28 describes in detail what members of the new priesthood are to wear and concludes with the following:

> You shall also make for them linen trousers to cover their nakedness; they shall extend from the hips to the thighs. They shall be worn by Aaron and his sons when they enter the tent of meeting or when they approach the altar to officiate in the sanctuary, so that they do not incur punishment and die. It shall be a law for all time for him and for his offspring to come. (Exodus 2.8:42–43, translation by the author)

In the ancient Near East, both men and women regularly wore kilts or skirt-like garments. But the preceding passage requires the new priesthood to wear trousers at the altar to avoid any inadvertent exposure of nakedness in the divine presence. This requirement can be dated only after trousers (breeches) came into use by Persians. Art historians have documented breeches and trousers in Persian reliefs of the 6th century B.C.E., precisely when Jews began coming into contact with that empire.[141] This means that the story in the Torah crediting the institution of the Aaronide priesthood to Moses in Exodus 28 cannot be any earlier than the 6th century B.C.E.

The fall of the northern kingdom in 720 BCE forced the migration of northern kingdom inhabitants into the southern kingdom, bringing their positive tales about Aaron/Jeroboam into the region. However, writers from the southern kingdom regarded Jeroboam I as an upstart who divided the kingdom two centuries before—they did not view him as a hero. Southern writers distorted the Aaron/calf tradition of 1 Kings 12–13. The story was rewritten to create the impression that Jeroboam I had been an idolater and that the northern kingdom had never recovered from the original sin of its foundation. We can date the southern distortion almost within a decade, thanks to the continuation of the calf story in 1 Kings:

> While Jeroboam was standing by the altar to offer incense, a man of God came out of Judah, by the word of God, to Bethel and proclaimed against the altar by the word of God. He said, "O altar, altar, thus says the Eternal: 'A son shall be born to the house of David, Josiah by name, and he shall sacrifice on you the priests of the high places who offer incense on you, and human bones shall be burned on you.'" (1 Kings 13:1–2, translation by the author)

If you stated in the 10th century B.C.E. that a man named Josiah would come along in the 7th century B.C.E. and disparage your legacy by defiling an altar you used, that would be quite a prophecy indeed! 2 Kings 23 tells us the ultimate fate of the altar at Bethel:

> As Josiah turned, he saw the tombs there on the mount, and he sent and took the bones out of the tombs and burned them on the altar and defiled it, according to the word of the Eternal that the man of God proclaimed [or "who prophesied this word"] when Jeroboam stood by the altar at the festival; he turned and looked up at the tomb of the man of God who had predicted these things. Then he asked, "What is that monument that I see?" The people of the city told him, "It is the tomb of the man of God who came from Judah and predicted these things that you have done against the altar at Bethel." (2 Kings 23:16–17, translation by the author)

For anyone who does not read the Bible as a fundamentalist, it is difficult to accept the storyline of a detailed prophecy that came true centuries later. Instead, it is much more defensible that the story of the "prophecy" and its fulfillment was created later, during the reign of King Josiah. Josiah began his religious reform about 622 B.C.E. and was assassinated by Pharaoh Necho at Megiddo in 609 B.C.E. This means that the story that relegates Jeroboam's actions in inaugurating the calves to a sin, while elevating Josiah by predicting their destruction, must be dated between 622 and 609 B.C.E. This would also have been the time that the formerly positive images of Aaron as a priest—and forerunner to the actions of Jeroboam— underwent the negative editing that marked a low point for Aaron as an allegorical figure.

60. Centralized Priesthood

What you leave behind is not what is engraved in stone monuments,
but what is woven into the lives of others.
Pericles (495–429 B.C.E.), statesman

The northern stories of the hero/king Jeroboam I were based in some reality. The split between the kingdoms provided opportunities for new, and sometimes conflicting, traditions. The Hebrew Bible, which contains writings spanning at least eight centuries, gives us a glimpse at the herculean effort undertaken by the leadership of the community to preserve Jewish culture. But, in words attributed to the French Revolution figure Maximilien Robespierre (1758–1794), "history is written by the victors."

The "victors" in this case were the southerners. They wrote "history" favorable to themselves or rewrote earlier traditions with a goal of vindicating themselves. The older, northerner traditions with positive realistic and allegorical representation of Jeroboam I— through the ancestral hero-stories of Jacob and Joseph, as well as through the stories of Aaron the good priest—were distorted to vilify the northerners while validating the superiority of the southerners. Contemporary readers seeking to get closer to the facts must extract the original favorable stories from the present polemical contexts in which they are embedded.

The passage we have been focusing on, which deals with Jeroboam's creation of places of worship in the northern kingdom, was edited to a point that descends into absurdity. The account claims that Jeroboam made the calves so that the northerners would not "return to their lord, to Rehoboam ... then they will kill me" (1 Kings 12:27). We are led to believe that Jeroboam is a hypocrite who only cares for himself, while telling his people that he is concerned for them. These do not sound like the actions of a man who had been specifically singled out by Rehoboam's father, Solomon, because he "saw how highly capable the young man was, for Jeroboam was a man of great ability" (1 Kings 11:28).

Also, the writer claims that Jeroboam actually said to his people, "O Israel, the gods [plural] who brought you up out of Egypt are right here" (1 Kings 12:28). This statement makes a mockery of the opening line of the Ten Commandments, which begins, "I am the Eternal, your God, who took you out of the land of Egypt" (Exodus 20:2 and Deuteronomy 5:6, translation by the author). The southern, Judahite writer parodies the Commandment in order to compound Jeroboam's sin: having just learned that Jeroboam was a hypocrite, we are encouraged to believe that he was an idolater as well.

And finally in the same passage, we are told that Jeroboam "made priests from all segments of the people who were *not* [emphasis added] descendants of Levi" (1 Kings 12:31). Given that the Levites were set aside to serve God, if Jeroboam had selected Levite priests to serve in the temple with the calves, it would have legitimated the calves as symbols of God. By indicating that non-Levites were made priests, the writer delegitimates the calves as part of his larger program to delegitimate Jeroboam I. (The writer leads the legacy of Jeroboam into a no-win situation: Non-Levite priests are offensive, but Levite priests in a temple with calves is abhorrent!)

We have established that the Korahite and the Zadokite priesthoods existed, and we know that there were several places of worship for the people to makes sacrifices to their god. After the Assyrian invasion of the northern kingdom of Israel (circa 720 B.C.E.) many Israelites migrated south to Judah. We do not know the actual impetus that inspired someone to attempt to centralize the priesthood, but we know that, about 100 years after the fall of northern Israel, King Josiah tried it.

Part IV of this book describes the "finding" of a set of laws regarding religious observance and rituals, as well as regulations for military, criminal and civil law. Understandably, since there was a concerted effort to diminish the position of Aaron/Jeroboam, the codes make no mention of the Aaronide priesthood. However, Josiah's reform had been in effect for barely a decade when the king met his death circa 609 B.C.E. The reform probably did not survive his death, and surely not the fall of Judah to the Babylonians, culminating in the 586 B.C.E. exile. Yet, Aaron remains important to the Jewish community to this day.

61. Aaron Rehabilitated

"The rules!" shouted Ralph, "you're breaking the rules!"
"Who cares?"
William Golding (1911–1993), from *Lord of the Flies*

In 539 B.C.E., Cyrus of Persia defeated the Babylonians and welcomed the Israelites (mostly known by this time as "Jews") to return to an area now called Yehud—the Aramaic form of Judah (Hebrew: *Yehudah*). Yehud was a Persian administrative district that covered less territory than the earlier Judah, but in Yehud the Jewish people were allowed to rebuild the sanctuary devoted to their god. Construction of this second temple was completed in the late 6th century B.C.E. (circa 515 B.C.E.), about a hundred years after the death of Josiah.

The sanctuary was the only sanctuary in Yehud devoted to the worship of the Eternal. This meant that only a small number of contenders for the priestly office could actually serve as priests. It was at this point that the image of Aaron the High Priest was rehabilitated. Religious reformers have often depicted their innovations as restorations. Both Martin Luther and the founder of Reform Judaism claimed that they were returning to the true meaning of their respective religions—which, they claimed, had been betrayed. For spiritual ancestors, Luther looked beyond the teachings of Roman Catholic Christianity to (his understanding) of those of Jesus and Paul. Jewish reformers of the 19th century saw themselves as heirs of the ancient Hebrew prophets. Something similar happened in biblical times.

The members of the faction that eventually succeeded to the priesthood found their ancestor in Aaron, one of the heroes of the Exodus story. As I observed earlier, the tale of Korah and his disastrous rebellion in Numbers 16 was meant to demonstrate that only the "sons of Aaron" could serve as legitimate priests. This claim that the true priesthood derived from ancient times masked the fact that it was a radical innovation. The Torah's story of the Korahites' unsuccessful challenge to Aaron, which resulted in their horrifying death, was meant to illustrate the fate of all who would challenge the new order. That Korah and his followers were swallowed up alive:

> ... was a reminder to the Israelites to ensure that
> no outsider, that is, one not of the legitimate seed
> of Aaron, would ever come close to the Eternal's
> presence to offer incense and become like Korah
> and his community. (Numbers 17:5, translation
> by the author)

To become "like Korah and his community" meant suffering a public, unnatural death.

Outside of the Torah, only the books of Ezra, Nehemiah and Chronicles claim that direct descendants of Aaron are the only legitimate priests. All three books are dated by scholars as having been created in the 5th/4th century B.C.E., at the earliest. Even though those texts are some of the latest in the Bible, their claim of Aaronide priesthood has stood the test of time, so let's take a closer look at them.

Ezra was active approximately during the years 480–440 B.C.E. and was known as both Ezra the Priest and Ezra the Scribe. The fact that Ezra was both a priest and a scribe made him unusual. The literacy rate was very low in biblical times, making a person proficient in reading and writing an important part of society. Scribes were employed in the courts of kings (who were typically illiterate) and were available for hire in places of commerce to create business records. As a priest, Ezra claimed descent from the seventeenth generation after Aaron.

Historically, we know that Cyrus the Great, founder of the Persian Empire, defeated the Babylonians in 539 B.C.E. The Bible goes on to tell us that Cyrus invited exiled Jews to return to their homeland and rebuild their temple. About a century later, under the rule of King Artaxerxes*, Ezra returned from Babylon as a man with a mission:

---

* Pronunciation: ar-tah-ZURK-seez

> For Ezra had dedicated himself to study the
> Teaching (Torah) of the Eternal so as to observe
> it, and to teach laws and rules to Israel . . . King
> Artaxerxes gave Ezra the priest-scribe [a letter
> stating] . . . "For you are commissioned by the
> king and his seven advisers to regulate Judah and
> Jerusalem according to the law of your God."
> (Ezra 7:10–14)

Nehemiah, a contemporary of Ezra, also returned to Jerusalem. While Ezra was intent on rebuilding the religious foundation of the Israelites, Nehemiah was more interested in literal, architectural rebuilding. Nehemiah returned to repair the damaged city walls in order to provide protection to the Israelites living there. Although the book of Ezra does not mention Nehemiah, the book of Nehemiah mentions Ezra and supports the role that Ezra set for himself.

Chronicles also identifies the "sons of Aaron" as the only true priests. A lengthy text originally requiring two scrolls, Chronicles 1 and Chronicles 2, Chronicles is a retelling of the history of the origins of the Jewish people, starting with Adam and ending with King Cyrus of Persia's proclamation that the Israelites should rebuild a temple to their god. Chronicles notably does not make mention of the Exodus.

Because of the characters mentioned in the texts, scholars know that the books of Ezra, Nehemiah and Chronicles could not have been written before the $5^{th}/4^{th}$ century B.C.E. And it is from the $5^{th}/4^{th}$ century B.C.E. and onward that all claimants to the priesthood of Israel must base their claim on descent from Aaron.

The figure of Aaron has been used both positively and negatively to serve the purposes of the writer. But inconsistencies in his storyline, historical anathemas, linguistic evidence of later dating, and glaringly obvious parallels with actual figures in history lay bare the fact that Aaron never actually existed.

The use of fictional figures to serve a politicize purpose has been used to great effect throughout history. The wisdom of the 6th century B.C.E. Chinese general and military strategist Sun Tzu was collected in the book, *The Art of War*, which still today is listed on the recommended reading list for students of the United States Military Academy at West Point. However, whether Sun Tzu actually existed is debated, with many scholars believing the work is a compilation reflecting the wisdom of many generals and strategists. The 14th century marksman William Tell of Switzerland was forced by a tyrannical local official to use an arrow to shoot an apple off his own son's head. Following that successful shot, Tell took a stand against the official—which became a rallying tale for Swiss people fighting against tyrannical foreign rule. Although William Tell is a compelling figure, there is no evidence that he actually existed and the scenario with the apple has echoes from older, Norse mythology. "Tokyo Rose" was the name American servicemen used for female, South Pacific radio personalities who taunted American servicemen during World War II by suggesting that, while they were battling far from home, their wives were being comforted by other men. In 1949, Japanese-American Iva Toguri D'Aquino (1916–2006) was accused of being the "real" Tokyo Rose and convicted of treason against the United States, serving six years of a ten-year sentence. History has shown that D'Aquino's conviction was based on fabricated evidence and the character of Tokyo Rose was a "mere wartime myth."[142] Stories of Sun Tzu, William Tell, and Tokyo Rose were used for political purposes. The historicity of Sun Tzu and William Tell is debated. The legend of Tokyo Rose is proven to be mythological.

Aaron, the 14th/13th century B.C.E. priest, is likewise a fictional character.

Summary – Part IX

- Aaron is described as the older brother of Moses in many biblical passages, but other passages disagree with that description. His high status, though, is not in dispute.

- The story of Aaron creating the golden calf casts aspersions on Aaron, but it may be a misreading of the text. Bovine imagery was widely used in the ancient Near East and the story originally meant that a golden calf was miraculously fashioned by God.

- Although the Bible says not to make images for use in the cult, there are many instances in the Bible where the heroes do just that.

- Using linguistic clues, we reveal that the 14th/13th B.C.E. century setting of the story of Moses and Aaron in the wilderness could not have been written any earlier than the 9th century B.C.E.

- The parallels between the actions of Aaron and Jeroboam I, the first king of the northern kingdom of Israel, make clear that the Aaron story is an allegory of Jeroboam I.

- The Korahite priesthood (the Sons of Korah) has been evidenced by archaeological finds. But a competitor to the allegorical Aaron would have been problematic; the Bible nicely puts Korah in his place.

- By analyzing passages in the Bible and looking at archaeological and art history clues, we are able to state confidently that the Korah passages, which are set in the 14th/13th century B.C.E. and put Aaron securely in a prominent position, could not have been written any earlier than the 6th century B.C.E.

- There were two efforts to centralize worship of God. The first to do it on the basis of a book was by Josiah in the 7th century B.C.E., but that effort was interrupted—either by the death of Josiah circa 609 B.C.E., or by the Babylonian destruction of Judah and the subsequent exile (this point is still debated by scholars).

- In 539 B.C.E. the Persians defeated the Babylonians and invited the Israelites to return and rebuild their temple. The land given to the Israelites was significantly smaller and—owning to the acceptance of the notion that sacrificial worship should be centralized—only one temple would be built, but there were many claimants to the role of priest. This necessitated the second effort to centralize worship.

- The fictional character Aaron was used either positively or negatively depending on the party using him. When the Bible was canonized, the final editors gave Aaron a place as the High Priest and considered all his (male) descendants priests as well. This fiction holds true today.

PART X
MOSES & SAUL

Overview: The first king of Israel, Saul, united the tribes into one kingdom and identified the Eternal as the national god of the Israelite people. Obvious parallels between the traditions of Saul in the Bible and Moses in the Torah lead us to conclude that the character Moses began as a positive allegory celebrating the military, political, and cultic successes of Saul's government. The House of Saul produced only one ruler after Saul before the throne was usurped by David, who founded the House of David—a dynasty that would rule for more than 400 years. Most traditions preserved in the Bible attempt to tamp down the history of Saul and elevate David's position instead. However, enough information about Saul remains so that we can glean information about the pivotal role Saul played in the formation of the Israelite religion and the worship of the Eternal.

62. Moses

Don't let worry get you down. Remember, Moses started out as a basket case. unknown

For Jews the world over, Moses was the greatest prophet. The Bible tells us that Moses was born to a Levite father and mother, adopted by the daughter of a pharaoh, and raised as an Egyptian prince—with all the privileges that conveyed. Tradition goes on to tell us that Moses was chosen by God to lead the Israelites out of 400 years of bondage to Egypt. In order to persuade Pharaoh that God wanted the Israelites to be released, nine plagues (frogs, locusts, diseased livestock, boils on people, etc.) were brought upon the Egyptian people. Pharaoh did not capitulate until the tenth plague—the death of the first-born, which included the death of Pharaoh's own child. The Israelites were released from bondage and led away by Moses. Their first significant stop was at Mt. Sinai where God gave Moses the "teaching and commandments" (Exodus 24:12).

After receiving God's law, the people continued on their journey toward the Promised Land of Canaan. However, the Israelite people proved to be fickle complainers during their wanderings. In his vexation, God declared that none of the former slaves would enter Canaan. Instead, they would wander in the wilderness for forty years; approximately the amount of time it would take for the generation of former slaves to die out. At the age of 120, Moses was allowed to glimpse the Promised Land from a mountain top, but even he was not allowed to journey into Canaan. The Promised Land would be entered by the free-born children of the Israelites (with exceptions for Joshua and Caleb, whom God allowed to enter Canaan). And:

Never again did there arise in Israel a prophet like
Moses. (Deuteronomy 34:10)

The first edition of John Bright's, *A History of Israel*, was published in 1959 but, because of the flow of new information discovered by archaeologists, a second edition (1972) was necessary. We saw earlier that Bright's book was popular in circles of religious moderates for its attempt to balance the critical study of Israelite history with respect and reverence for the biblical tradition. In the 1972 edition, Bright wrote:

> The events of exodus and Sinai require a great
> personality behind them. And a faith as unique as
> Israel's demands a founder as surely as does
> Christianity—or Islam for that matter. To deny
> that role to Moses would force us to posit another
> person of the same name.

In its time, the argument offered by John Bright for the historicity of Moses would have been compelling to most scholars. The year 1972 was still too early to dismiss the historicity of the traditions of the Exodus, and the traditions of the sojourn in Sinai with which they are often linked in the Torah. If there really was an Israelite Exodus from Egypt, someone must have led it. Inasmuch as the Bible supplied that leader with a name, and a good Egyptian name at that, why not accept it?

As we have seen, the very basis of that argument has been removed, or at the very least seriously called into doubt, by the archaeological evidence that the group called "Israel" arose in Canaan. The Exodus and the consequent tales of Israel at Sinai and wandering through the desert would appear to be unhistorical. But already in 1962, R. Francis Johnson (1923–2000), who taught at Connecticut College, wrote:

> Since large blocks of the Old Testament pass over
> Moses in silence, suspicion is raised about the
> historicity of this mighty figure . . . Perhaps his
> dominant position (in the Pentateuch) results
> from the piety of later generations of Israelites. If
> they have not actually created the figure of the
> nation's founder, perhaps they have magnified his
> importance and pictured him in such a way as to
> derive sanction for their own practices and
> values.[143]

In other words, it seems most likely that the writers of the Torah, in

Johnson's words, "actually created the figure of the nation's founder."

If Moses was not a historical figure but an allegory from which later Israel could "derive sanctions and values," we must attempt to find the model, or models, for the allegory. There is one thread that runs through all the different Moses traditions: Moses is the prophet who unites the people of Israel under the banner of his God. He is also a royal or quasi-royal figure who stands above every Israelite institution. This means that Moses originated as an allegorical representation of the royal historical figure who united Israel under the banner of God and who claimed sovereignty over all competing institutions. The prime candidate for this figure is Saul, the first king of Israel.

63. Saul

The old Romans all wished to have a king over them because they had not yet tasted the sweetness of freedom.
Livy (59 B.C.E. – 17 C.E.), Roman historian

The founders of the United States of America saw monarchy as an instrument of oppression and fought a bloody war to replace it with a republican form of government. The biblical book of Judges, in contrast, describes what life in Israel was like before Saul became king. The narrative in the book of Judges mentions the state of kingless-ness four times (Judges 17:6, 18:1, 19:1 and 21:25), and comments that in the absence of a king, "everyone did as he pleased" (Judges 21:25 and 17:6).

In illustration, the book of Judges provides one particularly gruesome example of just how precarious Israelite life was in the time "when there was no king": A man was traveling with his concubine and stopped in the town of Gibeah. A townsman invited the man and his concubine to stay in his house to provide them safe shelter. However, the "depraved lot" that lived in Gibeah demanded that the man come out of the house so that the townspeople could "be intimate with him" (rape him). Instead, the man "seized his concubine and pushed her out to them. They raped her and abused her all night long until morning." The concubine subsequently died, then the man "picked up a knife, and took hold of his concubine and cut her up limb by limb into twelve parts. He sent them throughout the territory of Israel," in an effort to shock the people of the land into action against the lawlessness (Judges 19).

The narrative in the book of Samuel tells us that, to remedy this state of lawlessness, the elders of Israel approached the prophet Samuel and demanded "a king for us, to govern us like all other nations" (1 Samuel 8:5). The man chosen to be king was Saul, from the tribe of Benjamin, who was "an excellent young man; no one among the Israelites was handsomer than he" (1 Samuel 9:2).

Karel van der Toorn (born: 1956), a scholar of ancient religions who taught at the University of Leiden and later at the University of Amsterdam, presented two studies of Saul that may shed light on the significance of Saul in the Israelite narrative. In one study, van der Toorn called attention to the fact that the Eternal (*Yahweh*) is thus far not found in any Syrian or Palestinian pantheon other than Israel.[144]. In a second study, van der Toorn argued that Saul was responsible for the Eternal becoming Israel's official god:

> The changes occurring under Saul were first of all political. The founder of a territorial state, Saul put in place an administrative apparatus and a standing military force. By a system of grants and other privileges he succeeded in maintaining the support of several groups in which power was traditionally vested. In its religious politics too, however Saul's rule was an innovation. The god of the head of state was promoted to the rank of national god . . . [The] priesthood, sworn to loyalty, was expected to serve the king's best interests. They became the civil servants of state religion.[145]

Van der Toorn's claim that Saul, as head of state, made the Eternal into the national god is fully supported by the book of Samuel, in which Saul's zeal is well documented. Saul is never accused of the one sin attributed to all the "bad" kings of Israel: he never deserts the Eternal for other gods. And his piety to the Eternal is also reflected in the name of his oldest son, Jonathan (Hebrew: *Yeho-natan*, "The-Eternal-has-given"). It is made clear to readers that Saul, as the "anointed" one (Hebrew: *māšiaḥ*), was chosen by God because "there was none like him in the entire people" (1 Samuel 10:24, translation by the author).

Saul gives credit to God for the Israelite victory over the Ammonites (1 Samuel 11:13), as does his son Jonathan for victory over the Philistines (1 Samuel 14:12). In his total devotion to God, Saul wipes out forms of divination that the cult of the Eternal considered illicit:

> The woman said . . . "Surely you know what Saul has done, how he has cut off the mediums and the

wizards from the land." (1 Samuel 28:9,
translation by the author)

The following biblical tale illustrates the way Saul regulated worship in
the cult of the Eternal. After striking down the Philistines:

> ... the people were famished ... [they] took
> sheep and oxen and calves and slew them on the
> ground and ... ate them with the blood. Then
> Saul was told, "The people are sinning against the
> Eternal, by eating with the blood." He said, "You
> have dealt treacherously; roll a great stone to me
> here." Then Saul said, "Disperse yourselves
> among the people, and say to them, 'Let everyone
> bring his ox or his sheep and slay them here and
> eat. Do not sin against the Eternal by eating with
> the blood.'" So every one of the people brought
> his ox with him that night and slew them there.
> Then Saul built an altar to the Eternal; he was the
> first to build an altar to the Eternal. (1 Samuel
> 14:31–35, translation by the author)

This tale must be understood against the background of biblical
views of blood.[146] Because blood was identified with the life force,
biblical legislation allotted the blood to God alone, who was popularly
believed to consume it. All humans, including non-Israelites, were
forbidden to eat blood, but Israelites had an additional obligation: They
were required to abstain from eating the flesh of a slaughtered animal
with the blood still in it. Precisely because of blood's potency as a life
force, its consumption appealed to famished soldiers who would need
to revitalize themselves for battle. But in Saul's eyes, the consumption
of blood was a sin against God. By insisting that the animals be
slaughtered ceremonially at the great stone, Saul made sure that the
blood would be poured out and that the flesh would not be eaten "with
the blood."*

---

* Leviticus 19:26, "You shall not eat anything with its blood" and Genesis
9:4, "You must not, however, eat flesh with its life blood in it" and

The last verse in the biblical tale is particularly instructive. It reads, *'oto hehel libnot mizbeah l-YHWH* which I translate as:

He was the first to build an altar to the Eternal.

In contrast, most of the ancient, and the most common modern translations, translate the line as:

And Saul built an altar to the Eternal; it was the first altar that he built to the Eternal.

This is an intentional obscuring of the plain sense of the text in order to deal with a problem that arises when readers accept the historicity of the tales about Noah, Abraham, Isaac, Jacob, Moses, and Joshua. The following table uses accepted approximations of the biblical chronology:

Approximate Biblical Date	Biblical Character	Altar-Building Passage
2100 B.C.E, or earlier	Noah	Genesis 8:20 - "Then Noah built an altar to the Eternal"
1800 B.C.E.	Abram (Abraham)	Genesis 12:7 - "And he built an altar there to the Eternal who had appeared to him"
1700 B.C.E.	Isaac	Genesis 26:25 - "So he built an altar there and invoked the Eternal by name"

Deuteronomy 12:23, "But make sure that you do not partake of the blood; for the blood is the life, and you must not consume the life with the flesh." However, the prophet Isaiah and Psalms 50 questioned whether God really wanted these sacrificial offerings: see Isaiah 1:11, "'What need have I of all your sacrifices?' Says the Lord. 'I am sated with burnt offering of rams, and suet of fatlings, blood of bulls.'", and Psalms 50:13, "Do I eat the flesh of bulls, or drink the blood of he-goats?"

1700 B.C.E.	Jacob	Genesis 35:7 - "There he built an altar and named the site El-bethel"
14th/13th century B.C.E.	Moses	Exodus 17:15 – And Moses built an altar and named it Adonai-nissi"
Early 13th century B.C.E.	Joshua	Joshua 8:30 – "At that time Joshua built an altar to the Eternal, the God of Israel"

Jewish scholars of late antiquity and the medieval period understood the correct translation of the verse and used creative, mental gymnastics to solve the problem. What follows is drawn from the Midrash called Leviticus Rabbah:

> It is written: *wayyiben ša'ul mizbeaḥ l-YHWH 'oto heḥel libnot mizbeaḥ l-YHWH*—So many altars were built by the ancients—Noah, Abraham, Isaac, Jacob, Moses, and Joshua, and you [the verse] say *'oto heḥel* - "he was the first?" The rabbis say: *'oto heḥel* means "he was the first of the kings." But Rabbi Yudan said: Because he was prepared to give his life for this matter, Scripture assigned him as much credit as if he himself had been the first to build an altar to the Eternal.[147]

In this text there are three speakers: an anonymous questioner, a group of anonymous rabbis, and a named respondent—a rabbi of antiquity, Rabbi Yudan (circa 3rd century C.E.). All speakers agree that 1 Samuel 14:35 states, in the plain sense of the verse, that Saul was the first to build an altar to God. For those Rabbis featured in the midrash, this statement is problematic because it contradicts other biblical traditions set in the pre-monarchic period, which claim that "so many altars were built by the ancients."

Leviticus Rabbah is instructive because it shows two different attempts to resolve the biblical contradiction. In the midrash, the rabbis claim that Saul had set a royal precedent by being the first of the kings to build an altar to God. In contrast, Rabbi Yudan resolves the incongruity by treating the scriptural claim as hyperbole; we are not to accept the plain sense of the verse. According to Rabbi Yudan, Saul was not chronologically the first to build an altar to God, but because of the courage he showed in building it, he might as well have been the first. In any case, both the anonymous rabbis and Rabbi Yudan agree on the necessity of imposing some sort of larger context on the verse so that it doesn't contradict other biblical verses.

The discomfort with the implications of this particular text is not confined to what modern readers can find in Leviticus Rabbah: Medieval, Jewish scholars, like Levi b. Gershon (1288–1344), David Kimhi (1160–1235), Joseph Kara (circa 1065–1135), and Isaiah of Trani (circa 1180–1250) also commented in their writings on the dichotomy. Joseph Kara wrote the following:

> This would imply that he was the first in the
> world to build an altar, but that cannot be correct,
> for after all, many altars had earlier been built.
> Therefore what is written 'oto heḥel libnot mizbeaḥ
> must be understood as if it read 'oto mizbeaḥ heḥel
> libnot; that is, "this was the first altar he built."

Kara's problem is that the text cannot mean what it says. Therefore, it "must be understood as if it read" something other than it does.[148]

But the problem shared by Kara and his successors is not inherent in 1 Samuel 14:35. When we accept, as we must, the fact that the stories about the period prior to the unification of the tribes by King Saul have no historical value for that period, then we are free to consider seriously the tradition that Saul was the first to build an altar to God. Stories such as these would have been told in circles that revered Saul, and among people who shared his zeal for the worship of the Eternal.

64. Moses as Allegory of Saul

The people I was taught were heroes—Jacob or Moses or David— *were ambivalent figures, or worse. But that messiness was joyful and* *challenging; I loved having a Bible that I could argue with.* David Plotz (born: 1970), journalist, quoted from the *Political Gabfest* podcast

The links between the career of the historical Saul and that of the allegorical "Moses" are striking. In the last chapter, we observed that Saul regulated the cultic worship of the Eternal in the same way that Moses did, by building an altar and specifying proper animal sacrifice. And there were more similarities between these two men: First, both men were said to be prophets. Second, numerous Bible scholars have called attention to the linguistic resemblance between God's words to the prophet Samuel when he designated Saul to save the people, and God's direct words to Moses to, likewise, save the people. In both cases God acknowledged the cries and sufferings of the Israelites. Third, both Moses and Saul were called on to wipe out the people of Amalek, the ancient enemy of the Israelites:

<u>Moses as Prophet</u>
Never again did there arise in Israel a prophet like Moses. (Deuteronomy 34:10)

<u>Saul as Prophet</u>
The spirit of God possessed him, and he fell into a prophetic frenzy . . . When all who had known him before saw how he prophesied with the prophets, the people said to one another . . . "Is Saul also among the prophets?" (1 Samuel 10:9–11, translation by the author)

God said to Moses:

Then God said, "I have observed the misery of my people who are in Egypt; I have heard their cry on account of their taskmasters. Indeed, I know their sufferings. (Exodus 3:7, translation by the author)

God said to Samuel regarding Saul:

Tomorrow about this time I will send to you a man from the land of Benjamin, and you shall anoint him to be prince over my people Israel. He shall save my people from the hand of the Philistines, for I have seen the affliction of my people because their cry has come to me. (1 Samuel 9:16, translation by the author)

God instructs Moses to wipe out Amalek:

Then the Eternal said to Moses . . . "I will utterly blot out the memory of Amalek from under heaven!" (Exodus 17:14)
- and -
You shall blot out the memory of Amalek from under heaven. Do not forget! (Deuteronomy 25:19)

Samuel tells Saul that God demands the destruction of Amalek:

Thus said the Eternal of Hosts . . . Now go, attack the Amalek people and [put to death] all that belongs to them. Spare no one, but kill alike men and women, young children and nursing babies, oxen and sheep, camels and asses!
(1 Samuel 15:2–3)

In cult, prophecy, and the accounts of Israel's wars with Amalek, the biblical identification of the historical Saul is so similar to that of the "Moses" of allegory that it cannot be dismissed as coincidence. But, as the biblical scholar Joseph Blenkinsopp wrote, when it comes to Saul, "the modern historian finds himself . . . working against the grain of the sources."[149] The sources who compiled these traditions favored Saul's successor, King David, and they sought to diminish the role of Saul in the narrative. To recover the underlying traditions, we must proceed as we did earlier with regard to Jeroboam I, and for much the same reason—the traditions were transmitted within circles largely unsympathetic to their subject.

According to 1 Samuel 31, Saul and three of his sons died in battle against the Philistines. The assassination of his surviving son left the field to Saul's enemy David, who came to the throne and established a dynasty that ruled Judah for more than four hundred years. Because the writers of the Bible favored David, most of the traditions in the books of Samuel regarding Saul are unfavorable.

However, we find occasional positive traditions about Saul that are probably genuine because the writers and compilers who transmitted these traditions had no reason to invent them. Most likely, anything positive about Saul was passed on only because it was too well known to be ignored.

65. Recontextualizing

What is political discourse if not spiteful?
Ross Douthat (born: 1979), New York Times columnist,
quoted from *The Argument* podcast

Saul's time as God's chosen leader was brief. Here's a short timeline
of notable moments in his career:

1 Samuel 9	We are introduced to Saul as "an excellent young man."
1 Samuel 10	Saul is anointed by Samuel to be the first king of Israel, and the spirit of prophecy comes upon him.
1 Samuel 11	After a military victory, Saul is formally inaugurated as king.
1 Samuel 13	Saul acts as the cult leader by presenting the offering to God.
1 Samuel 14	Saul, having established his sovereignty, makes war against his enemies all around.
1 Samuel 15	Saul is assigned a straightforward task of proscribing [killing] all living things of the nation of Amalek. Instead, Saul spares the king of Amalek, and the choice livestock—which he plans to sacrifice to God. Because Saul does not follow the explicit instructions, God rejects Saul.
1 Samuel 16	David is anointed by Samuel to be the next king of Israel.

The rest of 1 Samuel relates the rise of David as Saul continues his
downfall, finally dying at the end of the book. Then the 400-year reign
of the House of David begins in full. The stories of Saul are essential
to the early development of the united kingdom of Israel. Saul was the
first king of the unified tribes, and Saul established the worship of the
national God of Israel: the Eternal. Saul died in battle against the
Philistines and his son Ishbosheth ruled only briefly before David
became ascendant. In a politically astute move, David built upon what

Saul had already established.

As long as there have been people jockeying for power, there have been people willing to bend the narrative to suit their needs. The writers of the Bible had to tweak well-known traditions of Saul, so that the readers would not look upon David as a usurper but instead look upon him as the "chosen one" because Saul had lost his way, and perhaps lost his mind!

The question of Saul's mental health is played out by using a known positive tradition and turning it into an embarrassing negative. First, the positive: In 1 Samuel 10, the prophet Samuel tells Saul that God has designated him to be Israel's ruler, and Saul is given "another heart." It is as if God has changed Saul from an ordinary human being into someone divinely chosen to lead Israel. The passage below details Saul's prophetic activity, which is narrated in a thoroughly positive light:

> As [Saul] turned away to leave Samuel, God
> (Hebrew: *elohim*) gave him another heart . . .
> When they were going from there . . . a band of
> prophets met him, and the spirit of God possessed
> him, and he fell into a prophetic frenzy along
> with them. When all who had known him before
> saw how he prophesied with the prophets, the
> people said to one another, "What has come over
> the son of Kish? Is Saul also among the
> prophets?" A man of the place answered, "And
> who is their father?" Therefore, it became a
> proverb, "Is Saul also among the prophets?"
> (1Sam 10:8–12, translation by the author)

The phrase, "Is Saul also among the prophets?" is referred to as a proverb—a phrase familiar to Israelites and apparently used to describe someone in an anomalous situation. In this case, the proverb expresses the awe or wonderment at the change in Saul that marked his transformation into a divinely selected leader.

However, it is possible to take a phrase and recontextualize it so that the repetition has a negative connotation, which is what the writers of 1 Samuel 19 did when they used the phrase "Is Saul also among the prophets?" to ridicule Saul. The setting of the second story is a period after the Eternal has forsaken Saul in favor of David. In the new setting, Saul tries to have David assassinated at home. After this attempt fails, Saul tries to hunt David down elsewhere:

> Saul was told, "David is at Naioth in Ramah."
> Then Saul sent messengers to take David. When
> they saw the company of the prophets in a frenzy,
> with Samuel standing in charge of them, the
> spirit of God came upon the messengers of Saul,
> and they also fell into a prophetic frenzy. When
> Saul was told, he sent other messengers, and they
> also fell into a frenzy. Saul sent messengers again
> the third time, and they also fell into a frenzy.
> Then he himself went to Ramah. He came to the
> great well that is in Secu; he asked, "Where are
> Samuel and David?" And someone said, "They
> are at Naioth in Ramah." He went there, toward
> Naioth in Ramah, and the spirit of God came
> upon him. As he was going, he fell into a
> prophetic frenzy, until he came to Naioth in
> Ramah. He too stripped off his clothes, and he too
> fell into a frenzy before Samuel. He lay naked all
> that day and all that night. That's why they say,
> "Is Saul also among the prophets?" (1 Samuel
> 19:19–24, translation by the author)

In this version, the king is found on the ground naked, in "a frenzy before Samuel." A very early Jewish translation (the Aramaic Targum) renders the word translated here as "naked" as "out of his mind" (Aramaic: *baršan*). Despite the general esteem in which prophets are held in the Bible, in some instances prophets are associated with madmen, and this is one of them.[*] Saul's inclusion among the prophets in these verses means that Saul is mad.

---

[*] Jeremiah 29:26 comments on the "madman who wants to play prophet." The young prophet sent by Elisha is described as a madman in 2 Kings 9:11. Hosea 9:7 describes a prophet who has been driven mad.

The fact that he is "naked" also is significant. When biblical writers wish to speak positively about the human anatomy they refer to a shapely figure or to specific beautiful parts of the body. The word translated as "naked" (Hebrew: *ʿārum*) is found only in contexts of "fear," "humiliation," "defeat," and sexual activity of which the writer disapproves.[150] The writers of 1 Samuel 19 disfigured Saul's inclusion among the prophets so that it now connotes Saul's utter unfitness for royal office.

The writers similarly disfigured the biblical traditions that describe Saul's presiding over cultic worship of God. Let us turn to 1 Samuel 13:8–14, an episode designed to show why, after having told the prophet Samuel to anoint Saul as king, God later changed his divine mind.

> He [Saul] waited seven days, the time appointed by Samuel, but Samuel did not come to Gilgal, and the people began to scatter away from him. So Saul said, "Bring the animal for the whole burnt offering here to me, and the offerings of well-being." He offered the whole burnt offering, but as soon as he had finished offering it, Samuel arrived. Saul went out to meet him and greet him. Samuel asked, "What have you done?" Saul replied, "When I saw that the people were scattering away from me and that you did not come within the days appointed and that the Philistines were mustering at Michmash, I said, 'Now the Philistines will come down on me at Gilgal, and I have not entreated the favor of the Eternal; so I composed myself and offered the whole burnt offering." (1 Samuel 13:8-12, translation by the author)

The word *scatter* (Hebrew: *wayyāpeṣ*), elsewhere used to describe the aimless movement of sheep and goats who have lost their shepherd, foreshadows Saul's downfall. The people are out of Saul's control, and the writer has Saul admit as much in verse 11 when he says, "I saw that the people were scattering away from me." In the same fashion, the verb that Saul uses in the phrase "I composed myself" (Hebrew: *wā'et'apaq*) is also used in the Joseph story (Genesis 43:31) to describe Joseph's attempt to recover from an unexpected outburst of tears. Although the detail is charming in the Joseph story, it denotes inappropriate royal behavior in Saul's circumstances. As king, he should not have been so upset in the first place. The story continues:

> Samuel said to Saul, "You have done foolishly;
> had you kept the commandment of the Eternal,
> your God, which he commanded you, the Eternal
> would have established your kingdom over Israel
> forever, but now your kingdom will not continue.
> The Eternal has sought out a man after his own
> heart, and the Eternal has appointed him to be
> ruler over his people because you have not kept
> what the Eternal commanded you." (1 Samuel
> 13:13–14, translation by the author)

It is not entirely clear what Saul did wrong. One explanation is that he should have been patient. He should not have disobeyed "the commandment of the Eternal," namely, the word of Samuel, who had told him to wait to offer the sacrifice until his arrival; never mind that Samuel was late (1 Samuel 10:8, and 13:8).

Another possibility has to do with the offering itself. Like many other ancient (and modern) warriors, the Israelites preferred to have divine sanction before going into battle. In Israel's sacrificial system, the *'olah*, a whole burned offering—or as generations before the Nazi murders called it, "holocaust"—was considered the most efficacious because it was selfless. The burned fat and smoke were a pleasing aroma to God, and no meat was left for human consumption. By offering this special sacrifice, Saul may have usurped a cultic function that, in the writer's opinion, belonged properly to priests or to prophets like Samuel, but not to kings.

In either case, this sin cost Saul the chance at a dynasty. The story surely does not date from Saul's time. From the anachronism that God has already sought out Saul's successor, we learn that the tradition originated no earlier than the reign of David.

As if this were not enough, there is a second account of how a cultic violation by Saul cost him the dynasty in 1 Samuel 15:

> Samuel said to Saul, "The Eternal sent me to anoint you king over his people Israel; now, therefore, listen to the words of the Eternal. Thus says the Eternal-of-Hosts, 'I will punish the Amalekites for what they did in opposing the Israelites when they came up out of Egypt. Now go and attack Amalek, and utterly destroy all that they have; do not spare them, but kill man and woman, child and infant, ox and sheep, camel and donkey.'"
> . . . Saul came to the city of the Amalekites and lay in wait in the valley. Saul said to the Kenites, "Go! Leave! Withdraw from among the Amalekites, or I will destroy you with them, for you showed kindness to all the people of Israel when they came up out of Egypt." So the Kenites withdrew from the Amalekites. Saul defeated the Amalekites . . . He took King Agag of the Amalekites alive but utterly destroyed all his people with the edge of the sword. Saul and his people showed pity to Agag and the best of the sheep, the cattle . . . and all that was valuable. These they refused to destroy utterly; whatever was despicable and worthless, they utterly destroyed. (1 Samuel 15:5–9, translation by the author)

The word translated here as "utterly destroyed" is *heherim*, literally, "subject to the practice of *herem*." When an enemy was put to the *herem*, the victorious soldiers did not share in the spoils, as was usually the case. Instead, as we know from the Bible and from a 9th century B.C.E. Moabite source in which Israel was a victim of the *herem*, the spoils of war were required to be destroyed as a way of consecrating them to the victorious deity.[151]

The writer of these verses sardonically describes how Saul and the people "showed pity" to the Amalekite king and to the valuable cattle and utterly destroyed only what was not worth keeping. As a result of this violation of the *ḥerem*:

> The word of God came to Samuel: "I regret that I
> made Saul king, for he has turned back from
> following me and has not carried out my
> commands." Samuel was angry, and he cried out
> to the Eternal all night. Samuel rose early in the
> morning to meet Saul, and Samuel was told,
> "Saul went to Carmel, where he set up a
> monument for himself, and on returning, he
> passed on down to Gilgal." (1 Samuel 15:10–12).

That the king "set up a monument to himself" verifies God's evaluation of Saul—that is, Saul cares more for his monument than for the divine command:

> When Samuel came to Saul, Saul said to him,
> "May you be blessed by God. I have carried out
> the command of the Eternal." But Samuel asked,
> "What, then, is this bleating of sheep in my ears
> and the lowing of cattle that I hear?" Saul said,
> "They have brought them from the Amalekites,
> for the people showed pity for the best sheep and
> cattle, to sacrifice to the Eternal, your God, but
> the rest we have utterly destroyed." Then Samuel
> said to Saul, "Stop! I will tell you what the
> Eternal said to me last night." He replied,
> "Speak." Samuel said, "Perhaps you are little in
> your own eyes (a reference to 1 Samuel 9:21, in
> which Saul modestly refers to his humble
> origins), but are you not head of the tribes of
> Israel? The Eternal anointed you king over Israel.
> And the Eternal sent you on a mission, saying,
> 'Go, utterly destroy the sinners, the Amalekites,

and fight against them until their final
annihilation.' Why, then, did you not obey the
voice of the Eternal? Why did you swoop down
on the spoil and do what was evil in the sight of
the Eternal?" (1 Samuel 15:13–19, translation by the
author)

Saul is portrayed here as weak and ineffectual. His claim to have
"carried out the command of the Eternal" is belied by the bleating of
animals. His reference to "the Eternal, your God" rather than "my
God" amounts to self-incrimination rather than the intended
exculpation. Worst of all, by blaming the people for his failure to carry
out the *ḥerem*, he shows himself unqualified to be "head of the tribes
of Israel." As scholars have shown, the traditional story that Saul failed
to annihilate the Amalekites is based on Deuteronomy 25:17-19, a 7th
century B.C.E. text where God tells Moses to destroy the nation of
Amalek. Moses serves as an allegory of Saul, the first king of Israel and
the scourge of Amalek. In other words, the *ḥerem* story is an attempt,
several centuries after the fact, to account for Saul's displacement by
David. Once again, a positive tradition concerning Saul was distorted
by writers sympathetic to David and his dynasty.[152]

66. The Kenites

We did not come to fear the future. We came to shape it.
Barack Obama (born: 1961), U.S. President, 2009-2017

Despite the character bashing of Saul in the tradition where he defeats the Amalekites, its introduction contains extremely valuable information linking Saul to the allegory of Moses as the founder of Israelite cult of the Eternal. Let's turn to that introduction once more:

> Saul came to the city of the Amalekites and lay in wait in the valley. Saul said to the Kenites, "Go! Leave! Withdraw from among the Amalekites, or I will destroy you with them, for you showed kindness to all the people of Israel when they came up out of Egypt." So the Kenites withdrew from the Amalekites. (1 Samuel 15:5-6, translation by the author)

In order to pursue the allegory of Moses and its origin in Saul, we must ask about Saul's connection with the group known as the Kenites. There is a persistent inner biblical tradition that the Kenites had not been part of the groups that coalesced as "Israel." In fact, according to the book of Genesis, they were one of the peoples whom Israel was supposed to dispossess:

> When the sun had gone down and it was dark, a smoking fire pot and a flaming torch passed between these pieces (of Abraham's animal sacrifices). On that day, God made a covenant with Abram, saying, "To your descendants I give this land, from the river of Egypt to the great river, the river Euphrates, the land of the Kenites, the Kadmonites, the Hittites, the Perizzites, and the Rephaim." (Genesis 15:17–20, translation by the author)

In the book of Exodus, the father-in-law of Moses is identified as the Midianite priest Jethro (Exodus 3:1). In the book of Judges, the father-in-law of Moses is identified as a Kenite who is named Hobab (Judges 4:11). Clearly there are different traditions at work. References such as these allow us to surmise that the "Kenites" in the book of Judges and the "Midianites" in the Torah are two identical groups, or at least are closely related.

The Kenites were a community whose ancestry was traced to an eponymous ancestor named Cain, best known to readers of the Bible for committing the world's first homicide by killing his brother, Abel. After the fratricide, Cain's life was spared, but God punished Cain by having him "become a ceaseless wanderer on earth" (Genesis 4:12). Cain became the patriarch of a line of offspring that included Tubal-Cain who was the ancestor of metalworkers, as well as Jabal who was the ancestor of farmers, and Jubal who was the ancestor of musicians. Thus, out of the murderous and destructive line of Cain, the descendants brought skills that are necessary for civilization.

The Kenites were a nomadic tribe of people who, through their trading and travels, brought new ideas and cultures to the people living in the communities to which they journeyed, including to Canaanite lands where Israelites lived among the people. Sometimes the Kenites were adversaries of the Israelites, and sometimes they offered friendly kindnesses. One "kindness" the Kenites showed to the Israelites is found in Judges 4, a grisly tale we will recount below—but first, a bit of background.

The book of Judges contains some of the oldest stories in the Bible. Although the finished book of Judges is probably dated to the 8th century B.C.E., some of its material is thought to be centuries older. A recurring motif in the book is that the Israelites, who are expected to worship only the Eternal, instead adopt Canaanite customs and worship Canaanite gods. Having been unfaithful to the Eternal, the Israelites lose the support of God and fall to their enemies. After they repent for their faithlessness, God sends a hero to lead them out of their oppression. But then the cycle repeats.

In Judges 4, we learn about Heber the Kenite who had separated from the other Kenites (Judges 4:11) and lived in an area known as Hazor. Heber the Kenite formed an alliance with King Jabin of Canaan, who had defeated the Israelites during one of their cycles of unfaithfulness to God. After 20-years of oppression, God heard the pleas of the Israelites and moved to free them from their subjugation to Jabin. God sent a warrior, Barak, to conquer the army of King Jabin, which was led by his commander, Sisera (Judges 4:7). With the might of God behind the Israelites again, Barak's army gained the upper hand and Sisera's men went into a panic, leading to a rout by the Israelites (Judges 4:15–16). Sisera survived the attack but not its aftermath, as we see in the tale's continuation:

> Now Sisera had fled away on foot to the tent of Jael, wife of Heber the Kenite, for there was an alliance between King Jabin of Hazor and the clan of Heber the Kenite. Jael came out to meet Sisera and said to him, "Turn aside [come here], my lord, turn aside to me; have no fear." So he turned aside to her into the tent, and she covered him with a rug. Then he said to her, "Please give me a little water to drink, for I am thirsty." So she opened a skin of milk and gave him a drink and covered him. He said to her, "Stand at the entrance of the tent, and if anybody comes and asks you, 'Is anyone here?' say, 'No.'" But Jael, wife of Heber, took a tent peg and took a hammer in her hand and went softly to him and drove the peg into his temple, until it went down into the ground—he was lying fast asleep from weariness—and he died. Then when Barak came in pursuit of Sisera, Jael went out to meet him and said to him, "Come, and I will show you the man whom you are seeking." So he went into her tent, and there was Sisera lying dead, with the tent peg in his temple. It was on that day that God subdued King Jabin of Canaan before the Israelites. (Judges 4:17–23, translation by the author)

The gory tale of Jael's impaling of Sisera has inspired painters, musicians, and authors over the centuries. Immediately following the tale, Bible readers will find the Song of Deborah, which also contains a connection to the Kenites. Scholars believe that the Song of Deborah is the oldest passage in the Bible, possibly dating to the 12th century B.C.E. The Song is a military victory hymn and includes the verse:

> O Eternal, when you came forth from Seir,
> Advanced from the country of Edom,
> The earth trembled (Judges 5:4)

This verse bolsters the theory that the worship of the Eternal originated with the Kenites, because scholars believe the Kenites moved north into the region of Canaan from southern locales, including Seir and Edom.

67. The Eternal in the Land

You can never reach the promised land. You can march towards it.
James Callaghan (1912–2005)
U.K. Prime Minister, 1976–1979

Having earlier examined the ramifications of Karel van der Toorn's study of Saul's role in uniting the people of Israel under the banner of the Eternal—making the Eternal into Israel's national god—we now turn to another study by him that influenced the conclusions presented in this book. As we saw earlier, van der Toorn called attention to the fact that the Israelite God is thus far not found in any Syrian or Palestinian set of gods, or pantheon, other than Israel. Unlike other gods mentioned in the Hebrew Bible, such as Kemosh, Baal, or Asherah, or gods like El with whom he is often identified, the Eternal does not belong to the traditional circle of west Semitic deities.

In ancient times, it was common for a place-name to refer to the home of the divinity who lived there; think of the name "Bethel" which means "House of El." Two Egyptian texts from the late 2nd millennium B.C.E. mention "the Eternal in the land of the Shosu bedouin" *(tȝ šȝsw yhwȝ)* as a place-name. The place-name *"Yhwȝ"* first appears in Egyptian sources of the late 2nd millennium B.C.E. and is probably short for *Beth-Yahweh*, or "House of the Eternal." One text comes from the first part of the 14th century B.C.E., another from the 13th century B.C.E. In the second text, from the reign of Ramses II, the place Seir is also mentioned, which was a mountainous region southeast of biblical Judah and north of ancient Egypt.

The Kenite Hypothesis, first proposed by Friedrich W. Ghillany (1807–1876), speculates that the Israelites had come into contact with Kenite/Midianite worshipers of the Eternal in the desert on their way up from Egypt during the Exodus. But now that we know that the entire episode of Israel in Egypt is allegorical, the Kenite/Midianite hypothesis must be modified. Biblical sources show us that these groups were not confined to the south. Genesis 37:28 tells us that Midianites were active as traders in the area between Canaan and Egypt. More important, Judges 4:11 locates the non-sedentary, tent-dwelling group of Heber the Kenite at Kedesh in northern Israel.

In the Bible, the Midianite father-in-law of Moses is identified as a priest, but the only god he ever mentions is the Eternal. According to a tradition in Exodus 18:12, he presides at a sacrificial meal attended by Moses, Aaron, and the elders of Israel. It is a segment that might be defined as just a "marginal" tale and glossed over. But because other parts of the Bible contain strong anti-Midianite traditions, this tradition where a Midianite priest officiated over a sacred meal attended by Moses and Aaron should give us pause. Over the years numerous scholars have realized that this "marginal" tradition needs to be taken seriously. This one passage suggests that, in this polytheistic society, the Midianite/Kenites were responsible for bringing the worship of the Eternal to the group that became Israel.

As van der Toorn points out, the Egyptian data converge with a number of marginal biblical traditions that indicate that Eternal came from Seir, Mount Paran, Teman, and Sinai—all in or near southern areas in which Midianite/Kenites might be found. In most cases, people who left their homeland left their gods behind, but there were significant exceptions. One such exception was the Kenite/Midianite traders who, it appears, brought the Eternal along with them into Transjordan and northern Israel along the caravan routes.[153]

When people marry across cultures, elements of both cultures are likely to appear in the new union. The same is true when groups of people live in proximity to each other. When two or more groups join to form a single unit, while still maintaining some autonomy, they have "federated." If we translate the in-law relation of Moses and the Kenites/Midianites, into the political language of clan federation, we may speak of the Kenites' federating with elements located in what was to become northern Israel.

The tradition of Moses marrying into a Midianite family, the head of which was a priest of the Eternal, is an allegory of Saul federating (marrying) his tribes with the tribes of the Kenites/Midianite. Saul was crucial to this process of federation because Saul was the first king to unite the formerly loosely banded tribes. In the process, the Eternal became an Israelite god, the god of what we described earlier as the *berît*, or "covenant." As the god of Saul, the nation builder of Israel, the Eternal became the national god of Israel, and a distinctively Israelite religion came into being.

In ancient times people believed that political/military victories were achieved by the people supported by the most powerful deities. Saul proved himself to be a powerful leader. Saul claimed the Eternal as his deity, and as the deity of Israel. Those who threw their lot in with Saul followed suit.

There are ample analogies in the history of religion to support this theory. Two that will resonate with today's readers are the rise of Christianity after the conversion of the Roman emperor Constantine the Great (306–337 C.E.), and the triumph of Islam over Arab paganism which resulted from the political successes of Muhammed (571–632 C.E.) In the period roughly contemporary with the rise of ancient Israel, King Nebuchadnezzar I of Babylon (reign: circa 1125–1104 B.C.E.) heralded his defeat of his hated Elamite enemies by elevating the Babylonian god Marduk to supremacy. In addition to Marduk's original supremacy over the city of Babylon, home of Nebuchadnezzar, Nebuchadnezzar now claimed for Marduk supremacy over all the other gods and over the entire land.[154]

Of special interest is that the elevation of Marduk was expressed in literature by the composition of the *Enuma Elish,* the great Babylonian epic of creation. In ancient Israel, the triumphs of Saul led to the beginnings of the composition of Israel's Torah literature for the elevation of the Eternal. In early Israel, traditions were created that used the figure of the historical Saul, zealous devotee of the religion of the Eternal, as the model for the allegorical figure of Moses. This is one reason why the traditions concerning David, even those that speak of the Exodus, make no reference at all to the figure of Moses.

In *Biblical Origins* we have tried to shed light on the political motivations of the writers who gave us what became the Hebrew Bible. We saw how these writers made use of allegorical figures, some drawn from history and others originating in myth, to further their agenda. Over the eight centuries that the Bible was written, compiled and edited, these allegorical figures continued to be adapted by newer writers to meet the ever-changing needs of their audiences. That process of adaptation continues to this very day.

Summary – Part X

- For Jews the world over, Moses is the greatest prophet. However, the absence of Moses from many Hebrew Bible passages calls into question if the man Moses ever existed. Our research leads us to conclude that Moses is an allegorical figure used to serve as the founder of the Israelite nation. The actual founder was Saul.

- Parallels between the Saul traditions and the Moses allegories are too similar to be coincidence.

- Saul was the first king of Israel who united the loosely banded tribes of Israel into one united kingdom. Although the biblical information about Saul is limited, and frequently presented in a negative light, there is enough positive information preserved so that we can surmise that Saul had a lasting impact on the Israelite people.

- Saul established the Eternal as the national God of the Israelite nation. According to the Bible, Saul was the "first to build an altar to the Eternal." This was problematic to traditional readers because it contradicted other biblical traditions that told of earlier altar builders. We have shown, however, that these earlier builders of altars to the Eternal were allegorical retrojections.

- Saul died in battle against the Philistines. David became ascendant.

- Well-known traditions about Saul needed to be acknowledged by the writers of the Bible. But those writers, who were supporters of the Davidic dynasty, distorted the Saul stories so that readers would not look upon David as a usurper—instead looking upon him as the "chosen one."

- The father-in-law of Moses, referred to as a Midianite in the Torah and as a Kenite in the books of Judges and Samuel, is called a priest. The only deity he ever mentions is the Eternal, and he even presides over a sacrificial meal to the Eternal. This reveals to us that the worship of the deity known as the Eternal came to the Israelites from the Kenite/Midianite clans. The allegory of Moses marrying into the Kenite/Midianite clan is an allegory of the Israelites relationship with the Eternal.

- The Kenites were a nomadic tribe of people, originally from a land south of Canaan and north of Egypt. This fact aligned nicely with a theory that the Israelite Exodus out of Egypt brought them into contact with the Kenites and their worship of the Eternal. However, now that we know the Exodus did not happen, we can still place the Kenites in proximity to the Israelites because we know that the Kenites/Midianites were active traders between Canaan and Egypt.

- Saul's achievement in selecting a deity and making it into a national god is not unique in the history of religion. Nebuchadnezzar I made Marduk into the national god of Babylonia. Constantine enabled Christianity to become an international religion. And Muhammed did the same for Islam.

- At the same time the Babylonians were creating their epic story of creation, the Israelite nation was starting to coalesce. It is not inconceivable that the Israelites borrowed from their Babylonian neighbors when drafting their own creation story.

AFTERWORD

I think that many confuse 'applicability' with 'allegory'; but the one resides in the freedom of the reader, and the other in the purposed domination of the author.   J.R.R. Tolkien (1892–1973), author

The Greek critics who commented on Homer and his successors conceived of three levels, or kinds, of literary reality: historia (describing what actually happened), plasma (relating imaginary events as if they were real), and mythos (telling what never happened). The classical scholar D. C. Feeney (born: 1955), professor at Princeton University, observed that readers who interpret mythos as if it were historia or plasma mistake the genre before them.[155] Applying those same Greek analytical categories, we found that the Torah contains plasma and mythos but no historia. What archaeology has demonstrated is that, despite some historical semblance, the Torah's narratives are not history in the sense of events occurring in the time and place in which the biblical writers set them.

The narratives of the Torah do not reflect the lives of the people who served the writers as protagonists. Instead, the stories in the Torah are allegories. They speak of the times in which they were written in the allegorical setting of a completely fictional past. However, by approaching the stories of the Torah as fiction we are not dismissing their historical significance. On the contrary, we are attempting to show how these politically charged texts provide historical evidence for the period in which they were composed.

In her groundbreaking study *Images, Power and Politics*, Barbara Nevling Porter shows that the royal inscriptions of Esarhaddon, king of Assyria, in the 8th century B.C.E., are precious historical artifacts precisely because they do not stick to the "facts."[156] Rather, as political documents, they reveal Assyrian attitudes, ideologies, and official policy. By identifying the different audiences to which the inscriptions were addressed, Porter is able, convincingly, to reconstruct the complexities of ancient Assyrian political life.[157]

We have tried to do something similar here, which led to the conclusion that the different writers of the Torah aimed their messages at particular audiences and constituencies. Their method was allegorical and their goals ideological. In other words, if we wish to know what the Torah is about, it is crucial to identify the method by which the writers attempted to achieve their goals and what those goals were. If we are correct in identifying the narratives of the Torah as allegories, then our task is to decode them.

The most prominent allegory in the Torah is that of the Eternal and what he did for Israel before it became a people in its own territorial states. The key to understanding what the narratives of the Torah tell us is to decode what the Eternal meant to the Torah's writers in their own age. Then we might see how they used the allegory of the Eternal's deeds in the past to comment on their contemporary situation.

For example, the 10th century B.C.E. King David found refuge with the Philistines, the hated enemies of the Israelites. In trying to foster support for the actions of the 10th century David, a writer might produce a story indicating that the 18th century B.C.E. "Abraham" also found refuge with the Philistines. Not only that, but "God was with Abraham in all he did." Because the allegorical 18th century B.C.E. Abraham got the stamp of approval from God, the 10th century B.C.E. David gets the stamp of approval from contemporary readers.

If 5th century B.C.E. dissenters to the "Aaronide" priesthood had taken issue with the elevated status of the descendants of "Aaron," a timely allegory would serve to blunt any dissent. Perhaps an allegory set in the $14^{th}/13^{th}$ century B.C.E. relaying how God personally made the earth open up to swallow Korah and his followers who sought to take the priesthood from Aaron. In short, understanding God requires understanding the ancient agenda of the writers.

Some readers may find irony in the allegorical interpretations suggested here and object that, since it is impossible to recover what really happened, my own reconstructions are themselves allegories. If so, at least I will have demonstrated the potential of my approach.

APPENDIX

Glossary

Canon: a collection of sacred books

Decalogue: the Ten Commandments

Eschatological: relating to end of time; last judgment; fate of individual souls.

Extra-biblical: content outside of the Bible

Gentile: any non-Israelite

Historicity: historical authenticity

Idol: any representation, either image or statue, of a god that can be used as an object of worship. This includes idols of the Israelite god, the Eternal (Hebrew: *Yahweh*).

Judahite: people living in the region of Judah

Laver: a priestly washing basin

Midrash: ancient, rabbinic commentary on the Hebrew scriptures, attached to the biblical text—or, stories created post-biblically to help answer any lingering questions not already covered by the text.

Pantheon: a set of gods

Pericope: extract from a text being studied, often referring to biblical text

Realia: objects and material found in everyday life

Stela: a stone monument with ancient writing, often describing a historical event

Tamarisk: a type of tree. Because trees are so long-lived, they often served as a lasting memorial to an oath.

Tithe: shares a root with the word "tenth." The Torah mandates a tenth of one's produce/earnings be given in support of the temple.

Typology: a classification system by "type"

Yahweh: the proper name of the Israelite god

Time Line

Following is a list of people/events/characters featured in this book. "Attested" data reflect specifics proved by archaeological and/or extra-biblical discoveries. "Widely Accepted" data are those specifics which many scholars are in general agreement that, although not evidentially proven, have enough circumstantial evidence to be compelling, and therefore believed to have occurred. These specifics are marked with an '*' and some have been arrived at through the author's own academic evaluations at the time of publication. The data are subject to revision as new evidence is discovered. All dates are approximate, with some dates still debated.

"Biblical Literalist Chronology" uses genealogies and timespans of biblical events to calculate dates corresponding to the modern civil calendar used in most of the world. This method assumes the infallibility of the biblical tales—an assumption with which the author does not agree. The premise of this book is that many of the biblical tales are allegories of political happenings at the time they were written but set at an earlier time in order to give the political situation authority by precedent.

	Attested and/or Widely Accepted History	**Biblical Literalist Chronology**
3100	Sumerian invention of writing	
2400	Akkadian Empire est. (fell c. 2200 BCE) significant ruler: Sargon the Great	
2100+		Noah
1900	1st Babylonian Empire established. Successive Babylonian empires survived until 539 BCE.	
18th century	Reign of Babylonian king, Hammurabi. Codification of laws	Abraham

18th century (cont'd)	Texts from Chagar Bazar and Mari, both in modern-day Syria, provide early evidence of the use of the names "Jacob" and "Ishmael"	
1700–1550	Hyksos, or "rulers of foreign lands," rule in Egypt	Joseph
1500 +/-		Job (book composed centuries later)
14th/13th century		Moses & the "Exodus"
1355–1325	Egyptian (Amarna) letters reference corvée	
1275		Entry into Promised Land
1220	Pharaoh Merneptah stela includes Victory Hymn with first attestation of a group called "Israel"	
1198–1166	Reign of Rameses III, king of Egypt. Battled the "Sea Peoples." 1st attestation of a group called "Philistines."	
1100	Earliest settlement of Beersheba/Beersheva	
1020–1000	*Reign of Saul	
1000–961	Reign of David (based on only one piece of evidence)	
961–922	*Reign of Solomon	
late 10th century	1st Temple built	Samuel (combination of texts of various ages)
922	*Revolt of Jeroboam: Division into Israel/Northern Kingdom (Jeroboam) and Judah (Rehoboam)	

922–901	*Reign of Jeroboam	
885–850	*Reign of Ahab (husband to Jezebel)	Elijah
840	Moabite Stone (Mesha Stela) 1st mention of Hebrew God "the Eternal"	
789–748	*Reign of Jeroboam II	
785–720	720 BCE: Fall of Israel/ Northern Kingdom (10 Lost Tribes)	Amos, Jonah, Hosea, and Isaiah (edited over centuries)
715–686	Reign of Hezekiah of Judah - witnessed destruction of Israel/Northern Kingdom & influx of refugees, repelled Assyrian invasion, mandated sole worship of the Eternal	
704–681	Reign of Sennacherib, king of Assyria	
640–609	*Reign of Josiah. 622 BCE - "finds" book, institutes religious reforms	
627–582		Jeremiah (edited over centuries)
605–540		Daniel (book composed centuries later)
6th century	*1st clear statement of monotheism in 2nd Isaiah (edited over at least 100 years)	
593–573		Ezekiel
586	Babylonian defeat of Judah 586 BCE - Destruction of the 1st Temple	
586–539	Babylonian Exile	
539–333	Cyrus of Persia defeats Babylon Jews under Persian Rule - "Postexilic" period	

520–515	Temple rebuilt	Malachi
5th/4th century	Activity of Ezra the Scribe. "Publication" of Torah, beginnings of Judaism as religion	Ezra reads the Law Nehemiah restores the Law
336–323	Alexander the Great (Greek) defeats Persia	
250	Torah (1st 5 books) written in final form *date is highly speculative*	
164	Maccabean (Hasmonean) Revolt	
- 0 -		
37–100	life of Josephus	
70	Destruction of 2nd Temple (by Rome)	
189	Mishnah compiled by Judah the Prince	
306–337	Reign of Constantine of Rome	
370	Jerusalem Talmud (Gemara)	
380	Rome adopts Christianity	
650	Babylonian Talmud (Gemara)	

- Judges – contains some of the oldest biblical material
- Psalms - contains prayers and songs from every Biblical period of Israel's history
- Song of Songs and book of Proverbs - collected (potentially) over 800 years, completed 2nd century BCE
- Joshua - likely composed 7th century BCE and edited over centuries
- Chronicles - post-exilic retelling of entire history
- Canonization of the entire Hebrew Bible is (speculatively) estimated to have happened in the 2nd century CE
- (inclusion of some Ketuvim, the Writings, was debated into the early common era)

Genealogy of the Kings of Ancient Israel and Judah

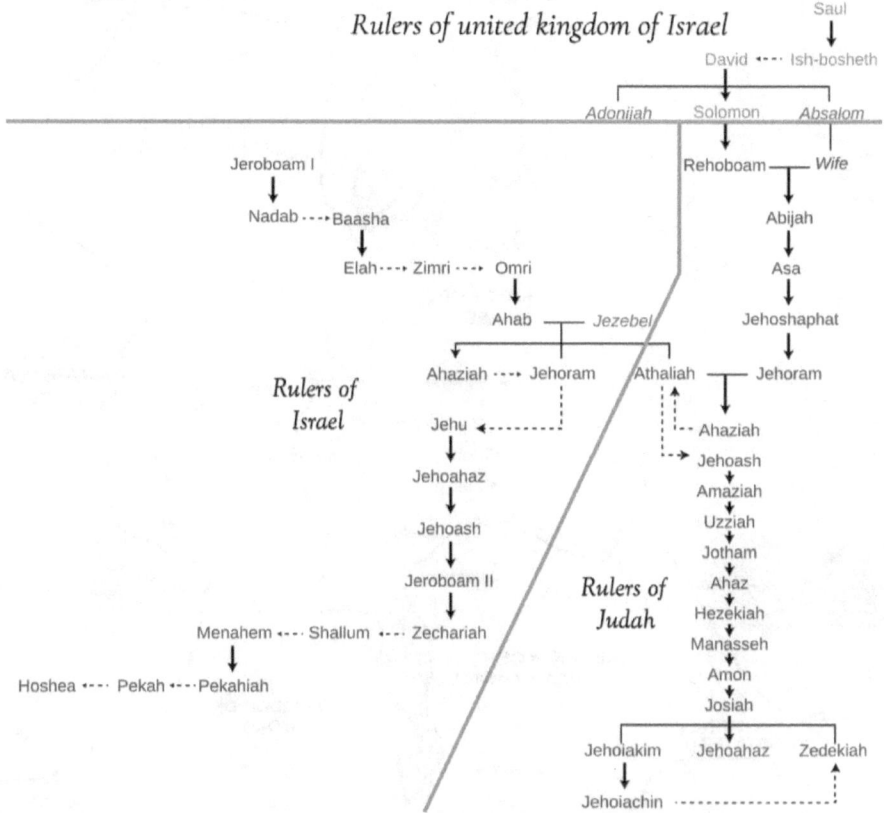

TKeiter/DSperling edited version of File:Genealogy_of_the_kings_of_Israel_and_Judah.png
Wikimedia.org/wikipediacommons User Mr. Absurd, recreated and based on an image of User FDuffy

Map of Ancient Israel and Judah

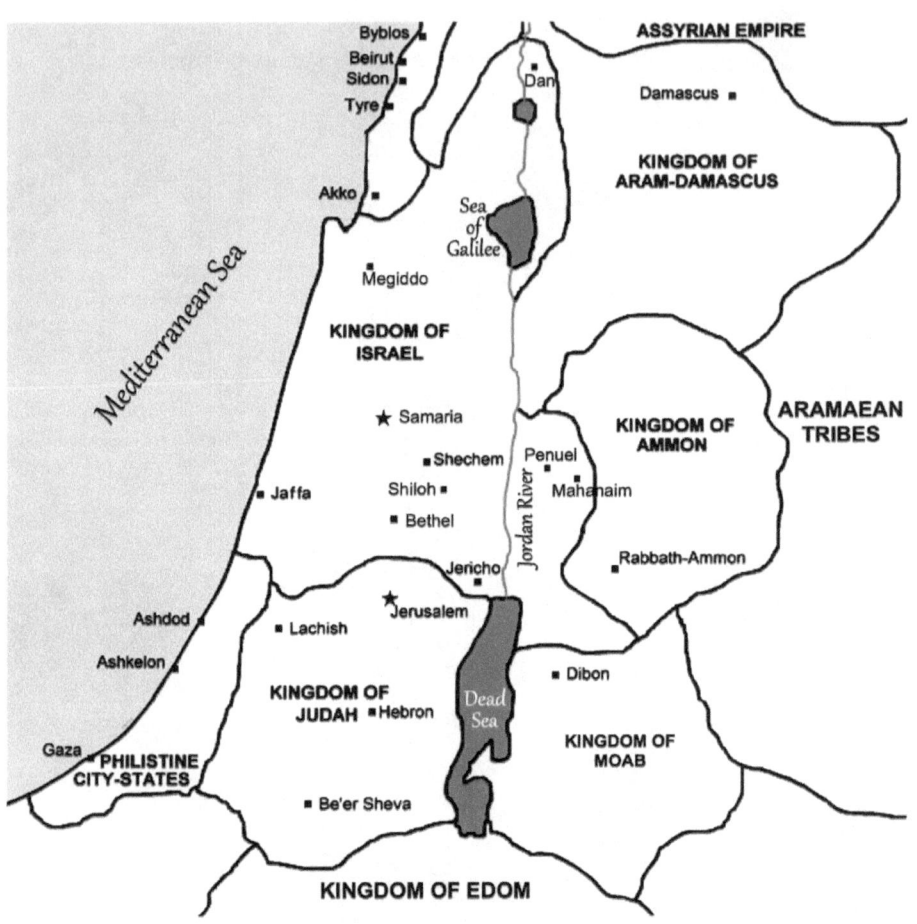

TKeiter/DSperling edited version of File: Levant 01.PNG
Wikimedia.org/wikipedia/commons User:ChrisRy5

ACKNOWLEDGMENTS

David Sperling writes: This present work has its genesis in my 1998 publication, *The Original Torah: The Political Intent of the Bible's Writers* (New York University Press). Inasmuch as *The Original Torah* appeared over twenty years ago, this 2022 revision is expanded and updated to incorporate more recent scholarship (noted in the endnotes).

Because this book would not exist if it were not for *The Original Torah*, I must once again thank those people who generously gave their time and expertise toward that publication: Heartfelt thanks to the staff of the library of the New York campus of Hebrew Union College-Jewish Institute of Religion (HUC-JIR), especially Mr. Henry Resnick and Mr. Julius Sperling (no relation).

As I did in the 1998 *Original Torah*, I will again mention my gratitude to several academic colleagues: Professor Leonard Kravitz (HUC-JIR, retired) who brightened many of my lunch hours at HUC-JIR with his extensive knowledge of the ways in which medieval Jewish philosophers read the Bible; Professor Elaine Pagels (Princeton University) and Professor Robert Seltzer (Hunter College/City University of New York CUNY, retired) who generously took the time to read early drafts of the manuscript; special thanks are owed to Professor James R. Russell (Harvard University) for his detailed criticisms and annotations; similarly, I thank Barbara Nevling Porter (Harvard University) for her thorough reading and acute suggestions.

Additional thanks to Professor Robert Seltzer for bringing my original manuscript to the attention of editors at NYU Press. I am grateful that my *Original Torah* remained in publication with NYU Press for over twenty years, serving the interest of numerous students and readers who strive to understand how the Torah came to be.

Regarding the 2022 version of the book, retitled as *Biblical Origins: The Political Intent of the Bible's Writers*, thanks are due to my wife, Rabbi Jennifer Jaech, Senior Rabbi at Temple Israel of Northern Westchester (Croton-on-Hudson, NY) who introduced my

Original Torah concepts as well as the book itself to her Saturday morning Torah Study members. Tara Keiter, a long-time Torah Study member, read the *Original Torah* and discussed with Jennifer that the book could be reworked for a wider audience. She bravely assumed the arduous task of decoding my academic jargon and rearranging the material into a more accessible form for which I am truly grateful.

Final thanks go to my HUC-JIR students from my 40+ years of teaching, as well as the congregants from Temple Israel of the City of New York and Temple Israel of Northern Westchester (Croton-on-Hudson, NY), who have provided me a ready ear when I wanted to test my hypotheses. I thank them for their intelligent and critical feedback.

This book is for my children, Sharon Sperling-Silber, Deborah Lewis Sperling, and Benjamin Lewis Sperling, and my grandchildren, Isaac, Sam and Becca.

David Sperling and Tara Keiter write: We are grateful to the early readers of *Biblical Origins,* especially Rabbi Janet Roberts for meticulously reviewing this project and insisting upon precision of words; Elizabeth Clubb for bravely being our first reader and suggesting improvements that led to greater clarity; Patsy Fawsett for her constructive criticism and thorough attention to detail, as well has her master class on punctuation; Larry Cohan for his thoughtful observations and questions; and Deborah Lewis Sperling for being our official editor who skillfully guided us toward a vastly improved final project.

Thanks also go to Professsor Maude Meisel (Pace University/Columbia University) for her concise summary of Virgil's *Aeneid,* which can be found in chapter 27; Eddie Pleasant for sharing our work with colleagues at the Stamford Church of Christ; Demetria Spinrad for sharing her digital marketing expertise; and to Robin Safarowic and Cheryl Riina at Temple Israel of Northern Westchester for their support of our project.

Tara Keiter writes: My first thanks must go to Professor S. David Sperling who graciously entrusted his *Original Torah* to me and patiently corrected my errors and misunderstandings. His passion and infectious enthusiasm for the Bible has inspired generations of rabbis and I count myself lucky for having worked with him on this book.

Special thanks go to my teacher and friend Rabbi Jennifer Jaech who introduced these concepts to me, as well as so much more about the Torah. Additionally, she suggested the new title for the book. Temple Israel of Northern Westchester has been fortunate that Rabbi Janet Roberts is a frequent guest Torah Study leader who brings her own dynamic and insightful instruction to the group, and from whom I am grateful to have learned a great deal. My thanks also go to Rabbi Helene Ferris, Rabbi Emerita at Temple Israel, whose perceptive instruction ignited my interest in Torah Study. And I thank my fellow Torah Study devotees with whom I have learned, shared and laughed for more than 20 years. I count myself lucky to be part of such an inspiring and intellectually curious group.

I am grateful for the encouragement and support that I received from so many people, especially my parents, Krishin (deceased) and Brenda Bhavnani, and my sister and brother-in-law, Reuki and Roger Schutt, and their extended family: Premela, Christopher, Gideon and Evander Deck; Anjali and Matthew Bayliss; and Sarojini Schutt. I am also grateful for my wonderful in-laws, Eileen Keiter, and Allan Keiter and Elizabeth Clubb. Thanks are also due to Patricia Chadwick, Jane Applegate, and Gina Constantine for sharing their insights into book publishing, and to Sue Feir for sharing her expertise as a librarian. And thank you to my dear friends, Liliana Ruiz and Josué Muñoz, and also to Heidi Bedell, for their enthusiasm when discussing this project with me.

Final thanks are for my family. To my husband, Eric H. Keiter, for his love and encouragement, as well as for his sage business advice and for being my own personal "help desk" when things go technically awry. And to our sons, Jack and George, who make everything worthwhile.

ENDNOTES

[1] An inscription discovered at Tel Dan in 1993 cites the "House of David" in reference to a king of Judah but not to King David himself. See Shmuel Ahituv, *Echoes from the Past* (Jerusalem: Carta, 2008), 467-469.

[2] H.G.M. Williamson, "How Many Isaiahs Were There?" [cited 14 Mar 2020]. Online: https://www.bibleodyssey.org:443/people/related-articles/how-many-isaiahs-were-there

[3] H.G.M. Williamson, "How Many Isaiahs Were There?" [cited 14 Mar 2020]. Online: https://www.bibleodyssey.org:443/people/related-articles/how-many-isaiahs-were-there

[4] For the Persian text, see Wilhelm Brandenstein and Manfred Mayrhofer, *Handbuch des Altpersischen* (Wiesbaden: Harrassowitz, 1964), 83.

[5] The same generally holds for the Christian New Testament as well. Only once do we find a claim for veracity: the conclusion of the Gospel of John (21:24) states that Jesus's beloved disciple "vouches for what is written. He it is who wrote it, and we know his testimony is true." But this statement stands out because of its singularity. By canonizing four Gospels, which often disagree about events and their chronology, rather than encouraging Gospel harmonization, the church seems not to have taken historicity as its primary criterion. See Luke T. Johnson, *The Real Jesus* (San Francisco: Harper, 1996), 148.

[6] For a concise outline of the life and thought of Nahmanides, with a bibliography, see Leonard Kravitz, "Mose ben Nahman," *Theologische Realenzyklopädie*, vol. 23, fasc. 3/4 (Berlin: de Gruyter, 1994): 362-364.

[7] Felicia R. Lee, "From Noah's Curse to Slavery's Rationale." in *The New York Times* November 1, 2003.

[8] H. L. Ginsberg, "Ugaritic Studies and the Bible," in David N. Freedman and Edward R. Campbell eds., *The Biblical Archaeologist Reader* (Garden City, NY: Anchor/Doubleday, 1964), 2:35-58, esp. 43-44.

[9] William F. Albright in Louis Finkelstein, ed., *The Jews, Their History, Culture and Religion* (New York: Harper, 1960), 6.

[10] John Bright, *A History of Israel*, 2nd Edition (Philadelphia: Westminster, 1972) 91.

[11] Joel Sweek, "The Babel-Bible Streit," ("The Babel-Bible Conflict") in Lowell K. Handy and Steven W. Holloway, eds., *The Pitcher is Broken: Memorial Essays for Gösta W. Ahlström* (Sheffield: Sheffield Academic Press, 1995), 401-19.

[12] Rolf Rendtorff, "Postexilic Israel in German Bible Scholarship," in Michael Fishbane and Emanuel Tov, eds. *Sha'arei Talmon Studies in the Bible, Qumran and the Ancient Near East Presented to Shemaryahu Talmon* (Winona Lake, Ind.: Eisenbrauns, 1992) 165-173, esp. 168, n. 10.

[13] John Bright, *A History of Israel*, 2nd Edition (Philadelphia: Westminster, 1972) 286. No doubt Bright's "deliverance" was inspired by Byron's poem "Jerusalem Delivered."

[14] For an up-to-date account of archaeological conclusions regarding the rise of the people Israel see William Dever, *Beyond the Texts. An Archaeological Portrait of Ancient Israel and Judah* (Atlanta: Society of Biblical Literature Press, 2017).

[15] Thanks are owed to the late Professor Moshe Greenberg of the Hebrew University for sharing his insightful article, "Did Job Really Exist? An Issue of Medieval Exegesis," in Michael Fishbane and Emanuel Tov, eds. *Sha'arei Talmon Studies in the Bible, Qumran and the Ancient Near East Presented to Shemaryahu Talmon* (Winona Lake, Ind.: Eisenbrauns, 1992) 3-11, in Hebrew. I have built upon his work but used my own translations, which differ marginally.

[16] Moshe Greenberg, ""Did Job Really Exist? An Issue of Medieval Exegesis," in Michael Fishbane and Emanuel Tov, eds. *Sha'arei Talmon Studies in the Bible, Qumran and the Ancient Near East Presented to Shemaryahu Talmon* (Winona Lake, Ind.: Eisenbrauns, 1992) 3-11.

[17] Moshe Greenberg, ""Did Job Really Exist? An Issue of Medieval Exegesis," in Michael Fishbane and Emanuel Tov, eds. *Sha'arei Talmon Studies in the Bible, Qumran and the Ancient Near East Presented to Shemaryahu Talmon* (Winona Lake, Ind.: Eisenbrauns, 1992) 3-11.

[18] From the introduction to Joseph ibn Kaspi's commentary (in Hebrew, translation by S. David Sperling) on Job, edited by Y. Last, cited by Greenberg in "Did Job Really Exist?" 9, n.26.

[19] Ephraim Kupfer, "Kaspi, Joseph ben Abba," in Cecil Roth and Geoffrey Wigoder, eds. *Encyclopaedia Judaica* (Jerusalem: Keter Publishing, 1972) 10:809-11

[20] Walter Burkert, Creation of the Sacred: Tracks of Biology in Early Religions (Harvard Univ. Press, 1996)

[21] Joseph Kaspi *Maskiyot Kesef*, apud Hannah Kasher and Moshe Kahan, "Joseph Kaspi", *The Stanford Encyclopedia of Philosophy* (Spring 2019 Edition), Edward N. Zalta (ed.), https://plato.stanford.edu/archives/spr2019/entries/kaspi-joseph/

[22] Hannah Kasher and Moshe Kahan, "Joseph Kaspi", *The Stanford Encyclopedia of Philosophy* (Spring 2019 Edition), Edward N. Zalta (ed.), https://plato.stanford.edu/archives/spr2019/entries/kaspi-joseph/

[23] David Stronach, "The Garden as a Political Statement: Some Case Studies from the Near East in the First Millennium B.C.," in *Bulletin of the Asia Institute* (1990): new series, vol 4, 171-80. See also A. Leo Oppenheim "On Royal Gardens in Mesopotomia," *Journal of Near Eastern Studies* 24/4 (1965): 328-333.

[24] Miguel Civil, Ignace J. Gelb, et al., eds., *The Assyrian Dictionary of the Oriental Institute of the University of Chicago* (Chicago: Oriental Institute, 1971) K, 406.

[25] Carlo Zaccagnini, "An Urartean Royal Inscription in the Report of Sargon's Eighth Campaign," in Mario Fales, ed., *Assyrian Royal Inscriptions: New Horizons* (Rome: Instituto per l'Oriente, 1981), 274.

[26] The identical word, in the form *giṣṣu daddaru*, can be found in the annals of Sargon II (722-705 B.C.E.); see, Ignace Gelb, Thorkild Jacobsen, et al., eds., *The Assyrian Dictionary of the Oriental Institute of the University of Chicago*. (Chicago: Oriental Institute, 1959) D, 17-18. The word *daddaru* seems restricted to Standard Babylonian, the dialect of the Assyrian annals, which provides further evidence for our hypothetical date.

[27] Benjamin R. Foster, "The Birth Legend of Sargon of Akkad," in William W. Hallo and Kyle Lawson Younger, Jr., eds., *The Context of Scripture vol. 1* (Leiden: Brill, 1997), 461.

[28] Hayim Tadmor, "Autobiographical Apology in the Royal Assyrian Literature," in Tadmor and Moshe Weinfeld, eds., *History, Historiography and Interpretation: Studies in Biblical and Cuneiform Literatures* (Jerusalem: Magnes Press, 1983) 36-57.

[29] See Frederick Mario Fales, "The Composition and Structure of the Neo-Assyrian Empire: Ethnicity, Language and Identities," in Giovanni B. Lafranche, Raija Mattila, Robert Rollinger eds., *Writing Neo-Assyrian History* (Helsinki: The Neo-Assyrian Corpus Text Project, 2019) 45-89.

[30] For the 8th century dating of Joshua 24, see David Sperling, "Joshua 24 Re-examined," *Hebrew Union College Annual* 58 (1987), 119-36; S. David Sperling, *Ve-Eileh Divrei Davd: Essays in Semitics, Hebrew Bible and History of Biblical Scholarship* (New York: Brill, 2017), 137-155.

[31] Trude Dothan and H. Jacob Katzenstein, "Philistines," in David N. Freedman, Gary Herion, et al., eds. *The Anchor Bible Dictionary* (New York: Doubleday, 1992), 5:333. Newer light is shed on the Philistines by an inscription of a ruler in northern Syria (!) who calls himself "King of Palastin" i.e., King of Philistine Land. For the inscription see J.D. Hawkins in K.L. Younger ed., *The Context of Scripture. Volume 4* (Leiden: Brill, 2017), 164-164.

[32] Amihai Mazar, "The Iron Age I" in Amnon Ben-Tor ed., *The Archaeology of Ancient Israel* (New Haven, CT: Yale University Press, 1992), 296; on Kadesh-Barnea, see p. 282.

[33] Robert Carroll, "Psalm LXXVIII: Vestiges of a Tribal Polemic." *Vetus Testamentum* 21, no. 2, (1971): 133–150.

[34] Amihai Mazar, "The Iron Age I" in Amnon Ben-Tor ed., *The Archaeology of Ancient Israel* (New Haven, CT: Yale University Press, 1992), 296; on Kadesh-Barnea, see p. 282.

[35] Peter Machinist, "The Question of Distinctiveness in Ancient Israel: An Essay," in Mordechai Cogan and Israel Eph'al, eds., *Ah, Assyria...Studies in Assyrian History and Ancient Near Eastern Historiography Presented to Hayim Tadmor* (Jerusalem: Magnes, 1991), vol. 33, 196-212.

[36] Peter Machinist, "Outsiders or Insiders: The Biblical View of Emergent Israel and Its Contexts," in Laurence Silberstein and Robert Cohn, eds., *The Other in Jewish Thought and History* (New York: NYU Press, 1994), 35-60.

[37] Peter Machinist, "The Question of Distinctiveness in Ancient Israel: An Essay," in Mordechai Cogan and Israel Ephal, eds., *Ah, Assyria...Studies in Assyrian History and Ancient Near Eastern Historiography Presented to Hayim Tadmor* (Jerusalem: Magnes, 1991), vol. 33, 196-212.

[38] Peter Machinist, "The Question of Distinctiveness in Ancient Israel: An Essay," in Mordechai Cogan and Israel Ephal, eds., *Ah, Assyria...Studies in Assyrian History and Ancient Near Eastern Historiography Presented to Hayim Tadmor* (Jerusalem: Magnes, 1991), vol. 33, 196-212.

[39] Peter Machinist, "The Question of Distinctiveness in Ancient Israel: An Essay," in Mordechai Cogan and Israel Ephal, eds., *Ah, Assyria...Studies in Assyrian History and Ancient Near Eastern Historiography Presented to Hayim Tadmor* (Jerusalem: Magnes, 1991), vol. 33, 196-212.

[40] For the minority biblical view that some important Israelite institutions originated outside the land of Israel, see Amos 5:25 and Joshua 24.

[41] Donald B. Redford, *Egypt, Canaan, and Israel in Ancient Times* (Princeton, NJ: Princeton University Press, 1992), 237.

[42] My own translations from the Ugaritic.

[43] Knut L. Tallqvist, *Akkadishe Götterepitheta* (Helsinki: Societas Orientalis Fennica, 1938) 456-58.

[44] James B. Pritchard, ed. *Ancient Near Eastern Texts Relating to the Old Testament*, 3rd Edition, with supplement, (Princeton, NJ: Princeton University Press, 1969) 159, 165.

[45] Erica Reiner Šurpu, A Collection of Sumerian and Akkadian Incantations (Graz, Austria, 1958), 13-16.

46 For the texts, see Raymond Faulkner, Ogden Goelet, and Eva von Dassow, *The Egyptian Book of the Dead: The Book of Going Forth by Day* (San Francisco: Chronicle, 1994).

47 Thomas L. Thompson, The Origin Tradition of Ancient Israel, The Literary Formation of Genesis and Exodus 1-23 (London: Bloomsbury, 1987), vol. 1, 80-101.

48 S. David Sperling, *Ve-Eileh Divrei David: Essays in Semitics, Hebrew Bible and History of Biblical Scholarship* (New York: Brill, 2017) see "Pants, Persians and the Priestly Source," 196-209. As we noted, trousers were likely invented in the 10th century B.C.E. in China, and worked their way to Persia. See Ulrike Beck, Mayke Wayner, Xiao Li, Desmond Durkin-Meisterernst, Pavel E. Tarasov, "The invention of trousers and its likely affiliation with horseback riding and mobility: A case study of late 2nd millennium BC find from Turfan in eastern Central Asia," *Quaternary International* (May, 2014) 348: 224-235.

49 The laws had a profound influence on laws in the Torah. See David P. Wright, *Inventing God's Law: How the Covenant Code of the Bible Used and Revised the Laws of Hammurabi* (New York: Oxford University Press, 2009).

50 Thomas L. Thompson, The Origin Tradition of Ancient Israel: The Literary Formation of Genesis and Exodus 1-23 (London: Bloomsbury, 1987), vol. 1, 80.

51 Andreas van Selms, "Temporary Henotheism," in Martinus A. Beek, ed., *Symbolae Biblicae et Mesopotamicae Francisco Mario Theodoro de Liagre Böhl dedicatae* (Leiden, Netherlands: Brill, 1973), 8-20.

52 Morton Smith, *Palestinian Parties and Politics That Shaped the Old Testament* (New York: Columbia University Press, 1971), 23.

53 Richard Washington, "Venezuela calls for mandatory labor in farm sector" for CNBC.com. July 29, 2016.

54 Anson Rainey, "Compulsory Labor Gangs in Ancient Israel," in *Israel Exploration Journal* 20/3-4 (1970).

55 Miriam Lichtheim, *Ancient Egyptian Literature, Volume II: The New Kingdom* (Berkeley and Los Angeles: University of California Press, 1976), 77.

56 Gösta W. Ahlström, *The History of Ancient Palestine* (Minneapolis, MN: Augsburg Fortress, 1993), 288-300.

57 Israel Finkelstein and Nadav Na'aman, eds., *From Nomadism to Monarchy: Archaeological and Historical Aspects of Early Israel* (Washington D.C.: Biblical Archaeological Society, 1994), 12.

[58] See Richard Hess for the identification of Caphtor in David N. Freedman, Gary Herion, et al., eds. *The Anchor Bible Dictionary* (New York: Doubleday, 1992), 1:869-70.

[59] Gösta W. Ahlström, *The History of Ancient Palestine* (Minneapolis, MN: Augsburg Fortress, 1993), 300-306.

[60] William Dever "Israel, History of (Archaeology and the Israelite 'Conquest')" in David N. Freedman, Gary Herion, et al., eds. *The Anchor Bible Dictionary* (New York: Doubleday, 1992), 3:553.

[61] Amihai Mazar, "The Iron Age I" in Amnon Ben-Tor ed., *The Archaeology of Ancient Israel* (New Haven, CT: Yale University Press, 1992), 282, 297: on Kadesh-Barnea, see p. 282. And, see Lawrence Geraty in David N. Freedman, Gary Herion, et al., eds. *The Anchor Bible Dictionary* (New York: Doubleday, 1992), 3:181-4.

[62] Samuel N. Kramer, *The Sumerians: Their History, Culture, and Character* (Chicago: University of Chicago Press, 1963), 45.

[63] Frank M. Cross, *Canaanite Myth and Hebrew Epic* (Cambridge, Mass.: Harvard University Press, 1973).

[64] Bertil Albrektson, *History and the Gods* (Lund, Sweden: Gleerup, 1967).

[65] God(s) and human(s) sacred marriage myth and ritual research has been published by, among others: Thorkild Jacobsen focusing on the Near East, especially Mesopotamian culture. Daniel Fleming focusing on Emar in Syria, and Walter Burkert on ancient Greece. It is misleading to speak of a "common pattern" in the sacred marriages of the ancient Near East. An additional resource with an extensive bibliography is Jacob Klein, "Sacred Marriage," in David N. Freedman, Gary Herion, et al., eds. *The Anchor Bible Dictionary* (New York: Doubleday, 1992) 5:866-70; Pirjo Lapinkivi, *The Sumerian Sacred Marriage in the Light of Comparative Evidence* (Finland: University of Helsinki, 2004).

[66] Found in Hans Goedicke & Jimmy Jack McBee Roberts, eds. *Unity and Diversity* (Baltimore,MD: Johns Hopkins University Press, 1975), 66-67.

[67] John Gibson, *Canaanite Myth and Legends* (Edinburgh: T and T Clark, 1987), 72.

[68] Michael D. Coogan, "Canaanite Origins and Lineage: Reflections on the Religion of Ancient Israel," 115-24; and Jo Ann Hackett, "Religious Traditions in Israelite Transjordan," 125-36; both in Patrick Miller Jr., Paul Hanson, S. Dean McBride, eds., *Ancient Israelite Religion: Essays in Honor of Frank Moore Cross,* (Philadelphia, PA: Fortress, 1987); also, Jo Ann Hackett in David N. Freedman, Gary Herion, et al., eds. *The Anchor Bible Dictionary* (New York: Doubleday, 1992) 1:569-572; also Jacob Hoftijzer and Gerrit van der Kooij, eds. *The Balaam Text from Deir Alla Re-Evaluated* (Leiden, Netherlands: Brill, 1991).

[69] Donald B. Redford, *Egypt, Canaan, and Israel in Ancient Times* (Princeton, NJ: Princeton University Press, 1992), 275.

[70] Noah Feldman, "Religion and the Earthly City," in Arien Mack, ed., (The New School for Social Research), *Social Research: An International Quarterly* (Baltimore, MD: The Johns Hopkins University Press, 2009), vol. 76, n.4, 989-1000.

[71] We lack detailed information about cult and myth in Moab, Ammon, and Midian. It is entirely possible that the cults of these nations, which were closely related to Israel in language and culture, emphasized the political activities of their gods.

[72] On Judges 9 see especially Edward Campbell, "Judges 9 and Biblical Archeology," in Carol Meyers and Michael O'Connor, eds., *The Word of the Lord Shall Go Forth: Essays in Honor of David Noel Freedman in Celebration of His Sixtieth Birthday* (Winona Lake, IN: Eisenbrauns, 1983), 263-71.

[73] Lawrence E. Toombs, "Shechem (Place)," in David N. Freedman, Gary Herion, et al., eds. *The Anchor Bible Dictionary* (New York: Doubleday, 1992) 5:1175-86.

[74] Dennis McCarthy, *Treaty and Covenant* (Rome: Pontifical Biblical Institute, 1978), 222, with the literature cited in n.20; and Kenneth Kitchen, "Egypt, Ugarit, Qatna and Covenant," in *Ugarit Forschungen* (Münster, Germany: Ugarit-Verlag, 1979), 11:453–64: Theodore Lewis, "Baal-Berith," in David N. Freedman, Gary Herion, et al., eds. *The Anchor Bible Dictionary* (New York: Doubleday, 1992) 1:550–1.

[75] George Mendenhall, "Covenant Forms in Israelite Tradition," *Biblical Archaeologist* 17/3, Sept. 1954, 50-76. Until recently, treaties from the early 2nd millennium were unavailable. For more on "suzerainty treaties," see Dominique Charpin and Francis Joannés, eds. *Marchands, diplomates et empereurs: Études sur la civilisation mésopotamienne offertes á Paul Garelli* (Paris: Éditions recherche sur les civilizations, 1991). Mendenhall expands upon the fundamental discontinuities between the Bronze Age suzerainty treaties and the Assyrian loyalty oaths in David N. Freedman, Gary Herion, et al., eds. *The Anchor Bible Dictionary* (New York: Doubleday, 1992) 1:1182-83. We now have the monumental, three-volume collection Kenneth Kitchen and Paul J.N. Lawrence, *Treaty, Law and Covenant in the Ancient Near East* (Wiesbaden: Harrassowitz Verlag, 2012).

[76] See Genesis 22:2, Leviticus 18:21, Leviticus 20:2-3, Judges 11:30-35, 2 Kings 3:27, 2 Kings 16:3, 2 Kings 17:17, 2 Kings 21:6, 2 Kings 23:10, Jeremiah 19:5, Jeremiah 32:35, Ezekiel 16:36, Ezekiel 23:37 & 39, Micah 6:7, Psalms 106:37, 2 Chronicles 28:3, and 2 Chronicles 33:6.

[77] Moshe Held, "The Root ZBL/SBL in Akkadian, Ugaritic and Biblical Hebrew," *Journal of the American Oriental Society* 88/1 (1968): 94, n.81. For the text and its date, see Rykle Borger, "Gott Marduk und Gott-König Šulgi als Propheten," *Bibliotheca Orientalis* 28/1-2 (1971): 3–24.

[78] Samuel Greengus, "The Old Babylonian Marriage Contract," *Journal of the American Oriental Society* 89/3 (1969): 505-32. For references to *riksu* and *rikistu* see Erica Reiner, Martha Roth, et al., eds. *The Assyrian Dictionary of the Oriental Institute of the University of Chicago.* (Chicago: Oriental Institute, 1999) R, 345-355.

[79] George Mendenhall and Gary Herion, "Covenant," in David N. Freedman, Gary Herion, et al., eds., *The Anchor Bible Dictionary* (New York: Doubleday, 1992) 5:1179-1202 with bibliography. Mendenhall and Herion allow that "these traditions also bear the marks of later 'creative writers' who embellished and reworked the tradition from the radically different perspective of the monarchic period." Quotations from George Mendenhall, "Covenant Forms in Israelite Tradition," *Biblical Archaeologist*, September 1954, 56.

[80] George Mendenhall, "Biblical History in Transition," in G. Ernest Wright, ed., *The Bible and the Ancient Near East* (Garden City, N.Y.: Doubleday, 1965), 40.

[81] Moshe Weinfeld in G. J. Botterweck and H. Ringgren, eds. *Theological Dictionary of the Old Testament.* (Grand Rapids, Mich.: Eerdmans, 1974–2018) 2: 278.

[82] David Sperling, "Rethinking Covenant in Late Biblical Books," *Biblica* 70/1(1989): 50–73. "An Arslan Tash Incantation: Interpretations and Implications." *Hebrew Union College Annual* 53 (1982): 1–10; S. David Sperling, *Ve-Eileh Divrei Davd: Essays in Semitics, Hebrew Bible and History of Biblical Scholarship* (New York: Brill, 2017), 60-69.

[83] Naphtali H. Tur-Sinai, *The Language and the Book II* (in Hebrew) (Jerusalem: Bialik, 1959), 327; see also, Hans Wolff, *Hosea* (Philadelphia: Fortress Press, 1974), 105.

[84] Albert T. Olmstead, *History of the Persian Empire* (Chicago: University of Chicago Press, 1948), 1-2.

[85] A. D. H. Mayes, "The Covenant on Sinai and the Covenant with David." *Hermathena*, no. 110 (1970): 41.

[86] Translation by Rabbi Dr. H. Freedman.

[87] Meindert Dijkstra, "Abraham." in Karel van der Toorn, Bob Becking, and Pieter W. van der Horst, eds. *Dictionary of Deities and Demons in the Bible* (Leiden, Netherlands: Brill, 1995), 6-10.

[88] Thomas Thompson, *The Historicity of the Patriarchal Narratives* (Berlin: de Gruyter, 1974), 2.

[89] John van Seters, *Abraham in History and Tradition*. (New Haven, CT: Yale University Press, 1975).

[90] Ephraim A. Speiser, "The Wife-Sister Motif in the Patriarchal Narratives," in Jacob Finkelstein and Moshe Greenberg, eds., *Oriental and Biblical Studies: Collected Writings of E.A Speiser* (Philadelphia: University of Pennsylvania Press, 1967), 62-82.

[91] See especially Samuel Greengus, "Sisterhood Adoption at Nuzi and the 'Wife-Sister' in Genesis," *Hebrew Union College Annual* 46 (1975): 5-31.

[92] For references to Speiser's reconstruction and the critical response, see S. David Sperling, *Students of the Covenant: A History of Jewish Biblical Scholarship in North America* (Atlanta: Scholars Press, 1992), 84, nn. 19, 21.

[93] Elizabeth Dias, "The Mystery of the Bible's Phantom Camels" in *Time*, February 11, 2014.

[94] Morton Smith, "The Present State of Old Testament Studies," in *Journal of Biblical Literature* 78/1 (1969): 20.

[95] Alan R. Millard, "Abraham" in David N. Freedman, Gary Herion, et al., eds. *The Anchor Bible Dictionary* (New York: Doubleday, 1992) 1:40.

[96] Nahum Sarna, *JPS Torah Commentary:* Genesis (Philadelphia, PA: Jewish Publication Society, 2001) 38.

[97] Hermann Gunkel, *The Legends of Genesis* (1901; reprint, New York: Schocken Books, 1964), 19.

[98] William F. Albright, "The Smaller Beth-Shan Stele of Sethos I (1309-1290 B.C.)," in *Bulletin of the American Schools of Oriental Research*, February 1952, 29.

[99] Moshe Weinfeld, "The Davidic Empire – Realization of the Promises to the Patriarchs," in *Eretz Israel* 24 (1993): 87-92.

[100] Joseph Fitzmyer, *The Genesis Apocryphon of Qumran Cave I* (Rome: Pontifical Biblical Institute, 1966), 54.

[101] Julius Theodor and Chanoch Albeck, eds., *Midrash Bereshit Rabba* (reprint, Jerusalem: Wahrmann, 1965), 385. Compare, also, the statement attributed to Rabbi Levi: "The Holy, be he blessed, gave Abraham a sign, so that whatever happened to him happened to his children," See Salomon Buber, ed., *Midrash Tanhuma* (reprint, Jerusalem: Ortsel, 1964), 70.

[102] For a detailed review and critique of scholarship on the chapter , see John A Emerton, "Some Problems in Genesis xiv," in *Vetus Testamentum Supplements* 41 (1990): 73-102.

[103] Yohanan Muffs, "Abraham the Noble Warrior: Patriarchal Politics and Laws of War in Ancient Israel," *Journal of Jewish Studies* (1982), 82.

[104] Lawrence J. Mykytiuk, *Identifying Biblical Persons in Northwest Semitic Inscriptions of 1200–539 B.C.E.* (Atlanta, GA: Society of Biblical Literature, 2004), 113.

[105] Yehoshaphat Nebo, The Commentaries to the Torah by Rabbi Joseph Bekhor Shor. Jerusalem: Mossad Harav Kook, 1994.

[106] Dale Manor, "Kadesh-Barnea," in David N. Freedman, Gary Herion, et al., eds. *The Anchor Bible Dictionary* (New York: Doubleday, 1992) 4:1-3.

[107] On these criticisms, see Hayim Tadmor, "The People and the Kingship in Ancient Israel: The Role of Political Institutions in the Biblical Period," in *Cashiers d'histoire mondiale* II (1968): 46-68; see also, Peter Machinist, "Hosea and the Ambiguity of Kingship in Ancient Israel," in Chaim Stern, ed., *Signs of Democracy in the Bible* (Chappaqua, NY: Temple Bethel of Northern Westchester, 1994), 25-63.

[108] John van Seters, "The Terms 'Amorite' and 'Hittite' in the Old Testament," in *Vetus Testamentum* 22/1 (1972): 64-81; see also, S. David Sperling, "Joshua 24 Re-examined," in *Hebrew Union College Annual* 58 (1987), 125-26; S. David Sperling, *Ve-Eileh Divrei Davd: Essays in Semitics, Hebrew Bible and History of Biblical Scholarship* (New York: Brill, 2017), 137-155.The ancient textual versions differ over the cities named. See R. Kyle McCarter Jr., *I Samuel* (AB) (New York: Doubleday, 1980), 142.

[109] I thank my lawyer friend Alan Appelbaum for apprising me of this term. Had Abraham not resolved the condition precedent, he could have forfeited the opportunity to raise it once the covenant was concluded.

[110] Hermann Gunkel, *The Legends of Genesis* translated by W.H. Carruth (Chicago: The Open Court Publishing Co, 1901), 20.

[111] Dale Manor, "Beer-sheba," in David N. Freedman, Gary Herion, et al., eds. *The Anchor Bible Dictionary* (New York: Doubleday, 1992), 1: 641-5.

[112] Language about disloyalty to future generations occurs in an 8th century Aramaic treaty. See Joseph Fitzmyer, *The Aramaic Inscriptions of Sefire* (Rome: Pontifical Biblical Institute, 1967), 12.

[113] See, for example, II Samuel 3:10, 17:11, and 24:2.

[114] See, for example, Lansing Hicks, "Melchizedek," in George A. Buttrick, ed., *Interpreter's Dictionary of the Bible* 3 (Nashville: Abingdon, 1962), 343; see also, John A. Emerton, "The Riddle of Genesis xiv," in *Vestus Testamentum* 21/4 (1971): 403-39.

[115] Ernst A. Knauf, "King Solomon's Copper Supply," in Edward Lipiński, ed., *Phoenicia and the Bible* (Leuven: Peeters, 1991), 183.

[116] George Ramsey, "Zadok," in David N. Freedman, Gary Herion, et al., eds. *The Anchor Bible Dictionary* (New York: Doubleday, 1992), 6: 1034-36

[117] George Ramsey, "Joshua (Person)," in David N. Freedman, Gary Herion, et al., eds. *The Anchor Bible Dictionary* (New York: Doubleday, 1992), 3: 999-1000.

[118] For examples, see Thomas Thompson, *The Historicity of the Patriarchal Narratives* (Berlin: de Gruyter, 1974), 43-50.

[119] Stanley Gevirtz, "Of Patriarchs and Puns: Joseph at the Fountain, Jacob at the Ford," in *Hebrew Union College Annual* (1975), 46: 51, 52.

[120] Bustenay Oded, apud Gershon Galil and Ephraim Stern, eds., *Melakim Aleph* (Olam Ha-tanakh vol. 10) (Tel Aviv: Davidson-Attai, 1994), 133.

[121] Gösta W. Ahlström, *The History of Ancient Palestine* (Minneapolis, MN: Augsburg Fortress, 1993), 550-54.

[122] Amihai Mazar, "The Iron Age I," in Amnon Ben-Tor ed., *The Archaeology of Ancient Israel* (New Haven, Conn.: Yale University Press, 1992), 293.

[123] H.L. Ginsberg, "Hosea's Ephraim, More Fool Than Knave (A New Interpretation of Hosea 12:1-14)," in *The Journal of Biblical Literature* (Atlanta, GA: Society of Biblical Literature, 1961), 80: 339-47.

[124] Martin Rose, "Names of God in the OT," in David N. Freedman, Gary Herion, et al., eds. *The Anchor Bible Dictionary* (New York: Doubleday, 1992), 4:1001-11; see further, Nadav Naaman, "Jeroboam's Polytheism According to IKings 12:28-29," in *The Journal of Northwest Semitic Languages,*" 46 (2020), 35-45.

[125] Donald Redford, *Egypt, Canaan and Israel in Ancient Times* (Princeton, N.J.: Princeton University Press, 1992), 108, 427-429 n. 57.

[126] Anson R. Rainey in Anson Rainey and R. Steven Notley, *The Sacred Bridge: Carta's Atlas of the Biblical World* (Jerusalem: Carta, 2006), 185-189.

[127] Tremper Longman III, "The Autobiography of Idrimi," in William Hallo and K. Lawson Younger, Jr. eds. *The Context of Scripture* (Leiden, Netherlands: Brill, 1997), vol. 1, 479-480; Jacob Lauinger, "Discourse and Meta-Discourse in the Statue of Idrimi and Its Inscription," in *MAARAV, A Journal for the Study of the Northwest Semitic Languages and Literatures* 23 (2019): 19-38.

[128] Mordechai Cogan and Hayim Tadmor, *II Kings (The Yale Anchor Bible Commentaries),* (New York: Doubleday, 1988), 311, 328-330.

[129] Mordechai Cogan and Hayim Tadmor, *II Kings (The Yale Anchor Bible Commentaries),* (New York: Doubleday, 1988), 152-164.

[130] John R. Spencer, "Aaron," in David N. Freedman, Gary Herion, et al., eds. *The Anchor Bible Dictionary* (New York: Doubleday, 1992) 1:1-6.

[131] For a bibliography, see John R. Spencer, "Golden Calf" in David N. Freedman, Gary Herion, et al., eds. *The Anchor Bible Dictionary* (New York: Doubleday, 1992) 2:1065-9.

[132] Knut L. Tallqvist *Akkadische Götterepitheta* (Helsinki: Societas Orientalis Fennica, 1938) 18.

[133] Stanley Gervirtz, "*ḥeret* in the Manufacture of the Golden Calf," in *Biblica 65* (1984): 377-81.

[134] Samuel E. Loewenstamm, *Comparative Studies in Biblical and Ancient Oriental Literatures* (Kevelaer, Germany: Butzon & Bercker, 1980), 242-45, 510.

[135] For the possible connection between cherubim (Hebrew: *kerubim*) and Mesopotamian sphinxes (Mesopotamian: *kāribu*) known in mythology and art, see Tryggve N.D. Mettinger, "Cherubim," in Karel van der Toorn, Bob Becking, and Pieter W. van der Horst, eds. *Dictionary of Deities and Demons in the Bible* (Leiden, Netherlands: Brill, 1995), 189-192.

[136] John Brinkman, "Political Covenants, Treaties, and Loyalty Oaths in Babylonia and between Assyria and Babylonia," in Carlo Zaccagnini ed., *Trattati*, (Rome: "L'Erma" di Bretschneider, 1990) 81-111. There is an apparent discovery of *adê* some five centuries earlier in a broken context (82), but that has no bearing on the historicity of the story.

[137] Moses Aberbach and Leivy Smolar, "Aaron, Jeroboam and the Golden Calves," in *Journal of Biblical Literature* (Atlanta, GA: Society of Biblical Literature, 1967), 86:129-40. The quotation is from p. 129. Some of their comparisons are drawn from biblical traditions concerning Jeroboam and Aaron outside these two chapters.

[138] Bustenay Oded, apud Gershon Galil and Ephraim Stern, eds., *Melakim Aleph* (Olam Ha-tanakh vol.10) (Tel Aviv: Davidson-Attai, 1994), 138.

[139] For the terminology of "braiding" as well as the general treatment of the story, see Baruch Levine, *Numbers 1-20 (The Anchor Yale Bible Commentaries)* (New York: Doubleday, 1993), 405-32.

[140] For a survey of Arad discoveries, see Gary Herion and Dale Manor, "Arad," in David N. Freedman, Gary Herion, et al., eds. *The Anchor Bible Dictionary* (New York: Doubleday, 1992) 1:331-6.

[141] S. David Sperling, *Ve-Eileh Divrei David: Essays in Semitics, Hebrew Bible and History of Biblical Scholarship* (New York: Brill, 2017) see "Pants, Persians and the Priestly Source" 196-209. Note that trousers were likely invented in the 10th century B.C.E. in China, and worked their way to Persia. See Ulrike Beck, Mayke Wayner, Xiao Li, Desmond Durkin-Meisterernst, Pavel E. Tarasov, "The invention of trousers and its likely affiliation with horseback riding and mobility: A case study of late 2nd millennium BC find from Turfan in eastern Central Asia," in *Quaternary International* (May, 2014) 348: 224-235.

[142] Richard Goldstein. "D'Aquino, Linked to Tokyo Rose Broadcasts, Dies." *The New York Times*, September 27, 2006.

[143] Robert Francis Johnson, "Moses" in *The Interpreter's Dictionary of the Bible* (Nashville, TN: Abingdon Press, 1962) vol 3: 441.

[144] Karel van der Toorn, "Yahweh," in Karel van der Toorn, Bob Becking, and Pieter W. van der Horst, eds. *Dictionary of Deities and Demons in the Bible* (Leiden, Netherlands: Brill, 1995), 1712-30 (with bibliography).

[145] Karel van der Toorn, "Saul and the Rise of Israelite State Religion," in *Vetus Testamentum* 43 (Brill: Netherlands, 1993): 519-42

[146] S. David Sperling, "Blood," in David N. Freedman, Gary Herion, et al., eds. *The Anchor Bible Dictionary* (New York: Doubleday, 1992), 1:763-5.

[147] Mordecai Margulies, ed., *Midrash Wayyikra Rabbah* (New York: Jewish Theological Seminary, 1993), p.586.

[148] For alternative ways of saying in biblical Hebrew, "this was the first altar that he built," see V. Philips Long, *The Reign and Rejection of King Saul* (Atlanta: Scholars Press, 1989), 122.

[149] Joseph Blenkinsopp, "The Quest of the Historical Saul," in James W. Flanagan and Anita W. Robinson, eds., *No Famine in the Land, Studies in Honor of John L. McKenzie* (Missoula, Mont.: Scholars Press, 1975), 93. For a summary and bibliography of scholarship relating to Saul, see Diana Edelman, "Saul," in David N. Freedman, Gary Herion, et al., eds. *The Anchor Bible Dictionary* (New York: Doubleday, 1992), 5:989-99.

[150] Sharon R. Keller, "Aspects of Nudity in the Old Testament" in *Source: Notes in the History of Art* (Chicago, IL: University of Chicago Press, 1993), Vol 12, No 2. p 32-36.

[151] For details, see Philip Stern, *The Biblical Ḥerem: A Window on Israel's Religious Experience* (Atlanta: Scholars Press, 1991).

[152] For the contrary view that the tale is early, see Philip Stern, *The Biblical Ḥerem: A Window on Israel's Religious Experience* (Atlanta: Scholars Press, 1991), 165-77.

[153] Karel van der Toorn, "Yahweh," in Karel van der Toorn, Bob Becking, and Pieter W. van der Horst, eds. *Dictionary of Deities and Demons in the Bible* (Leiden, Netherlands: Brill, 1995), 1716-17 (with bibliography).

[154] Wilfred G. Lambert, "The Reign of Nebuchadnezzar I: A Turning Point in the History of Ancient Mesopotamian Religion," in William S. McCullough, ed., *The Seed of Wisdom: Essays I Honour of Theophile J. Meek* (Toronto: University of Toronto Press, 1964), 3-13. Compare William W. Hallo, "Exodus and Ancient Near Eastern Literature," in Gunther Plaut, ed., *The Torah: A Modern Commentary* (New York: Union of American Hebrew Congregations, 1981), 373.

[155] D.C. Feeney, The Gods in Epic: Poets and Critics of the Classical Tradition (New York: Oxford University Press, 1991).

[156] Barbara Nevling Porter, *Images, Power and Politics: Figurative Aspects of Esarhaddon's Babylonian Policy* (Philadelphia: American Philosophical Society, 1993).

[157] See especially Barbara Nevling Porter, *Images, Power and Politics: Figurative Aspects of Esarhaddon's Babylonian Policy* (Philadelphia: American Philosophical Society, 1993), chaps 4, 5, 6; see also Peter Machinist, "Literature as Politics: The Tukulti-Ninurta Epic and the Bible" in *Catholic Biblical Quarterly* (Washington D.C.: Catholic Biblical Associate of America) 38 (1976): 455-82; see also, Peter Machinist, "Assyrians on Assyria in the First Millennium B.C.," in Kurt Raaflaub, ed., *Anfänge politischen Denkens in der Antike* (Munich: Oldenbourg, 1993), 77-104.

BIBLIOGRAPHY

Aberbach, Moses and Leivy Smolar. "Aaron, Jeroboam and the Golden Calves." *Journal of Biblical Literature* 86 (1967): 129–40.

Abrams, Morris H. *A Glossary of Literary Terms*. New York: Holt, Rinehart and Winston, 1971.

Aharoni, Yohanan, Michael Avi-Yonah, Anson F. Rainey, and Ze'ev Safrai. *The Macmillan Bible Atlas*. Rev. 3rd ed. New York: Macmillan, 1993.

Ahituv, Shmuel. *Echoes from the Past*. Jerusalem: Carta, 2008.

Ahlström, Gösta W. *The History of Ancient Palestine*. Minneapolis, MN: Augsburg Fortress, 1993.

Albrektson, Bertil. *History and the Gods*. Lund: Gleerup, 1967.

Albright, William F. "The Role of the Canaanites in the History of Civilization." In *The Bible and the Ancient Near East*, edited by G. Ernest Wright, 438–87. Garden City, NY: Doubleday, 1965.

———. "The Smaller Beth-Shan Stele of Sethos I (1309–1290 B.C.)." In *Bulletin of the American Schools of Oriental Research* (February 1952) 24–32.

Althann, Robert. "Josiah." In *The Anchor Bible Dictionary* 3, edited by David N. Freedman, Gary Herion, et al., 1015–18. New York: Doubleday, 1992.

Amir, Yehoshua. "Authority and Interpretation in the Writings of Philo." In *Mikra*, edited by Martin Mulder, 421–53. Philadelphia: Fortress Press, 1988.

Assman, Jan. "Aton." In *Lexikon der Ägyptologie* I (Wiesbaden: 1974) 526–40.

Auerbach, Erich. *Scenes from the Drama of European Literature*. New York: Meridian, 1959.

Barr, James. "The Literal, the Allegorical, and Modern Scholarship." *Journal for the Study of the Old Testament* 14, no. 44 (June 1989): 3–17.

Bartlett, John R. "The Conquest of Sihon's Kingdom: A Literary Re-examination." *Journal of Biblical Literature* 97/3 (1978): 347–51.

Beck, Ulrike; Mayke Wayner, Xiao Li, Desmond Durkin-Meistererernst, Pavel E. Tarasov. "The invention of trousers and its likely affiliation with horseback riding and mobility: A case study of late 2nd millennium BC find from Turfan in eastern Central Asia." *Quaternary International* 348 (May 2014): 224–235.

Blenkinsopp, Joseph. "The Quest of the Historical Saul." In *No Famine in the Land, Studies in Honor of John L. McKenzie*, edited by James W. Flanagan and Anita W. Robinson, 75–99. Missoula, MT: Scholars Press, 1975.

Borgen, Peder. "Philo of Alexandria." In *The Anchor Bible Dictionary* 5, edited by David N. Freedman, Gary Herion, et al., 333–42. New York: Doubleday, 1992.

Borger, Rykle. "Gott Marduk und Gott-König Šulgi als Propheten." *Bibliotheca Orientalis* 28/1–2 (January-March, 1971): 3–24.

Boyce, Mary. *The Early Period.* Vol I of *A History of Zoroastrianism.* Leiden: Brill, 1975.

Brandenstein, Wilhelm and Manfred Mayrhofer. *Handbuch des Altpersischen.* Wiesbaden: Otto Harrassowitz, 1964.

Brewer, David I. *Techniques and Assumptions in Jewish Exegesis before 70 C.E.* Tübingen: Mohr, 1992.

Bright, John. *A History of Israel,* 2nd edition. Philadelphia: Westminster, 1972.

Brinkman, John. "Political Covenants, Treaties, and Loyalty Oaths in Babylonia and between Assyria and Babylonia." In *Il Trattati nel mondo antico forma ideologia funzione,* edited by Luciano Canfora, Mario Liverani, and Carlo Zaccagnini, 81–111. Rome: "L'Erma" di Bretschneider, 1990.

Buber, Salomon, ed., *Midrash Tanhuma* (reprint). Jerusalem: Ortsel, 1964.

Büchsel, Hermann. "allēgoreō." In *Theological Dictionary of the New Testament* 1, edited by Gerhard Kittel and Gerhard Friedrich, 260–63. Grand Rapids: Eerdmans, 1974–76.

Burkert, Walter. *Creation of the Sacred: Tracks of Biology in Early Religions.* Cambridge: Harvard Univ. Press, 1996.

———. *Homo Necans.* Berkeley and Los Angeles: University of California Press, 1983.

Burton, Ernest. *A Critical and Exegetical Commentary on the Epistle to the Galatians.* Edinburgh: T and T Clark, 1921.

Carroll, Robert. "Psalm LXXVIII: Vestiges of a Tribal Polemic." *Vetus Testamentum* 21/2 (1971): 133–150.

Campbell, Edward. "Judges 9 and Biblical Archeology." In *The Word of the Lord Shall Go Forth: Essays in Honor of David Noel Freedman in Celebration of His Sixtieth Birthday,* edited by Carol Meyers and Michael O'Connor, 263–271. Winona Lake, IN: Eisenbrauns, 1983.

Charpin, Dominique. "Un Traité entre Zimri-Lim de Mari et Ibâl-pî-El II d'Ešnunna." In *Marchands, diplomates et empereurs: Études sur la civilisation mésopotamienne offertes á Paul Garelli,* edited by Dominique Charpin and Francis Joannés, 139–66. Paris: Éditions recherche sur les civilizations, 1991.

Civil, Miguel, Ignace J. Gelb, et al., eds. *The Assyrian Dictionary of the Oriental Institute of the University of Chicago* K. Chicago: Oriental Institute, 1956–2006.

Clark, Gordon. *The Word Hesed in the Hebew Bible*. Sheffield: Sheffield Academic Press, 1993.

Clements, Ronald. *The World of Ancient Israel*. Cambridge: Cambridge University Press, 1989.

Cogan, Mordechai and Hayim Tadmor. *II Kings (The Anchor Yale Bible Commentaries)*. New York: Doubleday, 1988.

Cohen, Chaim. "Genesis 14:1–11 – An Early Israelite Chronographic Source." In *The Biblical Canaan in Comparative Perspective* (Scripture in Context IV), edited by K. Lawson Younger, William Hallo, and Bernard F. Batto, 67–107. Lewiston: Edwin Mellen, 1991.

Cohen, Martin A. "The Role of the Shilonite Priesthood in the United Monarchy of Ancient Israel." *Hebrew Union College Annual* 46 (1965): 59–98.

Coogan, Michael D. "Canaanite Origins and Lineage: Reflections on the Religion of Ancient Israel." In *Ancient Israelite Religion: Essays in Honor of Frank Moore Cross*, edited by Patrick Miller Jr., Paul Hanson, S. Dean McBride, 115–24. Philadelphia: Fortress, 1987.

Cooper, Alan, and Bernard Goldstein. "Exodus and Maṣṣot in History and Tradition." *MAARAV, A Journal for the Study of the Northwest Semitic Languages and Literatures* 8 (1992): 15–37.

———. "The Festivals of Israel and Judah and the Literary History of the Pentateuch." *Journal of the American Oriental Society* (January–March 1990) 19–31.

Cross, Frank M. *Canaanite Myth and Hebrew Epic*. Cambridge: Harvard University Press, 1973.

Day, John. "Pre-Deuteronomic Allusions to the Covenant in Hosea and Psalm LXXVIII." *Vetus Testamentum* 36/1 (1986): 1–12.

Dever, William. "Archaeology, Syro-Palestinian and Biblical." In *The Anchor Bible Dictionary* 1, edited by David N. Freedman, Gary Herion, et al., 354–67. New York: Doubleday, 1992.

———. *Beyond the Texts: An Archaeological Portrait of Ancient Israel and Judah*. Atlanta: Society of Biblical Literature Press, 2017.

———. "The Contribution of Archaeology to the Study of Canaanite and Early Israelite Religion." In *Ancient Israelite Religion: Essays in Honor of Frank Moore Cross*, edited by Patrick Miller Jr., Paul Hanson, S. Dean McBride, 209–47. Philadelphia: Fortress, 1987.

———. "Israel, History of (Archaeology and the Israelite 'Conquest')." In *The Anchor Bible Dictionary* 3, edited by David N. Freedman, Gary Herion, et al., 553. New York: Doubleday, 1992.

Dias, Elizabeth. "The Mystery of the Bible's Phantom Camels." *Time*, February 11, 2014.

Dijkstra, Meindert. "Abraham." In *Dictionary of Deities and Demons in the Bible*, edited by Karel van der Toorn, Bob Becking, and Pieter W. van der Horst, 6–10. Leiden: Brill, 1995.

Dothan, Trude and H. Jacob Katzenstein, "Philistines." In *The Anchor Bible Dictionary* 5, edited by David N. Freedman, Gary Herion, et al., 333. New York: Doubleday, 1992.

Drews, Robert. *The End of the Bronze Age: Changes in Warfare and the Catastrophe ca. 1200 B.C.* Princeton, N.J.: Princeton University Press, 1993.

Durand, Jean-Marie. *Archives épistolaires de Mari*. Paris: Éditions recherche sur les civilisations, 1988.

Edelman, Diana. Review of *Joshua 24 as Poetic Narrative*, by William Koopmans. *Journal of Near Eastern Studies* 52/4 (1993): 308–10.

———. "Saul." In *The Anchor Bible Dictionary* 5, edited by David N. Freedman, Gary Herion, et al., 989–99. New York: Doubleday, 1992.

Eidem, Jesper. "An Old Assyrian Treaty from Tell Leilan." In *Marchands, diplomates et empereurs: Études sur la civilization mésopotamienne offertes à Paul Garelli*, edited by Dominique Charpin and Francis Joannés, 185–207. Paris: Éditions recherche sur les civilisations, 1991.

Emerton, John A. "The Riddle of Genesis xiv." *Vetus Testamentum* 21/4 (1971): 403–39.

———. "The Site of Salem, the City of Melchizedek (Genesis XIV 18)." *Vetus Testamentum Supplements* 41 (1990): 45–71.

———. "Some Problems in Genesis xiv." *Vetus Testamentum Supplements* 41 (1990): 73–102.

Evans, Carl. "Naram-Sin and Jeroboam: The Archetypal *Unheilsherrscher* in Mesopotamiam and Biblical Historiography." In *Scripture in Context II*, edited by William W. Hallo, James C. Moyer, and Leo G. Perdue, 94–124. Winona Lake, IN: Eisenbrauns, 1983.

Fales, Frederick Mario. "The Composition and Structure of the Neo-Assyrian Empire: Ethnicity, Language and Identities." In *Writing Neo-Assyrian History*, edited by Giovanni B. Lafranche, Raija Mattila, Robert Rollinger, 45–89. Helsinki: The Neo-Assyrian Corpus Text Project, 2019.

Faulkner, Raymond, Ogden Goelet, and Eva von Dassow. *The Egyptian Book of the Dead: The Book of Going Forth by Day*. San Francisco: Chronicle, 1994.

Feeney, D.C. *The Gods in Epic: Poets and Critics of the Classical Tradition*. New York: Oxford University Press, 1991.

Feldman, Noah. "Religion and the Earthly City." *Social Research: An International Quarterly* 76 (2009): 989–1000.

Finkelstein, Israel. *The Archaeology of the Israelite Settlement.* Jerusalem: Israel Exploration Society, 1988.

Finkelstein, Israel and Nadav Na'aman, eds. *From Nomadism to Monarchy: Archaeological and Historical Aspects of Early Israel.* Washington D.C.: Biblical Archaeological Society, 1994.

Finkelstein, Louis, ed. *The Jews, Their History, Culture and Religion.* New York: Harper, 1960.

Fishbane, Michael, and Emanuel Tov, eds. *Sha'arei Talmon Studies in the Bible, Qumran, and the Ancient Near East Presented to Shemaryahu Talmon.* Winona Liake, IN: Eisenbrauns, 1992.

Fitzmyer, Joseph. *The Aramaic Inscriptions of Sefire.* Rome: Pontifical Biblical Institute, 1967.

———. *The Genesis Apocryphon of Qumran Cave I.* Rome: Pontifical Biblical Institute, 1966.

Fleming, Daniel. *The Installation of Baal's High Priestess at Emar.* Atlanta: Scholars Press, 1992.

Foster, Benjamin R. "The Birth Legend of Sargon of Akkad." In *The Context of Scripture vol. 1* edited by William W. Hallo and Kyle Lawson Younger, Jr., 461. Leiden: Brill, 1997.

Frankena, Rintje. "The Vassal Treaties of Esarhaddon ad the Dating of Deuteronomy." *Oudtestamentische Studiën* 14 (1965): 122–54.

Friedman, Richard E. *Who Wrote the Bible?* New York: Harper & Row, 1989.

Galil, Gershon and Ephraim Stern, eds., *Melakim Aleph* (Olam Ha-tanakh vol. 10). Tel Aviv: Davidson-Attai, 1994.

Gelb, Ignace, Thorkild Jacobsen, et al., eds. *The Assyrian Dictionary of the Oriental Institute of the University of Chicago* D, 17–18. Chicago: Oriental Institute, 1956–2006.

Geller, Markham. Review of *Sin and Sanction in Israel and Mesopotamia*, by Karen van der Toorn. *Journal of Cuneiform Studies* 42/1 (1991): 105–17.

Geller, Stephen. "The Struggle at the Jabbok: The Uses of Enigma in a Biblical Narrative." *Journal of the Ancient Near Eastern Society* 14 (1982): 37–60.

Geraty, Lawrence. "Heshbon." In *The Anchor Bible Dictionary*, edited by David N. Freedman, Gary Herion, et al. New York: Doubleday, 1992.

Gervirtz, Stanley. "ḥeret in the Manufacture of the Golden Calf." *Biblica 65* (1984): 377–81.

———. "Of Patriarchs and Puns: Joseph at the Fountain, Jacob at the Ford." *Hebrew Union College Annual* 46 (1975): 51, 52.

Gibson, John. *Canaanite Myth and Legends.* Edinburgh: T and T Clark, 1987.

Ginsberg, H. L. "Hosea, Book of." *Encyclopaedia Judaica* 8, edited by Cecil Roth and Geoffrey Wigoder, 1010–23. Jerusalem: Keter Publishing, 1972.

———. "Hosea's Ephraim, More Fool Than Knave (A New Interpretation of Hosea 12:1–14)." *The Journal of Biblical Literature* 80/1 (1961): 339–47.

———. *The Israelian Heritage of Judaism*. New York: Jewish Theological Seminary, 1982.

———. "Ugaritic Studies and the Bible." In *The Biblical Archaeologist Reader* vol. 2, edited by David N. Freedman and Edward R. Campbell, 35–58. Garden City, N.Y.: Anchor/Doubleday, 1964.

Gnoli, Gherardo. "Mithra." *Encyclopedia of Religion* 9, edited by Mircea Eliade, 579–80. New York: Macmillan, 1987.

Goedicke, Hans & Jimmy Jack McBee Roberts, eds. *Unity and Diversity*. Baltimore: Johns Hopkins University Press, 1975.

Goldstein, Richard. "D'Aquino, Linked to Tokyo Rose Broadcasts, Dies." *The New York Times*, September 27, 2006.

Gottwald, Norman. *The Tribes of Yahweh*. Maryknoll, N.Y.: Orbis, 1979.

Greenberg, Moshe. "Did Job Really Exist? An Issue of Medieval Exegesis." In *Sha'arei Talmon Studies in the Bible, Qumran and the Ancient Near East Presented to Shemaryahu Talmon*, edited by Michael Fishbane and Emanuel Tov, 3*–11*. Winona Lake, IN: Eisenbrauns, 1992.

Greengus, Samuel. "The Old Babylonian Marriage Contract" *Journal of the American Oriental Society* 89/3 (1969): 505–32.

———. "Sisterhood Adoption at Nuzi and the 'Wife-Sister' in Genesis." *Hebrew Union College Annual* 46 (1975): 5–31.

Greenstein, Edward, and David Marcus. "The Akkadian Inscription of Idrimi." *Journal of the Ancient Near Eastern Society* 8 (1976): 59–96.

Gunkel, Hermann. *The Legends of Genesis*. Translated by W.H. Carruth. Chicago: The Open Court Publishing Co, 1901: 1964 reprint.

Hackett, Jo Ann. "Religious Traditions in Israelite Transjordan." In *Ancient Israelite Religion: Essays in Honor of Frank Moore Cross*, edited by Patrick Miller Jr., Paul Hanson, S. Dean McBride, 125–36. Philadelphia: Fortress, 1987.

———. "Balaam." In *The Anchor Bible Dictionary* 1, edited by David N. Freedman, Gary Herion, et al., 569–72. New York: Doubleday, 1992.

Hallo, William W. "Biblical Abominations and Sumerian Taboos." *Jewish Quarterly Review* 76/1 (1985): 21–40.

———. "Exodus and Ancient Near Eastern Literature." In *The Torah: A Modern Commentary*, edited by Gunther Plaut, 367–77. New York: Union of American Hebrew Congregations, 1981.

Halpern, Baruch. *The First Historians*. New York: Harper & Row, 1988.

Hasel, Gerhard F. "Sabbath." In *The Anchor Bible Dictionary* 5, edited by David N. Freedman, Gary Herion, et al., 849–56. New York: Doubleday, 1992.

Hasel, Michael G. "*Israel* in the Merneptah Stele." In *Bulletin of the American Schools of Oriental Research* 296 (1994) 45–61.

Hawkins, J.D. "Aleppo 6." In *The Context of Scripture* 4, edited by K.L. Younger, 164. Leiden: Brill, 2017.

Held, Moshe. "The Root ZBL/SBL in Akkadian, Ugaritic and Biblical Hebrew." *Journal of the American Oriental Society* 88/1 (1968): 90–96.

Herion, Gary and Dale Manor. "Arad." In *The Anchor Bible Dictionary* 1, edited by David N. Freedman, Gary Herion, et al., 331–6. New York: Doubleday, 1992.

Hess, Richard. "Caphtor." In *The Anchor Bible Dictionary* 1, edited by David N. Freedman, Gary Herion, et al., 869–70. New York: Doubleday, 1992.

———. "Early Israel in Canaan: A Survey of Recent Evidence and Interpretations." *Palestine Exploration Quarterly* 125 (1993): 125–42.

Hicks, Lansing "Melchizedek." In *Interpreter's Dictionary of the Bible* 3, edited by George A. Buttrick, 343. Nashville: Abingdon, 1962.

Hillers, Delbert. *Covenant: The History of a Biblical Idea*. Baltimore: Johns Hopkins University Press, 1969.

———. *Treaty Curses and the Old Testament Prophets*. Rome: Pontifical Biblical Institute, 1964.

Hodgson, Marshall G.S. "Bāṭiniyya." *Encyclopedia of Islam* 1 (New edition), edited by Hamilton A. R. Gibb, Johann Hendrik Kramers, Évariste Lévi-Provencal, and Joseph Schacht, 1098–1100. Leiden: Brill, 1960.

Hoffman, Yair. *The Doctrine of the Exodus in the Bible*. Tel Aviv: Tel Aviv University Press, 1983.

———. "A North Israelite Typological Myth and a Judaean Historical Tradition: The Exodus in Hosea and Amos." *Vetus Testamentum* 39/2 (1989): 169–82.

Hoftijzer, Jacob and Gerrit van der Kooij. *The Balaam Text from Deir Alla Re-Evaluated*. Leiden: Brill, 1991.

Jacobsen, Thorkild. "Religious Drama in Ancient Mesopotamia." In *Unity and Diversity*, edited by Hans Goedicke and Jimmy Jack McBee Roberts, 65–97. Baltimore: Johns Hopkins University Press, 1975.

———. *The Treasures of Darkness*. New Haven, Conn.: Yale University Press, 1976.

Japhet, Sara. *I and II Chronicles*. Louisville: Westminster, 1993.

Joannés, Francis. "Le Traité de vassalité d'Atamrum d'Andarig envers Zimri-Lim de Mari." In *Marchands, diplomates et empereurs: Études sur la civilisation mésopotamienne offertes á Paul Garelli*, edited by Dominique Charpin and Francis Joannés, 166–77. Paris: Éditions recherche sur les civilizations, 1991.

Johnson, Luke T. *The Real Jesus.* San Francisco: Harper, 1996.

Johnson, Robert Francis. "Moses." In *The Interpreter's Dictionary of the Bible* 3, edited by George A. Buttrick, 441. Nashville, TN: Abingdon Press, 1962.

Josephus: The Complete Works, Chapter 9. *How, After the Death of Antiochus, Hyrcanus made an Expedition Against Syria, and Made a League with the Romans. Concerning the Death of King Demetrius and Alexander.* Paragraph 1.

Kamin, Sarah. *Jews and Christians Interpret the Bible.* Jerusalem: Magnes, 1991.

Kasher, Hannah and Moshe Kahan. "Joseph Kaspi." In *The Stanford Encyclopedia of Philosophy* (Spring 2019 Edition), Edward N. Zalta (ed.), https://plato.stanford.edu/archives/spr2019/entries/kaspi-joseph/

Kempinski, Aharon. "How Profoundly Canaanized Were the Early Israelites?" *Zeitschrift des deutschen Palästina-Vereins* 108/1 (1992): 1–6.

Keller, Sharon R. "Aspects of Nudity in the Old Testament." *Source: Notes in the History of Art* 12, no. 2 (1993): 32–36.

Kennedy, James. "Peasants in Revolt: Political Allegory in Genesis 2–3." *Journal for the Study of the Old Testament* 47 (1990): 3–14.

Kitchen, Kenneth, "Egypt, Ugarit, Qatna and Covenant." In *Ugarit Forschungen* 11 (1979): 453–64. Münster, Germany: Ugarit-Verlag.

Kitchen, Kenneth and Paul J.N. Lawrence. *Treaty, Law and Covenant in the Ancient Near East.* Wiesbaden: Harrassowitz Verlag, 2012.

Klein, Jacob. "Sacred Marriage." In *The Anchor Bible Dictionary* 5, edited by David N. Freedman, Gary Herion, et al., 866–71. New York: Doubleday, 1992.

Klein, Jacob, and Yitschak Sefati. "The Concept of 'Abomination' in Mesopotamian Literature and the Bible." *Beer Sheba 3* (1990): 131–48.

Knauf, Ernst A. "El Šaddai – Der Gott Abrahams?" *Biblische Zeitschrift* 29/1 (1985): 97–103.

———. "King Solomon's Copper Supply." In *Phoenicia and the Bible*, edited by Edward Lipiński. Leuven: Peeters, 1991.

Koopmans, William. *Joshua 24 as Poetic Narrative.* Sheffield: Journal for the Study of the Old Testament, 1990.

Kramer, Samuel N. *The Sumerians: Their History, Culture, and Character.* Chicago: University of Chicago Press, 1963.

———. *The Sacred Marriage Rite.* Bloomington: Indiana University Press, 1969.

Kravitz, Leonard. "Mose ben Nahman." In *Theologische Realenzyklopädie*, vol. 23, fasc. 3/4, edited by Gerhard Krause and Gerhard Muller, 362–64. Berlin: de Gruyter, 1994.

Kupfer, Ephraim. "Kaspi, Joseph ben Abba." In *Encyclopaedia Judaica* 10, edited by Cecil Roth and Geoffrey Wigoder, 809–11. Jerusalem: Keter Publishing, 1972.

Kupper, Jean-Robert. "Zimri-Lim et ses vassaux." In *Marchands, diplomates et empereurs: Études sur la civilisation mésopotamienne offertes á Paul Garelli*, edited by Dominique Charpin and Francis Joannés, 139–66. Paris: Éditions recherche sur les civilizations, 1991.

Lambert, Wilfred G. "Morals in Ancient Mesopotamia." *Jaarbericht van het Voorasiatisch-Egyptisch Genootschaap "Ex Oriente Lux"* 15 (1957–58): 184–96.

———. "The Reign of Nebuchadnezzar I: A Turning Point in the History of Ancient Mesopotamian Religion." In *The Seed of Wisdom: Essays I Honour of Theophile J. Meek*, edited by William S. McCullough, 3–13. Toronto: University of Toronto Press, 1964.

Landsberger, Benno. "Die babylonische Termini für Gesetz und Recht." In Symb. Koschaker: 219–34.

Lang, Bernhard. *Monotheism and the Prophetic Minority*. Sheffield: Almond, 1982.

Lapinkivi, Pirjo. *The Sumerian Sacred Marriage in the Light of Comparative Evidence*. Finland: University of Helsinki, 2004.

Lauinger, Jacob. "Discourse and Meta-Discourse in the Statue of Idrimi and Its Inscription." *MAARAV, A Journal for the Study of the Northwest Semitic Languages and Literatures* 23 (2019), 19-38.

Leach, Edmund. "Anthropological Approaches to the Bible during the Twentieth Century." In *Humanizing America's Iconic Book*, edited by Gene Tucker and Gordon Knight, 75–94. Chico, CA: Scholars Press, 1980.

Lee, Felicia R. "From Noah's Curse to Slavery's Rationale." *The New York Times* November 1, 2003.

Lemche, Niels. *The Canaanites and Their Land*. Sheffield: Journal for the Study of the Old Testament, 1991.

———. *Early Israel*. Leiden: Brill, 1965.

———. "Habiru, Hapiru." In *The Anchor Bible Dictionary* 3, edited by David N. Freedman, Gary Herion, et al., 6–10. New York: Doubleday, 1992.

———. "Israel, History of (Premonarchic Period)." In *The Anchor Bible Dictionary* 3, edited by David N. Freedman, Gary Herion, et al., 526–45. New York: Doubleday, 1992

Levine, Baruch. "The Epilogue to the Holiness Code; A Priestly Statement on the Destiny of Israel." In *Judaic Perspectives on Ancient Israel*, edited by

Ernest Frerichs, Baruch Levine, and Jacob Neusner, 9–34. Philadelphia: Fortress Press, 1987.

———. *Numbers 1–20 (The Anchor Yale Bible Commentaries)*. New York: Doubleday, 1993.

———. "The Triumphs of the Lord." *Eretz Israel* 20 (1989): 202–14.

Lewis, Brian. *The Sargon Legend: A Study of the Akkadian Text and the Tale of the Hero Who Was Exposed at Birth*. Cambridge: American Schools of Oriental Research, 1980.

Lewis, Theodore. "Baal-Berith." In *The Anchor Bible Dictionary* 1, edited by David N. Freedman, Gary Herion, et al., 550–1. New York: Doubleday, 1992.

Licht, Jacob. "Biblical Historicism." In *History, Historiography and Interpretation*, edited by Hayim Tadmor and Moshe Weinfeld, 107–20. Jerusalem: Magnes, 1983.

Lichtheim, Miriam. *Ancient Egyptian Literature, Volume II: The New Kingdom*. Berkeley and Los Angeles: University of California Press, 1976.

Lieberman, Saul. *Hellenism in Jewish Palestine*. New York: Jewish Theological Seminary, 1950.

Lieberman, Stephen. "A Mesopotamian Background for the So-Called *Aggadic* 'Measures' of Biblical Hermenetics." *Hebrew Union College Annual* 58 (1987): 137–225.

Liverani, Mario. *The Politics of Abdi-Ashirta of Amurru*. Malibu, CA: Undena, 1979.

Loewenstamm, Samuel E. *Comparative Studies in Biblical and Ancient Oriental Literatures*. Kevelaer: Butzon & Bercker, 1980.

Long, Burke. Review of *The Origin Tradition of Ancient Israel*, by Thomas Thompson. *Journal of Biblical Literature* 108 (1989): 327–30.

Long, V. Philips. *The Reign and Rejection of King Saul*. Atlanta: Scholars Press, 1989.

Longman III, Tremper. "The Autobiography of Idrimi." In *The Context of Scripture* 1, edited by William Hallo and K. Lawson Younger, 479–80. Leiden: Brill, 1997.

Machinist, Peter. "Assyrians on Assyria in the First Millennium B.C." In *Anfänge politischen Denkens in der Antike*, edited by Kurt Raaflaub, 77–104. Munich: Oldenbourg, 1993.

———. "Hosea and the Ambiguity of Kingship in Ancient Israel." In *Signs of Democracy in the Bible*, edited by Chaim Stern, 25–63. Chappaqua: Temple Bethel of Northern Westchester, 1994.

———. "Literature as Politics: The Tukulti-Ninurta Epic and the Bible." *Catholic Biblical Quarterly* 38/4 (1976): 455–82.

———. "The Question of Distinctiveness in Ancient Israel: An Essay." In *Ah, Assyria…Studies in Assyrian History and Ancient Near Eastern Historiography Presented to Hayim Tadmor* (Scripta Hierosolymitana 33), edited by Mordechai Cogan and Israel Eph'al, 196–212. Jerusalem: Magnes, 1991.

———. "Outsiders or Insiders: The Biblical View of Emergent Israel and Its Contexts." In *The Other in Jewish Thought and History*, edited by Laurence Silberstein and Robert Cohn, 35–60. New York: NYU Press, 1994.

Manor, Dale. "Beer-sheba." In *The Anchor Bible Dictionary* 1, edited by David N. Freedman, Gary Herion, et al 641–45. New York: Doubleday, 1992.

———. "Kadesh-Barnea." In *The Anchor Bible Dictionary* 4, edited by David N. Freedman, Gary Herion, et al, 1–3. New York: Doubleday, 1992.

Manor, Dale, and Gary Herion. "Arad." In *The Anchor Bible Dictionary* 1, edited by David N. Freedman, Gary Herion, et al., 331–6. New York: Doubleday, 1992.

Margulies, Mordecai. *Midrash Wayyikra Rabbah*. New York: Jewish Theological Seminary, 1993.

Marty, Martin. "America's Iconic Book." In *Humanizing America's Iconic Book*, edited by Douglas Knight and Gene Tucker, 1–23. Chico, CA: Scholars Press, 1980.

Mayes, A. D. H. "The Covenant on Sinai and the Covenant with David." *Hermathena*, no. 110 (1970): 41.

Mazar, Amihai. "The Iron Age I." In *The Archaeology of Ancient Israel*, edited by Amnon Ben-Tor, 258–301. New Haven: Yale University Press, 1992.

Mazar, Benjamin. *World History of the Jewish People III*. Givatayim: Jewish History Publications and Rutgers University Press, 1971.

McCarter Jr., R. Kyle. *I Samuel (The Anchor Bible)*. New York: Doubleday, 1980.

McCarthy, Dennis. *Treaty and Covenant*. Rome: Pontifical Biblical Institute, 1978.

Mendenhall, George. "Biblical History in Transition." In *The Bible and the Ancient Near East*, edited by G. Ernest Wright, 27–58. Garden City, N.Y.: Doubleday, 1965.

———. "'Change and Decay in All Around I See': Conquest, Covenant and The Tenth Generation." In *Biblical Archaeologist* 39/4 (1987): 152–57.

———. "Covenant Forms in Israelite Tradition." In *Biblical Archaeologist* 17/3 (1954): 50–76.

———. "The Hebrew Account of the Conquest of Palestine." In *Biblical Archaeologist* 25/3 (1962): 66–87.

———. *The Tenth Generation: The Origins of the Biblical Tradition*. Baltimore: Johns Hopkins University Press, 1973.

Mendenhall, George and Gary Herion. "Covenant." In *The Anchor Bible Dictionary* 1, edited by David N. Freedman, Gary Herion, et al., 1182–83. New York: Doubleday, 1992.

Mettinger, Tryggve N.D. "Cherubim." In *Dictionary of Deities and Demons in the Bible*, edited by Karel van der Toorn, Bob Becking, and Pieter W. van der Horst. 189-192. Leiden, Netherlands: Brill, 1995.

Millard, Alan R. "Abraham." In *The Anchor Bible Dictionary* 1, edited by David N. Freedman, Gary Herion, et al., 40. New York: Doubleday, 1992.

Miller, J. Maxwell. "The Israelite Journey through (around) Moab and Moabite Toponymy." *Journal of Biblical Literature* 108/4 (1989): 577–99.

———. "Moab." In *The Anchor Bible Dictionary* 4, edited by David N. Freedman, Gary Herion, et al., 882–93. New York: Doubleday, 1992.

Moran, William. *The Amarna Letters*. Baltimore: Johns Hopkins University Press, 1992.

Morris, Jenny. "The Jewish Philosopher Philo." In *Emil Schürer, the History of the Jewish People in the Time of Jesus Christ*. Vol 3, edited by Geza Vermes and Fergus Millar, 809–89. Edinburgh: T and T Clark, 1987.

Muffs, Yohanan. "Abraham the Noble Warrior: Patriarchal Politics and Laws of War in Ancient Israel." *Journal of Jewish Studies* 33 (1982), 81–107.

Mulder, Martin. "Baal-Berith." In *Dictionary of Deities and Demons in the Bible*, edited by Karel van der Toorn, Bob Becking, and Pieter W. van der Horst, 266–72. Leiden, Netherlands: Brill, 1995.

Mykytiuk, Lawrence J. *Identifying Biblical Persons in Northwest Semitic Inscriptions of 1200–539 B.C.E.* Atlanta: Society of Biblical Literature, 2004.

Na'aman, Nadav. "The 'Kenite Hypothesis' in the Light of Excavations at Horvat 'Uza." In *Not Only History*, edited by Gilda Bartoloni and Maria Giovanna Biga, 171-182. Winona Lake, IN: Eisenbrauns, 2016.

———. "Jeroboam's Polytheism According to IKings 12:28-29." In *The Journal of Northwest Semitic Languages*," 46 (2020), 35-45.

Nebo, Yehoshaphat. *The Commentaries to the Torah* by Rabbi Joseph Bekhor Shor. Jerusalem: Mossad Harav Kook, 1994.

Nicholson, Ernest. *God and His People, Covenant and Theology in the Old Testament*. Oxford: Oxford University Press, 1986.

Nielsen, Eduard. *Shechem, a Traditio-Historical Investigation*. Copenhagen: Gad, 1969.

Nikiprowetzky, Valentin. "Ethical Monotheism." *Daedalus*, Spring 1975, 69–89.

Oden, Robert. "Myth and Mythology." In *The Anchor Bible Dictionary* 4, edited by David N. Freedman, Gary Herion, et al, 946–56. New York: Doubleday, 1992.

———. "The Place of Covenant in the Religion of Israel." In *Ancient Israelite Religion Essays in Honor of Frank Moore Cross*, edited by Patrick D. Miller Jr., Paul D. Hanson, and S. Dean McBride, 429–47. Philadelphia: Fortress Press, 1987.

Oded, Bustenay, apud *Melakim Aleph* (Olam Ha-tanakh vol.10), edited by Gershon Galil and Ephraim Stern, eds., 138. Tel Aviv: Davidson-Attai, 1994.

Oller, Gary. "Idrimi." In *The Anchor Bible Dictionary* 3, edited by David N. Freedman, Gary Herion, et al, 381–82. New York: Doubleday, 1992.

Olmstead, Albert T. *History of the Persian Empire*. Chicago: University of Chicago Press, 1948.

Oppenheim, A. Leo. "On Royal Gardens in Mesopotamia." *Journal of Near Eastern Studies* 24/4 (1965): 328–333.

Pagels, Elaine. *The Gnostic Gospels*. New York: Random House, 1979.

———. *The Origin of Satan*. New York: Random House, 1995.

Perlitt, Lothar. *Bundestheologie im Alten Testament*. Neukirchen-Vluyn: Neukirchener Verlag, 1969.

Plaut, W. Gunther, ed. *The Torah: A Modern Commentary*. New York: Union of American Hebrew Congregations, 1981.

Porter, Barbara Nevling. *Images, Power and Politics: Figurative Aspects of Esarhaddon's Babylonian Policy*. Philadelphia: American Philosophical Society, 1993.

Pritchard, James B., ed. *Ancient Near Eastern Texts Relating to the Old Testament*, 3rd Edition, with supplement. Princeton: Princeton University Press, 1969.

Rainey, Anson F. "Compulsory Labor Gangs in Ancient Israel." *Israel Exploration Journal* 20/3–4 (1970): 191–202.

———. *El Amarna Tablets, 359–379*. Neukirchen-Vluyn: Neukirchener Verlag, 1978.

———. "Remarks on Donald Redford's Egypt, Canaan and Israel in Ancient Times." In *Bulletin of the American Schools of Oriental Research* (August 1994) 81–85.

———. Review of *The Tribes of Yahweh*, by Norman Gottwald. *Journal of the American Oriental Society* 107/3 (1987) 541–43.

———. "Uncritical Criticism." *Journal of the American Oriental Society* 115/1 (1995) 101–4.

Rainey, Anson and R. Steven Notley. *The Sacred Bridge: Carta's Atlas of the Biblical World* Jerusalem: Carta, 2006.

Ramsey, George. "Joshua (Person)." In *The Anchor Bible Dictionary* 3, edited by David N. Freedman, Gary Herion, et al, 999–1000. New York: Doubleday, 1992.

———. "Zadok." In *The Anchor Bible Dictionary* 6, edited by David N. Freedman, Gary Herion, et al, 1034–35. New York: Doubleday, 1992.

Redford, Donald B. "Akhenaten." In *The Anchor Bible Dictionary* 1, edited by David N. Freedman, Gary Herion, et al, 135–37. New York: Doubleday, 1992.

———. *Egypt, Canaan, and Israel in Ancient Times*. Princeton: Princeton University Press, 1992.

Reiling, Jannes. "Melchizedek." In *Dictionary of Deities and Demons in the Bible*, edited by Karel van der Toorn, Bob Becking, and Pieter W. van der Horst, 1057–53. Leiden, Netherlands: Brill, 1995.

Reiner, Erica. *Šurpu, A Collection of Sumerian and Akkadian Incantations*. Graz, Austria, 1958: 13–16.

Reiner, Erica, Martha Roth, et al., eds. *The Assyrian Dictionary of the Oriental Institute of the University of Chicago*. Chicago: Oriental Institute, 1999.

Rendtorff, Rolf. "Postexilic Israel in German Bible Scholarship." In *Sha'arei Talmon Studies in the Bible, Qumran and the Ancient Near East Presented to Shemaryahu Talmon* 10, edited by Michael Fishbane and Emanuel Tov, 165–73. Winona Lake, IN: Eisenbrauns, 1992.

Ringgren, Helmer. *Israelite Religion*. Philadelphia: Fortress Press, 1966.

Rofé, Alexander. "The Battle of David and Goliath: Folklore, Theology, Eschatology." In *Judaic Perspectives on Ancient Israel*, edited by Jacob Neusner, Baruch A. Levine, and Ernest S. Frerichs, 117–51. Philadelphia: Fortress, 1987.

———. "Ephraimite versus Deuteronomistic History." In *Storia e tradizioni di Israele scritti in onore di J. Alberto Soggin*, edited by Daniele Garrone and Felice Israel, 221–35. Brescia: Paidea, 1991.

Röllig, Wolfgang. "Bethel." In *Dictionary of Deities and Demons in the Bible*, edited by Karel van der Toorn, Bob Becking, and Pieter W. van der Horst, 332–33. Leiden, Netherlands: Brill, 1995.

Römer, Willem. "Einige Überlegungen zur 'Heiligen Hochzeit' nach altorientalischen Texten." In *Von Kanaan bis Kerala: Festschrift für Prof. Mag. Dr. Dr. J. P. M. van der Ploeg O.P. zur Vollendung des siebzigsten Lebensjahres am 4. Juli 1979: überreicht von Kollegen, Freunden und Schulern*, edited by Wilhelmus Delsman, 411–28. Neukirchen-Vluyn: Neukirchener Verlag, 1982.

Rose, Martin. "Names of God in the OT." In *The Anchor Bible Dictionary* 4, edited by David N. Freedman, Gary Herion, et al, 1001–11. New York: Doubleday, 1992.

Rosenberg, Joel. *King and Kin: Political Allegory in the Hebrew Bible*. Bloomington: Indiana University Press, 1986.

Sarna, Nahum. *JPS Torah Commentary: Genesis*. Philadelphia: Jewish Publication Society, 2001.

Sasson, Jack. "On M. H. Pope's Song of Songs [AB7C]." *MAARAV, A Journal for the Study of the Northwest Semitic Languages and Literatures* 1/2 (1979): 177–96.

———. Review of *The Tenth Generation*, by George E. Mendenhall. *Journal of Biblical Literature* 93/2 (1974): 294–96.

Scullion, John. "God in the OT." In *The Anchor Bible Dictionary* 2, edited by David N. Freedman, Gary Herion, et al, 1041–48. New York: Doubleday, 1992.

Seeligmann, Isaac L. "A Pre-monarchic Hymn." In *I. L. Seeligmann Studies in Biblical Literature*, edited by Avi Hurvitz, Sara Japhet, and Emanuel Tov, 189–204. Jerusalem: Magnes, 1992.

Selms, Andreas van. "Temporary Henotheism." In *Symbolae Biblicae et Mesopotamicae Francisco Mario Theodoro de Liagre Böhl dedicatae*, edited by Martinus A. Beek, 8–20. Leiden: Brill, 1973.

Smith, Morton. "The Common Theology of the Ancient Near East." *Journal of Biblical Literature* 71/3 (1952): 135–47.

———. *Palestinian Parties and Politics That Shaped the Old Testament*. New York: Columbia University Press, 1971.

———. "The Present State of Old Testament Studies." *Journal of Biblical Literature* 78/1 (1969): 19–35.

Soden. Wolfram von. "Religion und Sittlickeit nach den Anschauungen der Babylonier." *Zeitschrift der deutschen morgenländischen Gesellschaft* 89/2 (1935): 143–69.

———, editor. *Akkadisches Handwörterbuch*. Wiesbaden: Harrassowitz, 1965–1981 (3 vols.)

Speiser, Ephraim A. "Authority and Law in Mesopotamia" and "The Wife-Sister Motif in the Patriarchal Narratives." In *Oriental and Biblical Studies: Collected Writings of E.A Speiser*, edited by Jacob Finkelstein and Moshe Greenberg, 313–23 and 2–82. Philadelphia: University of Pennsylvania Press, 1967.

———, editor. *World History of the Jewish People*. Vol I. Tel Aviv: Massadah, 1964.

Spencer, John R. "Aaron." In *The Anchor Bible Dictionary* 1, edited by David N. Freedman, Gary Herion, et al., 1–6. New York: Doubleday, 1992.

——— "Golden Calf." In *The Anchor Bible Dictionary* 2, edited by David N. Freedman, Gary Herion, et al., 1065–69. New York: Doubleday, 1992.

Sperling, S. David. "An Arslan Tash Incantation: Interpretations and Implications." *Hebrew Union College Annual* 53 (1982): 1–10.

———. "Blood." In *The Anchor Bible Dictionary* 1, edited by David N. Freedman, Gary Herion, et al., 763–65. New York: Doubleday, 1992.

———. "God in the Hebrew Scriptures." *Encyclopedia of Religion* 6, edited by Mircea Eliade, 1–8. New York: Macmillan, 1987.

———. "Israel's Religion in the Ancient Near East." In *Jewish Spirituality from the Bible through the Middle Ages*, edited by Arthur Green, 5–31. New York: Crossroad, 1986.

———. "Joshua 24 Re-examined," *Hebrew Union College Annual* 58 (1987): 119–36.

———. "Rethinking Covenant in Late Biblical Books." *Biblica* 70/1 (1989): 50–72.

———. *Students of the Covenant: A History of Jewish Biblical Scholarship in North America.* Atlanta: Scholars Press, 1992.

———. *Ve-Eileh Divrei David: Essays in Semitics, Hebrew Bible and History of Biblical Scholarship.* New York: Brill, 2017.

Spinoza, Benedict Baruch. *A Theologico-Political Treastise*, translated by Robert H. M. Elwes. Reprint. New York: Dover, 1951.

Stern, Philip. *The Biblical Ḥerem: A Window on Israel's Religious Experience.* Atlanta: Scholars Press, 1991.

Stronach, David. "The Garden as a Political Statement: Some Case Studies from the Near East in the First Millennium B.C." *Bulletin of the Asia Institute* new series, 4 (1990): 171–80.

Sweek, Joel. "The Babel-Bible Streit." In *The Pitcher is Broken: Memorial Essays for Gösta W. Ahlström*, edited by Lowell K. Handy and Steven W. Holloway, 401–19. Sheffield: Sheffield Academic Press, 1995.

Tadmor, Hayim. "Autobiographical Apology in the Royal Assyrian Literature." In *History, Historiography and Interpretation: Studies in Biblical and Cuneiform Literatures*, edited by Tadmor and Moshe Weinfeld, 36–57. Jerusalem: Magnes Press, 1983.

———. "The People and the Kingship in Ancient Israel: The Role of Political Institutions in the Biblical Period." In *Cashiers d'histoire mondiale* II (1968): 46–68.

Talmage, Frank. "Apples of Gold: The Inner Meaning of Sacred Texts in Medieval Judaism." In *Jewish Spirituality from the Bible through the Middle Ages*, edited by Arthur Green, 313–55. New York: Crossroad, 1986.

Tallqvist, Knut L. *Akkadishe Götterepitheta.* Helsinki: Societas Orientalis Fennica, 1938.

Tate, Jonathan. "Allegory, Greek." In *Oxford Classical Dictionary* 2nd ed.,
    edited by Nicholas G. L. Hammond, and Howard H. Schullard, 45–46.
    New York: Oxford University Press, 1970.

Teixidor, Javier. *The Pagan God Popular Religion in the Greco-Roman Near East.*
    Princeton, NJ: Princeton University Press, 1977.

Theodor, Julius and Chanoch Albeck. *Midrash Bereshit Rabba* (reprint).
    Jerusalem: Wahrmann, 1965.

Thiel, Winfried. "Omri." In *The Anchor Bible Dictionary* 5, edited by David N.
    Freedman, Gary Herion, et al., 17–20. New York: Doubleday, 1992.

Thompson, Thomas. *The Historicity of the Patriarchal Narratives.* Berlin: de
    Gruyter, 1974.

———. "Historiography (Israelite)." In *The Anchor Bible Dictionary* 3, edited
    by David N. Freedman, Gary Herion, et al., 206–12. New York:
    Doubleday, 1992.

———. *The Origin Tradition of Ancient Israel. Vol. I: The Literary Formation of
    Genesis and Exodus 1–23.* Sheffield: Journal for the Study of the Old
    Testament, 1987.

Toombs, Lawrence E. "Shechem (Place)." In *The Anchor Bible Dictionary* 5,
    edited by David N. Freedman, Gary Herion, et al., 1175–86. New York:
    Doubleday, 1992.

Toorn, Karel van der. "Migration and the Spread of Local Cults." In
    *Immigration and Emigration within the Ancient Near East: Festschrift Edward
    Lipiński* (OLA 65), edited by Karel van Leberghe and Antoon Schoors,
    365–77. Leuven: Peeters, 1995.

———. "Saul and the Rise of Israelite State Religion." *Vetus Testamentum*
    43/4 (1993): 519–42.

———. *Sin and Sanction in Israel and Mesopotamia.* Maastricht: van Gorcum,
    1985.

———. "Yahweh." In *Dictionary of Deities and Demons in the Bible*, edited by
    Karel van der Toorn, Bob Becking, and Pieter W. van der Horst, 1712–
    30. Leiden, Netherlands: Brill, 1995.

Tucker, Gene, and Douglas Knight, eds. *Humanizing America's Iconic Book.*
    Chico, CA: Scholars Press, 1980.

Tur-Sinai, Naphtali H. *The Language and the Book II* (in Hebrew). Jerusalem:
    Bialik, 1959.

Van Seters, John. *Abraham in History and Tradition.* New Haven, CT: Yale
    University Press, 1975.

———. "Joshua 24 and the Problem of Tradition in the Old Testament." In
    *In the Shelter of Elyon: Essays in Honor of Gösta W. Ahlström, Journal for the
    Study of the Old Testament Supplement Series* 31, edited by W. Boyd Barrick

and John R. Spencer, 139–58. Sheffield: Journal for the Study of the Old Testament, 1984.

———. "Once Again – The Conquest of Sihon's Kingdom." *Journal of Biblical Literature* 99/1 (1980): 117–19.

———. "The Terms 'Amorite' and 'Hittite' in the Old Testament." *Vetus Testamentum* 22/1 (1972): 64–81.

de Vaux, Roland. *Ancient Israel.* New York: McGraw-Hill, 1965.

Veyne, Paul. *Did the Greeks Believe in Their Myths?* Chicago: University of Chicago Press, 1988.

Wallace, Howard. "Eden, Garden of." In *The Anchor Bible Dictionary* 2, edited by David N. Freedman, Gary Herion, et al., 281–83. New York: Doubleday, 1992.

Washington, Richard. "Venezuela calls for mandatory labor in farm sector" for *CNBC.com.* July 29, 2016.

Weinfeld, Moshe. "Berîth." In *Theological Dictionary of the Old Testament* 2, edited by Botterweck, G. Johannes, and Helmer Ringgren, 253–79. Grand Rapids.: Eerdmans, 1974–2018.

———. *The Book of Genesis with a New Commentary.* Tel Aviv: Gordon, 1975.

———. "The Common Heritage of Covenantal Traditions in the Ancient World." In *I Tratatti nel mondo antico. Forma, ideologia, funzione*, edited by Luciano Canfora, Carlo Zaccagnini, Mario Liverani, 175–91. Rome: L'Erma di Bretschneider, 1990.

———. "The Covenant of Grant in the Old Testament and in the Ancient Near East." *Journal of the American Oriental Society* 90/2 (1970) 184–203.

———. "Covenant Terminology in the Ancient Near East and Its Influence on the West." *Journal of the American Oriental Society* 93/2 (1973) 190–99.

———. "The Creator God in Genesis I and in the Prophecy of Deuter-Isaiah. *Tarbiz* 37/2 (1968): 105–32.

———. "The Davidic Empire: Realization of the Promises to the Patriarchs." *Eretz Israel* 24 (1993): 87–92.

———. *Deuteronomy and the Deuteronomic School.* Oxford: Clarendon Press, 1972.

———. "The Pattern of the Israelite Settlement in Canaan." *Vetus Testamentum Supplements* 40 (1988): 270–83.

———. "The Promise to the Patriarchs and Its Realization: An Analysis of Foundation Stories." In *Society and Economy in the Eastern Mediterranean ca. 1500–1000 B.C.*, edited by Michael Heltzer and Edward Lipiński, 353–69. Leuven: Peeters, 1988.

———. Review of *God and His People*, by Ernest Nicholson. *Revue biblique* 98/3 (1991): 431–36.

Wellhausen, Julius. *Prolegomena to the History of Ancient Israel.* Reprint. Gloucester, MA: Peter Smith, 1973.

Wernberg-Møller, Preben. Review of *Treaty Curses and the Old Testament Prophets*, by Delbert Hillers. *Catholic Bible Quarterly* 27/1 (1965): 68–69.

Whitelam, Keith. "Israel's Tradition of Origin: Reclaiming the Land." *Journal for the Study of the Old Testament* 44 (1989): 29–36.

Williamson, H.G.M. "How Many Isaiahs Were There?" [cited 14 Mar 2020]. Online: https://www.bibleodyssey.org:443/people/related-articles/how-many-isaiahs-were-there

Wilson, John. "Egypt and the Bible." In *World History of the Jewish People.* Vol. I, edited by Ephraim A. Speiser, 338–41. Tel Aviv: Massadah, 1964.

Wolff, Hans. *Hosea.* Philadelphia: Fortress Press, 1974.

Wright, David P. *Inventing God's Law: How the Covenant Code of the Bible Used and Revised the Laws of Hammurabi.* New York: Oxford University Press, 2009.

Young, Gordon, ed. *Mari in Retrospect.* Winona Lake, IN: Eisenbrauns, 1992.

Yusa, Michiko. "Henotheism." *Encyclopedia of Religion* 6, edited by Mircea Eliade, 266–68. New York: Macmillan, 1987.

Zaccagnini, Carlo. "An Urartean Royal Inscription in the Report of Sargon's Eighth Campaign." In *Assyrian Royal Inscriptions: New Horizons*, edited by in Mario Fales, 274. Rome: Instituto per l'Oriente, 1981

ABOUT THE AUTHOR & CO-WRITER

Dr. S. David Sperling, Ph.D. retired in 2019 from a 40+ year career as a professor of Bible at Hebrew Union College-Jewish Institute of Religion (HUC-JIR) in New York City. He has also been a visiting professor at New York University, Syracuse University, the College of William and Mary and The Jewish Theological Seminary.

David has published three academic texts: *The Original Torah: The Political Intent of the Bible's Writers* (New York: NYU Press, 1998); *Students of the Covenant: A History of Jewish Biblical Scholarship in North America* (Atlanta, GA: Society of Biblical Literature, 1992); *Ve-Eileh Divrei David: Essays in Semitics, Hebrew Bible and History of Biblical Scholarship* (Leiden, The Netherlands: Brill, 2017). His current project is a book on the Hallel Psalms (Psalms 113-118).

David served as Consulting Editor to *The Haftarah Commentary* by W. Gunther Plaut, translated by Chaim Stern (URJ Press, 1996), and to *The Torah: A Modern Commentary by W. Gunther Plaut and David E.S. Stein* (URJ Press, 2005). Additionally, he has contributed to some 145 articles published in the *Encyclopaedia Judaica* (2007), as well as serving as Editor of the Bible section.

David currently serves as the Scholar-in-Residence at Temple Israel of Northern Westchester (Croton-on-Hudson, NY) where he frequently guest-lectures.

David was ordained as a rabbi by the Jewish Theological Seminary in 1967, following which he earned his Ph.D. in Ancient Semitic Languages from Columbia University. David is a member of the Central Conference of American Rabbis.

Co-Writer Tara S. Keiter graduated from the University of Massachusetts, Amherst in 1987 with a double degree in Economics and Sociology. After an 8-year career in the financial services industry in New York City, Tara left the workforce to raise her children.

Tara and her family have been members of Temple Israel of Northern Westchester since 1995. She is grateful that her work summarizing by blog (2014–2025) and podcast (2015–2023) Rabbi Jennifer Jaech's Torah Study sessions led her to involvement with this fulfilling project.

ABOUT THE TYPE

The main text of this book is set in Garamond, named for the 16th century engraver Claude Garamond and updated in the 1920s by Jean Jannon. The quotations in this book are set in High Tower Text, which is a 1994 update by Tobias Frere-Jones of the 15th century printing of Nicolas Jenson

The book cover is set in three fonts: IM FELL English SC (2010) by Igino Marini; MarcellusSC (2012) by Brian J. Bonislawsky; and, Cormorant Garamond (2015) by Christian Thalmann.

The publishing house logo is comprised of two fonts: Fleur De Leah (2008-2021) and Italianno (2009), both by Robert Leuschke.

All fonts available for use through SIL Open Font licensing.

www.ingramcontent.com/pod-product-compliance
Lightning Source LLC
Chambersburg PA
CBHW020432130626
46549CB00001B/109